Magpie

by

Bronwen Carson

Published by Unleash Press

unleashcreatives.net/press

Copyright © 2023 by Bronwen Carson

Printed in the United States of America

ISBN 978-1-737519485

to Mo, Jess, my beloved Isephene,
...and all who yearn for the whisper of trees

"I come into the peace of wild things
who do not tax their lives with forethought
of grief. I come into the presence of still water.
And I feel above me the day-blind stars
waiting with their light. For a time
I rest in the grace of the world and am free."

from "The Peace of Wild Things" by Wendell Berry

I'd like to thank the state of North Carolina, where I was able to slow down enough to remember the wildness within and where the whispers of trees reawakened a sense of belonging no amount of hustle ever could.

Deepest gratitude and acknowledgements to the exhaustive research of J.T. Garret whose book, The Cherokee Herbal, opened my eyes, mind, heart, and spirit in ways I'm still discovering. Through his book, I learned of the extraordinary phytochemical, pharmacological and often inherent psychopharmacologic properties of the more than 600 species of native medicinal plants used in Tsalagi (Aniyunwiya) traditional medicine. Much of this knowledge is sacred, passed to specific members to carry on as healers. Despite my wanting to learn as much as I could about their remedies and recipes, what I came to ultimately understand is curiosity doesn't determine right and appropriation often parades as education.

I'd be remiss if I didn't express my gratitude for Mx. Lindsey Ryan of GRASP, Dr. Selena Waite, and endless blogs written by insightful, formidable, hilarious, late diagnosis ASD women.

Lastly, I'd like to thank Isobel Carson, Jess Draper, Vieve Radha Price, Jamie Price, Audrey Rosenberg, Brooke Decker, and Peter Ho Davies for their encouragement to continue developing this story as well as their honest feedback, without which, I wouldn't have found the story that wanted to be told hiding within the story I thought I wanted to tell.

My hope is this book will act as a gentle reminder of our profound relationship with nature, that some mysteries are not for us to have, and how most answers we deem irrefutable truths are just collective agreements. I also hope with all my heart that the thoughts and experiences of an undiagnosed neurodivergent woman help unravel misperceptions and stereotypes about ASD.

Magpie

Bronwen Carson

1977 – Yadkin County, North Carolina

almost invisible

pale sky up n up n up thru Nathy's arms sky clouds leaves
sky clouds leaves he sounds like the ocean

swooshcreakrustleswoosh close my eyes match my breathin
with the breeze creamylemonspicysharp honeysuckle
rosemary earth like hot oil n wet skillets

hold my breath

holditholditholditholdit

then slowslow out my mouth almost invisible whistle a
soundvoice only Nathy can hear he says trees sing all the time
n invisible sounds can join he likes dark blue soundvoices best

almost sunset better go circle Nathy til my fingers r warm n
buzzy cross the crumbly paint on old barn watchin it fall into
a river of flecks from yestrday

n the day fore that   n the day fore that

last wave to Nathy soon wave not goodbye wave cause there'll
be tomorrow

n the tomorrow after that   n' the tomorrow after that

skip home shadow dancin soft n quick n long shadows know
lots of secrets whens n ifs n maybes won't ask her though
cause now's where I wanna be paint flecks tingly buzzy
fingers shadow secrets

Nathy's leaves n' dark blue waterwhispers in my chest

1

1

it's almost here

My office walls are covered in old windows and mirrors. Mercury, bottle, lead, wavy, bullseye. Different shapes and sizes. The frames are wood. No stained glass. No color. I've collected them over the past twenty years. My orphaned portals.

They're why I'm waiting. Not for their abbreviated opinions of my unimpressive reflection—I'm waiting for the few minutes each day when the sun bounces off the glass building across the street, through my windows and onto them, splitting the light into a cacophony that muffles the world for a few minutes. These few minutes each day are the only time I feel much of anything.

According to the Stoics, apatheia (*a* "without" *pathos* "suffering") was the defining characteristic of sages. I like to think about that whenever the dull and amorphous within me shifts in its dreamless sleep. I never thought I'd turn out to be the indifferent type. I guess no one thinks that. Six-year-olds running through sprinklers don't scream "When I grow up, I want to be an empty, purposeless shell! HURRAH!" It just happens. Apathy seeps in while running errands, having unmemorable sex, waiting for the train. It's still and quiet. Emptiness is too big to see coming. It's also peaceful. No attachments, no reasons to linger or prove or uphold. There's a beauty to nothingness. A purity.

A few years ago, I went to Seattle for a conference but ended up blowing it off because of the second verse, same as the first at those things. I opted for tourist traps; Pike Place Market, the Chihuly Glass Garden, the Pop Museum, hitting a bar between each stop. I wound up, of course, in the Space Needle, quipping to myself with that specific brand of faith in

one's wit inebriation brings, about how unimpressive Mt.
Rainier was because I couldn't find it anywhere on the horizon.
After few minutes a guide walked up to me, and quietly said,
"Not there," pointing to the distant mountain range I was
mocking. Then she lifted her finger past the thick clouds that
seemed perpetually draped over Seattle like dryer lint, and said,
"There."

I remember feeling heavy. Wobbly. Like my chest was
filled with cold, oily marbles. Mt. Rainier was too big. Too big,
and too quiet, and just waiting for me to see it. Or not. It didn't
care either way.

In that moment, a giant emptiness tore a hole through
my chest, and the cold oily remains of something vital slid out,
clattered to the ground, and rolled away. There was no
warning. No sign saying, 'Hey, Maggie, you're losing yourself to
the abyss.' Just an almost imperceptible atmospheric shift
towards a different direction. A tree grows through chain link
slowly. Until one day the fence can't be removed without
killing the tree.

When I came back from the conference, the constant
thrum of asphalt and steel here replaced the need to know
what had shifted that night in the Space Needle. Maybe the
need to know didn't return with me. Maybe it was never there
to begin with. Either way, there's not much of me that doesn't
belong to this city now.

Some people say New York is hard and cruel, but it's also
fair and honest. It doesn't care who you are. I like that about it.
It's also said everyone should live here once but leave before it
makes them too hard. But there are different levels of
hardness. Different strata. Some have hidden threads of gold.
A freshly torn orange on a stuffy train, blank eyes momentarily
reliving past anarchies, an unexpected 30 seconds of quiet amid
the relentless jack hammers and voices. But those are rare.

Mostly life here is one thing, then another. And the increments of time spent doing them.

Today's things consist of boiling two hundred hopeful interns down to ten who will receive an interview. I'll accomplish this by printing out all two hundred resumes, closing my eyes, and pulling ten randomly from the stack. I know it's callous. But a decision must be made somehow. I'm not much of a believer in destiny, mostly because it seems more about laziness than faith, but the egalitarian nature of the superposition principle? That, I can get behind. Between my hand and the stack, every potential intern both has and doesn't have an interview.

these fractals of hope   thin as frost
just as brittle

I reach for the tenth and final choice when the room fills with light. I sit back and stop. It's the only time I do. But something about it is different today. I can feel it passing through me. Illuminating other places and times. The shapes of forgotten things.

I have only one truly vivid memory from my childhood that feels like I was there. Most images my mind offers the few times I've let it drift back are like Polaroids of a childhood I'm told I lived. But the one I remember experiencing is about light. Bright, sparkling light, moving, and dancing. Where I am and who else might be there isn't clear, only the sense of being surrounded by light. I can't remember exactly what happy feels like, but when the light is in my office, in this way, I almost can.

The radiator in the corner hisses and for a moment it sounds like something else. Like most New Yorkers, I have a love/hate relationship with these mini dinosaurs—an admiration for their ability to scald with impunity, and an irritation for their dominant state of drooling tepid, rust-flecked water. But just now the gurgling water and steam sounded like something else. I close my eyes. Try to coax the faded shapes in my mind closer, but the gravity of forgetting is too strong.

"Sorry to disturb," my assistant says from the doorway.

Chelsea knows not to interrupt me during these few minutes each day so in her mind, it must be apocalyptic. In the three years she's been my assistant, the only thing I've been able to discern about her is a mysterious hatred for natural light. I make her wait in the glare as penance.

"Yes?" I ask.

"Your mother." Her mouth twitches, reverting to a grim dash. Water starts pooling along the crescents of her lower lids. Interruption officially atoned.

"Yes?" I ask.

"Again," she replies.

This one precious moment of something other than nothing has been stolen by my mother who despite being one of the most well-intended people you'll ever meet, is hyperventilated in almost everything she does.

She never left the town where she grew up. The town where she met my father when he moved there for "a quieter life" after being honorably discharged from the Army. She married him, raised me, my sister, and my brother all in that same town. If you can call the triangulation of livestock farms, unculled rhododendrons, and Dollar Generals a town.

Mom's one of those glue types that holds communities together. A person everyone recognizes as kind. I'm more like my father. Not that he isn't well intended or kind. He's just more self-contained.

Chelsea holds her ground, blinking monosyllabically. I offer my unblinking reply. This is a common interaction between us. She never wins, but I respect the effort.

"Take a message, please" I say, releasing my gaze back to the pitches on my desk awaiting a sagacity that was once available whenever I needed it. But discernment, along with most attributes I've held without noticing, has now atrophied. Chelsea disappears, door left ajar in her resentful wake.

I return my attention to the light, but it's been resorbed into the anemic film that passes as daylight in February. Mirrors and windows once again two-dimensional fragments of a fluorescent-lit office. I try to resist the grey-green undertow. Pull the thread of whatever my mind wanted to remember but the memory of light and water is gone.

"Five, four, three, two, one." I say to my dissected reflection. It's from a Ted talk I watched a few years ago about managing stress and refocusing by acknowledging things you see, touch, hear, smell, and taste descending from five things down to one. The whole process took too long, so I streamlined it.

"FIVE, FOUR, THREE, TWO, ONE."
I can't be broken hologram Maggie today.
"FIVE, FOUR, THREE, TWO, ONE."
The grey greenness continues to spread. Like a virus. One that causes neuropathy. Ghost limbs. You'd think knowing this about myself would change it. It doesn't.

The grey greenness usually settles into my hands. I don't have to look down to know my fingers are now glued together, thumb a strange attached-yet-separate entity, there only to grant the appearance of an ability to hold things. I've dubbed them my doll hands. Doll hands hold a limited number of objects. A book. Or a shelf. Maybe a taco.

I will my thumb to relax and fingers to separate enough to slide the folder of short-listed intern prospects to the center of my desk, press speakerphone, then #2. Mitchel's office.

Mitchel's a colleague, and for all intents and purposes, my best friend. Purposes being drinks after work and reciprocal bitching posts. Intents being we never encroach upon each other or demand regular attention. Topographical analysis of relationship dynamics usually reveals my overall lack of breadth and depth. Luckily, our mutual interests—binge watching *Supernatural*, *Fringe*, or *Stranger Things*, bourbon, Krispy Kreme, Scottish indie rock, a disdain for care posturing, and being unabashed workaholics with the combined emotional content of a thimble—keep in depth surveys of our friendship at bay.

He's also dousing rod, able to determine interns I should interview through the bestowal of wacky nicknames. If one rolls off his brain, that prospective intern gets an interview. If nothing comes to mind, that resume is returned to the stack and a new one is chosen. A few years ago, I interviewed an intern he couldn't nickname. It created a wormhole to a demonic dimension.

Mitchel picks up with an exaggerated "yyyyyoooooh."

"You wanted to be a Beastie Boy in your misunderstood youth, didn't you?"

"You get me," he drawls. Mitchel's from Mississippi. For the most part he submerges this fact.

One of the first things we bonded over was an oath to never again venture below the Mason Dixon. The other was his asking "Man-Man or Egg Shen?" upon seeing my Six Demon Bag Travel mug on his first day at the firm.

"I feel seen right now," he says. "It's a beautiful thing."

"Here for you in all the ways and means," I reply.

"Oh, you *are* the ways and means," he volleys back.

"Mitch-"

"Hey, you called me. Okay. Let's go. Nicknames."

I open the folder. Ten resumes whose sameness mirrors the manila folder that holds their indistinguishable futures.

second verse same as the first

"Ground Control to Major Mags…"

Mitchel's like a dog. Or a vacuum cleaner. You can't let him sense weakness.

"Contestant number one," I say with too much levity, "Bently Tashman. Talk about setting your kid up for trophy wives and cirrhosis."

Mitchel chuckles. "Mmmhmm, mmmhmm. Got it! Cool Breeze McHashlington."

"Okay, next is..." I pull out the next lucky resume. "Kimberly Graham."

"Butterfingers Fandango. Her friends call her Corkie."

"You stay up nights to come up with these, don't you?"

"I sleep like a baby in a fairytale."

"Babies in fairytales are cursed or meet untimely deaths."

"Yeeeeeexactly," he replies, "Next."

"Okay, but I have a question."

"I'm a smudged newspaper in the gutter of life."

"Mitch—"

"An illegible metaphor for all things lost in this tragic—"

"Shouldn't metaphors be at least metaphorically legible?"

"Potato, potaahto, pa-toe-toe."

"Pa-toe-toe?"

Mitchel's on an upcycle of Addy. My doctor refuses to refill my prescription until I "clean up my diet and stress act". She might as well ask me to disprove the third law of thermodynamics. We've been down this road before. She'll buckle under the weight of my insistence in about a week or I'll find someone else to prescribe it. It became a necessity a few years ago when double red eyes and No-Doz were no longer a match for Gen Z over-producing, over-achievers who see inevitable burnout looming, but leap like lemmings off the cliff anyway. I also thought it might help with the whole apathy thing, but instead of resembling a Dr. Scholl's gel insole, Adderall transforms me into one of those giant waving air puppets on used car lots. I still don't feel anything. But I resemble someone who does.

"Breaker-breaker 1-9, this is Taters Haaslebock sendin out a where's Alice, over."

"Sorry, Alice is..." I can't scrape together an end to this statement without veering too close to the truth, so I just say, "hanging up now."

"You'll be back." He's seamlessly switched from long-haul trucker to a perfect, dusky-voiced Crowley from *Supernatural*.

"You never get the accent right."

"I always get it right. Wack-a, wack-a."
A perfect Fozzie bear.

"Orshki-borshki," I say trying to one up him via the Swedish Chef. I hang up to his unimpeachable Kermit the Frog sings *Rock of Ages*.

"They're waiting," Chelsea says from the doorway.

She was listening. Again. She's a teeny sponge that can hold fifty times her weight in private conversations. Sometimes I wonder what she's planning to do with them. Write country songs? Ritualistic burnings under a full moon? It could go either way with her. She clears her throat.

"Oh, hello Chelsea, I didn't see you there."
She raises one sharply penciled brow, tilting her head crisply.
uh-oh might've broken her
I grab my *Surely Not Everybody Was Kung Fu Fighting* mug of heavily bourbon'd red eye. As I leave my office, the radiator hisses again. Something like water. Then it's gone.

****

The infotainment needs to be updated. It's been stuck on the same loop for a week. I still end up watching the eight-second bites flash across the screen as the elevator's milky muzak softens local and global tragedies. Microbes released by melting glaciers killing marine life by the hundreds, smoothed by an orchestral version of Michael Jackson's "Beat It". The

Bronwen Carson

unstaunchable flow of refugees from the Middle East, eased into resembling a critically acclaimed yet binge-worthy streaming series via the easy listening version of "Wish You Were Here" by Avril Lavigne.

me too Avril me too

Mitchel grunts. "Pointless to have something meant to keep us informed if it's always regurgitating last week's facts."

"If you can call them facts," I say, then add, "a few hand-picked incidents polished by—"

"The fat oligarchic fingers of the news machine?"

I chuff my admiration, expecting to find the wry grin that's usually drawn across his face when I compliment him, but it's blank. His eyes are on the screen. I start to say something but can't think of anything worthwhile or helpful so I return to the music video disasters on the tiny TV, hoping the flatness he's found will somehow smother me too.

Mitchel's usually my ladder out of tarpits, shallow ones at least, but it's his turn to be helped so I'm at a loss. Should I laugh? Toss out a Crowley quote? Shake him and yell 'Dammit, man! Snap out of it!', like they do in the movies?

The elevator slows to a stop.

hallelujah

We'll disassemble our new cellmate in secret code, and all will be well once more.

The doors slip open to the fourth floor, a self-organizing game development company where the omnipresent air of panicked sweat could be bottled and sold as chemical warfare. The smell of fear, now in an easy-to-use aerosol.

Unfortunately, no one is waiting. Whoever pushed the button more than likely fled the back-stabbing cabals by taking the stairs. Elevators in New York adhere to a space-time continuum all their own so taking the stairs is always a solid choice. I grope for something frothy to say but my brain isn't up to the task, so I just say some words.

10

"No patience. You know? Haha, you know? The game? Zip. Goose egg. Mitchel's not here right now, please leave a message.

I can't do breezy and hate women who lilt their voices to tackle the slightest evidence of male frailty, so I go with deadpan. "She's a piece of work. A drink is in order."

That one landed. He flicks his eyes to me, "At least one".

The she in question is Owsley Newton, freshly minted COO at The Bridge Group, the brand development firm I've been with for the past fifteen years, and Mitchel for the past eight. The why of the tension now clotting the elevator is more complex.

This entire day has been off, but it spiraled irretrievably down the drain at the meet-the-new-COO spitball. Initially, she was beneficence incarnate. Once everyone was sufficiently relaxed, the blood rites began.

"Embarrassing. Mediocre. Hack," she'd said, tossing pitch after pitch onto the seventeen-foot-long unfinished Amish barnwood conference table as the moat of Bridge Group employees incrementally crumpled. The phrase "Neil deGrasse Tyson couldn't quantify the tonnage of crap that is this one" seemed a particular favorite of hers. Somewhere around the ninth revisitation of it I diverted my remaining energy to conjuring a membrane between myself and the fervent need to please her that had filled the room with sulfured breath and greasy brows.

After another twenty minutes of something, something, very important something, she paused. It's one of the few moments I remember because the stillness had a clenched-ness to it. The vehement kind of dental impressions.

Newton was surveying us with such severity it was difficult not to exclaim *dun-dun-duuuuuuuun!* I almost did. But she broke the seal with disdainful insights into "Our soft serve lives of participation trophies and vanity degrees." Around her

11

"Dead weight, sinking ships" speech, I began to wonder if one could, in fact, die of boredom.

The real low point was when, after Mitchel's recap on our three top clients, Newton's eyes trickled down his orthotic braces. It was bizarre because Mitchel's the golden boy here. Clients love the PR bump they get for their token gesture of inclusion. Then, when they realize he's excellent at his job, go on to congratulate themselves on a prophetic acumen for spotting talent.

I'd said "Bitch" just loud enough to reach Newton who flicked her eyes to me, brows raised in what appeared to be approval, before unceremoniously dismissing us with a "We're done people."

A spaghetti of hands retrieved disemboweled pitches, gusts of ammonia-drenched air as all rushed the door. I tried to give Mitchel my best Scarlet O'Hara single eyebrow arch of defiance, but he was trying to get up smoothly under Newton's velociraptor gaze and one of his canes wasn't agreeing with the process. The smirk scratched across her face triggered a flare in my throat.

Now I'm standing in an elevator trying to figure out how real friends navigate vulnerability. Drinks. Friends have drinks. He'll vent. I'll say "uh-huh" and nod, adding a few colorful profanities, then we'll devise a coded language we'll roll out anytime she acts like an ass, which, if this afternoon is any indication, will be daily.

The slow, whirring churn of the pre-war elevator eases us past the remaining three floors to the lobby while the infotainment restarts its loop. As the doors slide open, a jumble of voices chanting something indistinguishable rushes in to meet us. Protesters. This building gets visitations at least once a week.

"Wonder who's on the pyre today?" I quip.

It's quite possibly us because The Bridge Group handles PR for a decent amount of capitalistic greed mongers, but we're not the worst offenders. The eighth floor is entirely populated by corporate lawyers.

We simultaneously say, "Death Star," a nickname we gave them last year. It takes a lot for PR people to cast stones, but corporate lawyers make us feel like fluffy unicorns who poop rainbows for the greater good.

Mitchel laughs, speeding towards the lobby doors. Even though I'd prefer finding an exit to slither through unnoticed, the reemergence of Mitchel's levity seems fragile, so I join him.

As we approach the doors, their signs come into focus.

Frack This!   *Big Oil will Spoil!*   *No Fracking Way!*

"Uh-oh, looks like mamma Newton's in truuuuhhh-ble," he says. "Let's see if we can get them to storm the castle."

"Uh-uh, no way."

"Your account, right?"

It is. A decade ago, I'd have fought tooth and nail for this account. Uphill battle, disastrous publics, the challenge of changing as many minds as I could. I don't feel that way anymore.

"She just gave it to me today. How did you-? Right. Chelsea."

He shrugs. Chelsea does love parceling out her pilfered information precisely when it will have the most impact. I wouldn't be surprised if she anonymously tipped off these protestors.

"Come on," I say trying to sound bored, "I'm not in the mood for angry Muppets."

"No?" he says, performing an annoyingly impressive angry Muppet impression, eliciting a barrage of challenges from the protesters. He waggles his eyebrows, and I cave because this is better than bleak, storm cloud Mitchel.

"Okay. Let's rumble," I say.

Mitchel lets out a West Side Story whistle and pushes through the doors. I follow, hoping the Muppets will give me some ideas, but find myself engulfed by a cacophony of feeble thought grenades.

"Rotten Roots, Rotten Grass!"

"Big green fracking fools!"

"Frack with the bull, you get the horns!"

The promise of cathartic arguments and campaign ideas disintegrates. It's cold. I'm bored. I want to go home. I shake my head and walk away, inciting a fresh ripple of paltry insults.

"Earth burner!"

"One day, you'll be sorry when—"

"Yep, already am," I say.

just not for this

poor Maggie   so broken

stop it

I focus on Mitchel and the sparring match that's sprung up between him and a protester holding a sign that reads *Only* **YOU** *Can Prevent Faucet Fires*. The sole clever slogan in the bunch. I feel an overwhelming need to meet this person. Perhaps congratulate them. I move closer.

"—is at the root of it," Mitchel says. He's using what he likes to call his prosecutorial 'voice of reason'.

"Root?" The protestor asks. "Good. Okay. Let's talk about that. About roots." The voice is strong and clear. Slight upward curl. Appalachian. It's been a long time since I've heard a voice like that. "Roots are an unseen system," the protestor continues, "critical, but usually taken for granted until it's too late."

My feet are still walking towards them, but the closer I get, the more untethered I feel. As if I'm unspooling.

"Come on, don't you think that's a bit reductive?" he asks. "The problem with you all-"

"*You all?*" The protestor asks pointedly.

"Idealists," he says. "Extremists-"

"No," the protestor says,   "Fine. *Extremism*" he says.

"your addiction to-"   "never accounts for,"

"convenience is the-"   "complex interdependent"

"problem that——"   "variables of——"

I can't hear Mitchel anymore. Or the protestor. There's no sound at all. Only the protestor's face. Her eyes.

June 1977

gonna be hot today cadas've already started close my eyes I
can hear em better that way like green whirls inside yellow
balloons hardta tell what they're sayin cause they all talk at the
same time somthin bout a trip round the world Nathy'll know
but seems right cause their voices r fast n far n already gone
cross the ocean giant blue whales peekin one huge eye through
the water at the cada voices hummin on their way to Spain
where a girl pulls em into her dream bout zebras eatin licorice
n marshmallows now they're in China silk worms curlin up in
their little houses cause the cadas r chatterin bout whales n
licorice n little girls dreamin WHOOSH now the cadas r over
the ocean again ridin waves now swirlin round trees wrapped
in fog blankets makin em wake up laughin cause the cada
voices r tickly now they're over the mountains n rivers n farms
n schools closed for summer they're almost back cada voices
almost back inside em prolly why they sing in waves their
voices r all the way outside em flyin cross the entire world n
they haveta wait 'til they come back before they can sing again
gonna go with em this time round the world

breathe in   hold it   wait til they start   wait   NOW

huuuuuuuuummmmmmmuuuuummmmmmm

my voice goes with em I can see Nathy n old barn n Dolly the
grey horse n the dollar general but their voices r too far n too
fast for me n I don't have any hum left gonna try every
mornin hum for longer n longer so I can go round the whole
world with em

today feels tingly not just cause of the cadas it's somthin else
like a million pop rocks fizzin inside me that always means
somethin special's gonna happen not sure why special days

feel fizzy they just do best part is tryin to figure out what the
special thing is it's different every time almost missed the last
one cause the special thing didn't happen til almost dark when
I found a blue-black raven feather leanin on a post on the way
home from Nathy n old barn looked like the night poured
itself into a feather when no-one was lookin maybe so it could
see all the daytime things without folks makin a fuss bout it

daddy made pancakes for breakfast YUM with extra syrup he
got me a winnie the poo plate for my birthday so the scrapple
doesn't touch the syrup anymore he always knows what
people really want even before they do after breakfast he gives
me a ride to the end of the driveway

popcrrrrrucnhpoppopcrrrrrrunch we say laughin

we say it every time cause the pops n crunches r the best with
daddy's truck it has big tires cause he drives through the mud a
lot n even up hills it has a big pine tree painted on the side he
works for the forest he takes care of trees n the pee-dee river

daddy stops n winks as I get out he always winks n he always
says *home by dark* n I always say *yep* then he drives away
popopcrrrrunchpoppop I turn round momma's lookin out
the window she watches us when daddy lets me ride in the
truck up the driveway she watches us but she thinks we don't
know not sure if daddy does prolly does I pretend not to see
momma seein me n walk real slow n skim the fence with my
hand like I'm not thinkin bout anythin just walkin haveta be
careful now cause she can see round corners n through trees n
she's watchin me lots more lately maybe cause last week at
Sunday school I snuck out n went to Ohma's instead n now
momma's eyes can see round trees n haveta wait til I'm sure
she thinks I'm just playin with dandelions

Bronwen Carson

almost   almostalmost   YAY

I start skippin higher n higher one day I'll touch the first big
branch of the tulip tree not yet it's not the fizzy thing I can
tell so I just keep skippin makin sure to stay in the middle of
the road cause even though the coppers mostly stay near the
grass sometimes they think the middle's nice

I get to spend today at Ohma's daddy said so the special fizzy
thing's prolly gonna be there she knows everythin bout
everythin but she loves plants n trees n wild things the most
daddy took me to her in the spring cause I got a few real bad
wasp stings n he said she'd be able to fix em better than any
doctor he said she's saa laa gee n that meant she knows lots of
secret stuff we don't know when I asked him what saa laa gee
was he just kinda smiled a smile I hadn't seen before n said
they're the people who were here first a long time ago n then he said
somethin bout how they belong to the earth n don't try to be
on top of it daddy knows lots of stuff like that cause he was
supposed to be a tree but somthin got mixed up n he ended up
a person instead

trees know lots n they remember everythin what the air is
gonna be like tomorrow n what songs birds were singin on a
tuesday a zillion years ago whenever we're drivin round or
walkin if he sees a branch that fell or split off cause of a storm
he always picks it up n takes it home to make a chair or a
picture frame sometimes he makes little wood birds with
wings that flap or ones that twirl round n round

I was nervous on the wasp sting day after he said what he said
cause I was gonna meet a person who maybe was growin up
out of the ground like a tree n the only tree I know how to talk
to is Nathy sometimes other trees but mostly Nathy I forgot

18

all bout bein nervous when we got there   the smell along the
way to Ohma's were the ones that r always round   dust pine
straw horse n cow poo   but close to her house new smells
came in the windows   new n old too like a memory that might
be a memory or maybe just somewhere I'd been when I was
dreamin sweet n sharp n bright n soft n strong n there but also
not there   all at the same time   it made my heart feel too big to
stay inside up til then my favorite smells were waffles n
honeysuckle n the way lichen's kinda minty when it hasn't
rained in a while   but Ohma's place smelled different   like
magic not stupid made-up glitter n plastic unicorns but real
magic so green it's almost black but also pale n shimmery too
like birch leaves in winter

her front yard was a giant garden bigger than I'd ever seen n
mostly wild out of a fairy tale forest with little fairies n
creatures that disappear if you look right at em   there were
plants n flowers n little trees in groups different shapes n sizes
n colors some were spindly with wispy arms some were round
n happy with bright orange freckles some were tall n bushy
with little dark purple berries n ones that wound round the
ankles of all the others carryin secret messages between em
there were butterflies n bees too I even saw a purple n green
humminbird with yellow wings that was laughin at secret jokes
the whole time I told myself to be a humminbird next time

there were a bunch of birdhouses in the yard too seemed like
they were all over the place now I know there r exactly four n
they each have a meanin n r part of a secret saa laa gee world
bout truth n nature n directions one looks like an old red boat
one that looks mostly like a black mountain but also like a wolf
one painted white that looks like a bear holdin a ball one looks
like a round fat house but also like a bonfire that one's yellow
the birdhouses r faded but when I first saw em it seemed they

19

musta been real bright a long time ago I was wrong bout that
too now I know I mostly don't know most things but Ohma
says not knowin's good that you learn lots more that way I
love bein round her soso much sometimes it makes me wanna
cry n laugh at the same time

I go to Ohma's most every day in the summer n on weekends
if all my homework's done she tells me bout how plants that
grow wild next to each other balance each other like nettles n
jewelweed or sunflowers n thyme she always says nature is
balance n we haveta remember that cause we're part of it
though we don't act like it she says it's why the medicine goes
in four directions n that directions always depend on where
you start

up the path round the back to where she hangs plants n
flowers n roots to dry she makes all kinda teas n medicines
out of em on the wasp stings day she put some salve from a
little jar on em then ran the dull side of a small knife on my
arm n the stingers came right out I could feel my heart
poundin inside the stings but the salve cooled em down it
smelled real strong but not in a bad way just lemon-y n pine-y
kinda bitter it stained my skin yellow for a few days n that was
pretty neat later on I found out it was made outta chickweed
cottonwood sap dandelion witch leaves goldenseal chamomile
flowers n somthin called comfrey Ohma says seven is a special
number

run round to the screen door Ohma's talkin sometimes
fireball the cat comes round n she talks to him bout secrets n
the best places for huntin fireball likes me n I like him so he
won't mind but she's not talkin to him cause her voice sounds
different today maybe she's helpin someone like she helped
me with the wasps lots of people come to her for help with

different stuff I wait outside n listen momma says I have wolf
ears n that I hear everythin in the county I try not to but I
can't stop em my ears do what they wanna do n they don't
much mind if they're supposedta hear stuff r not so I mostly
just let em do what they do I don't know the words Ohma's
sayin though they're more like sounds wrappin round each
other heavy n smooth like the rocks along the river but also
fast n light like dandelion seeds then I hear another voice
talkin in the same way the other voice is like mine I tiptoe
away from the door cause Ohma hasn't seen me yet I crouch
next to the window listenin to em n tryin see if I can figure
what they're sayin get real still but the fizzies r fillin my belly
with bees Ohma says somethin the other voice giggles   I
peek through the window n on the other side is a girl with huge
walnut-colored eyes lookin right at me n smilin a real big smile
like we've been friends a long time I know right away she's the
special fizzy thing Ohma chuckles at us n waves for me to
come in my stomach feels flip-floppy gonna meet a real-life
magical pixie

Ohma smiles at me then at the pixie then she says

   Maggie this is Dana

2

I look at the protester's eyes. I hear something ringing far away. Like a cellphone stuffed in a down jacket or car alarm in another borough. But it's me. Deep in my brain. Ringing, then spreading like ice water. Numbing my vocal cords. Flooding my veins like—

"M-Magpie?" she asks.

Then nothing. No ringing, no wind, no voices in protest, no traffic, no buildings, no ground, no Brooklyn, no me. Just a space where the world used to be, and my childhood nickname suspended in the air as if it's always been here, waiting for the years to pass—so we could finally catch up to it, waiting inside this moment. My heart doesn't seem to be able to pick a rhythm. But my eyes are steady. They watch her lower her sign.

"Maggie............***Morris***?" her voice asks.
My name doesn't sound right.

breathe Maggie Morris

My lungs pull in air. I tell the air leaving them to make sounds that make up the word that belongs to her.

"Dana." I meant it as a question but maybe she's transcended punctuation. Maybe the air leaving my lungs understands this.

"Mags? You okay? You're kinda—you look like you might..." That was Mitchel's voice. It bounces around in my head.

Mags?   *her eyes*
stones   *you okay?*   *likewalnuts*
      feathers   *okay you?*
kindaMags   *sparklers*
       youlookyoumight

I'm just a husk in the shape of someone called Maggie Morris, question mark, so even though this moment's been waiting for us to arrive, I'm not ready. Growth that was meant to happen so this moment could fit, or I could fit into it, hasn't happened. And any second now Dana's going to know it.

"I, uh, sorry. I-this is Dana," I sputter.

Mitchel's eyebrows knit into a caterpillar. I have the urge to laugh but if I start, I won't stop. I'll laugh until my corpse is donated as research. The woman who laughed inappropriately, and to death.

Dana's eyes are waiting.

"This is Mitchel" I add, "he-we-we work together at, uhm …"

Her eyes nod. I'm sure they're attached to her face, but they look suspended. Two glossy, sentient walnut-colored orbs, looking and nodding. Then they look over to the protest group. They're all watching us, shifting awkwardly as confusion and hypothermia battle it out under their eco-conscious hemp hats.

"I just need to…" she says, then walks over to them.

she's gonna leave

Mitchel scoots next to me. "Scale of one to ten, how freaked out are you right now?"

she's leaving

The protesters gather around her.

"So, that would be a ten then," he says.

again leaving again

Dana passes her sign to a tall woman hunkered deeply into an ankle length muddy green coat, wearing a green beanie. Dylan would've called the woman 'my asparagus', but she looks more like a sea cucumber to me.

Dylan's my—I don't know. He's Dylan. He ended up living with me not unlike a stray dog following someone home. He's a model—though he loathes being referred to as one. His real self (according to him) is life guru. I should have ended things the first time he said it. Proclamations about one's unicorn-level expertise, or self-realizations are always a little creepy. When we first started dating, the things he'd say sounded like jokes. Like deadpan ironic wit. Then, I realized he wasn't joking. I'm convinced our still being together can be chalked up to my overall laziness at life, and his believing my lack of fawning means I'm a deeply wise, magnificent creature underneath it all. Silly man.

"Hey, Mags," Mitchel says, nudging me, "hey ..."

oh right   not dreaming   actually happening

I look over at Dana and the sea cucumber, their heads leaning toward one other with unconscious ease. Emotional shorthand. A tidepool of spiky, oily things stirs in my stomach.

"I know you're spooked," Mitch continues, "but you need to snap out of it. This is your chance. Right?"

I've only mentioned Dana once to Mitchel that I can recall. During our getting to know the me I want you to see phase of friendship—the time when divulging catalytic moments in one's past as a way of appearing more interesting than one is. Not much makes me interesting outside of my childhood relationship with a Cherokee girl in my town and how one night she disappeared.

Dana leans closer to the sea cucumber, whose eyes snap to me, scanning for something. Evidence of worthiness probably. Dana gives her a kiss. This green beanie wearing Big Green Fracking Fools sign carrying person is in Dana's life. Dana has people in her life she's close to. She's slept and eaten and gotten sick and travelled and painted protest signs. Maybe loved people. Maybe hated some. The few times I've let her drift to the surface of my mind has been as a gauzy image of a girl through a window, with walnut-colored eyes, smiling.

The protesters unfurl, releasing Dana and resuming their kick line of watery thought grenades. As Dana walks back to us, the streetlamp banners and trees lining Bridge Park thrash and shudder behind her. It must be windy. I don't feel it. I think I hear it, but it doesn't sound right. The narrow streets of

Dumbo often make the wind sound like wailing—an immense saudade waiting in the periphery.

"Jesus," Mitchel whispers aggressively, "Pull it together. Life just handed you a win. How many times have you said you just wanted to know what happened?"

"I never said that."

Mitchel's eyebrows levitate. I ignore him. I don't want to think about stupid things I've said while drunk. Tonight holds great possibility for a repeat performance in that regard. I'll have to be careful. Drink just enough to seem relaxed. Just enough to wear my happy-go-lucky Maggie coat. Just enough to seem glad to see her. I don't know why I'm not actually glad to see her.

Dana approaches, wrapping her violet scarf snugly around her neck and ears, offering a tentative smile. "Would you want to maybe—?"

"Get a drink?" Mitchel pipes in, "Yes, Lord, please. Absolutely a get a drink moment in time, no?" He looks at me, green eyes insistent. Even though curiosity is driving him nuts, he's also offering me a mental perimeter. His southern roots, although the cause of a substantial amount of emotional damage, also instilled an impeccable ability to identify landmines.

Dana's waiting. She's very still, like one of those ancient trees on the Olympic Peninsula. Old growth. A glorious, strong, ancient, all-knowing redwood, looking at me, the husk in clown shoes.

she's starting to see it
starting to wonder
do something
something people do

I tell my mind to tell my neck to tell my head to nod. Mitchel's concerned brow smooths.

"Excellent! We were headed to the Zombie Hut."

"In Carroll Gardens?" Dana asks.

"You know it?" I ask, proud of a renewed ability to speak as the humans do.

Dana nods but looks confused.

"Nice!" Mitchel intercedes, "Mags, and I live near there—I mean in the neighborhood. We both live in the neighborhood."

After 9/11, I didn't want to live in Tribeca anymore. It felt too observed—a giant held breath of soot and snuffed out lives the city would never entirely be able to exhale. So, I joined a growing obstinacy of ex-pat buffalos grazing in gauzy-angered formations along the buckling sidewalks, artisanal cheese boutiques, renovated brownstones, and cramped subway platforms of Carroll Gardens, Brooklyn.

"Me too" Dana says.

wait what? me too what?

wait that's not poss--how long? howcouldshe howcouldwenot

The high-pitched buzz in my brain is back.

"No!" Mitchel exclaims. "Really? You hear that Mags? What are the odds?"

"So weird," I say.

whatthehellisgoingonrightnow?

"Got to love BoCoCa!" Mitchel laughs.

Mitchel saying BoCoCa is disturbing. We share a hatred of neighborhood acronyms. Almost as much as portmanteau couple names. The overall cool kids club about them.

It's quiet again. They're waiting. Mitchel, for a clear yes or no.

Dana, for an explanation of why her childhood friend champions rapacious planet destroyers.

Over the years, each time the girl with walnut eyes drifted through my mind, she became less of a real human, more a representation of misplaced possibilities. Now she's standing four feet away, nose running from the cold. Like she's some kind of person or something. One who is waiting for me to be or do or say something. Just like Mitchel. Just like my knees, and pancreas, and prefrontal cortex. All waiting. So, I nod.

"Excellent! I'll book an Uber." Mitchel says as Dana and I exchange glances.

say something

"So," I say.

Dana's eyes flick to the sea cucumber, then back to me, her hesitant smile scratching my enamel, reminding me we too were once inseparable.

"So weird," she says, picking up where I stalled, "and-"

"Shit!" Mitchel mutters. "45 minutes"

"There must be somewhere closer," Dana says.

"Well, we usually—"

"Mitchel and I don't do afterwork in this area. We uphold the separation of church and state," I say, determined not to slip back into the peripheral saudade.

"So, would that make the Zombie Hut church or state?" Dana chuckles.

"Definitely church." Mitchel says.

"Let me try," I say, pulling my phone out.

"Maggie has special ..." Mitchel says.

"...connections," I add.

The momentary reappearance of our banter revives me.

okay you can do this

just an old friend

just Dana

    like walnuts

who suddenly disappeared one night

                    feathers

who never wrote or called

                              sparklersparklers

who was fine all along

I look at my phone, hoping Mercury himself will inhabit my Uber app and manifest a damn car.

just a little sign that tonight isn't going to be...shit
"45 minutes" I say.

With a collective acceptance of defeat, we murmurate towards Water Street—not toward the subway (out of the 472 MTA stations, only 135 are disability accessible and neither York nor High Street are on that list). It's just after 7 so we might be able to snag a cab dropping off patrons of the arts who prefer St. Ann's Warehouse over Broadway.

"CAB!" Mitchel yells. "Hey! Hey, hey! CAB!"

The cab he's spotted is a block away. I take off towards it. Despite the belief every New Yorker is capable of a screeching whistle that can cross the Atlantic...

whales

           silkworms   *cicadas*

...no-one here actually does that. We yell.

"HEY! HEY! CAB! CAB!" I scream, waving my arms.

The cab grinds to a halt. A surge of conquering hero floods me. I turn to wave Mitchel and Dana over, but they're already on their way, effortlessly chatting as if they're the long-lost friends in this scenario.

oh let me make you laugh haha
oh aren't you just so charmed and laughing hahaha
I get into the cab.

"You gotta close the door, lady."

"My friends are coming."

"Uh-huh, I gotta start the meter, lady."

"Okay"

"Where to?"

yeahwell that's the question isn't it

"Lady, where?" The cabbie repeats.

corner of awkward and make it stop

"Lady—"

"Carroll Gardens. Sackett and Smith"

I pop my head out to check their progress. They're only a few yards away. My voice yells "Here, Mitchel, here!"

He gives me his *stop acting crazy* look as Dana slips into the middle seat, taking his canes and setting them next to her as if she's been doing so for decades. Mitchel eases into the far window seat next to her.

The cab takes off, the NY1-sponsored mini television blaring at us. I hug the door, anchoring my left elbow into my spleen. Just an inch of space. If she touches my arm, I'll scream.

"So, you were saying, five years," Mitchel says.

"Uh-huh," Dana replies.

"That's nuts! I mean, isn't that nuts, Mags? She's been on Degraw and Court five years!"

Dana glances at me. Maybe she's curious if I think it's nuts.

"Yeah. If nuts were, you know, a gryphon" I say.

She chuckles, warm and genuine. It makes me feel like I'm wearing my skin inside out.

"Of all the gin joints," I add pithily.

"In all the towns..." Mitchel pauses so Dana can finish the quote. Silence, followed by Mitchel again. "No? Really?"

"Sorry," Dana says flatly.

"You know. Casablanca?"

"I've heard of it"

"What is happening right now?" He demands. "How have you not seen Casablanca?"

so what if she hasn't seen Casablanca
she's been held hostage in an alternate dimension
without punctuation   or phones   or email

I should turn. Face her. Seem here. Engaged. Normal. But we're too close as it is, so all I can do is tilt and rotate my head, peering sideways, my elbow edging towards splenectomy.

"I never met anyone who hasn't seen Casablanca," Mitchel continues, unable to let it go.

"No-one?" She asks.

"Guess I should reevaluate my circle of acquaintances. Diversify. Bring some protesters into the mix"

"You should. Protesters are—" Dana starts.

"The spinach of the human world!" Mitchel quips.

the spinach of the what?

someone's a Pepper tonight isn't he?

stop it just be happy   be normal   be—

Dana laughs.

just a husk   just a husk   just a husk

NY1 takes over with "Now it's time for weather on the ones. Bundle up because it's going to be a frosty one. A cold snap is moving in with overnight lows dropping into the teens. The seven-day forecast—"

Mitchel mutes the volume. "You guys mind?"

"No, that'd be great," Dana says.

"Fine by me!" I say jovially.

Mitchel looks at me, eyebrows raised. He chuckles. I'm not in the mood to share in his amusement, so I turn and look through the window to a frosty bleakness that seems warmer than this overstuffed, overheated Prius prison. He can continue his infatuation over Dana with her huge walnut-colored eyes and her warm, easy voice. Her innate ability to know how to take his canes without seeming tactless or fussy. I look at him.

*hey, you're **my** friend, right?*

His eyes cloud over before turning to his window. Dana looks out the front windshield. I dig my elbow harder into my side. Other than tires crunching road salt and the scorched recirculation of Little Trees Black Ice air freshener and fabric embedded farts, the cab is deathly quiet.

My hands feel weird. Balloon-y. I glance at them. They're regular hand sized.

five four three two one   five four three two one

It's not working. I'll have to do the whole rigamarole.

FIVE things I can see
Cobble Hill Cinemas   stop light   The Chocolate Room
person walking Labradoodle   K&Y Market
Dana and Mitchel are chatting again, amicable. Unforced.
"Have you eaten at Stan's yet?" he asks.
"More of a Buddy's Burritos gal," she says.
"Aw, no, no! You have to go into Stan's! At least once. I
mean, for a real, old-school Brooklyn…"
FOUR things I can feel
seam of my coat   ridges of the rubber floor mat
pins and needles in my legs   cold metal seeping into my arm
"What about you Maggie?" Dana asks me.
"I'm sorry?" I ask.
"Favorite local restaurant?" she says. She's trying to
include me. She did that when we were kids too. I think.
"I, uhm, Buttermilk Channel," I say.
"Oh man," Mitchel says, "the—
"Rum banana pudding," the three of us say.
THREE things I can hear
Mitchel laughing bwaahaaaahhaaa
Dana laughing huuhuuhuuhhahaa
Maggie laughing ha-ha
We turn onto Smith Street.
finally

****

The Zombie Hut is a cross between a 1980's basement
game room and the Tiki Hut from Disneyland. Places like this
don't pick up until 10 p.m. when the young ones are on their
way home from 80 hour-a-week internships or disastrous dates.
Most come for the stiff drinks like the Gilligan (described on
the menu as "Rum, Rum, and Vodka") and retro board games

like Connect Four and Boggle. It's also a three stumble-drunk minute walk from my loft.

We search the empty tables, the question of where three people should sit in an almost vacant bar on par with splitting the atom.

"How about…?" I point to a table near the fake fire pit with a nice amount of distance between the seats. Perfect accommodations for unreconcilable force fields.

"Excellent choice, ma'am" Mitchel says, leaning heavily into his Mississippi roots.

Dana nods. "Sure". She glances at me, half smiles. The ringing in my head starts again.

click clack click clack

say something

     sprinklers

say something   *oak tree*

old barn   *feathers*

          her mom

say something   *sparklers*

"My treat" Mitchel says edging towards the bar where Drew, the latest in a string of would-be actors paying the bills by bartending is trying to memorize a script. "How often do you get to witness a reunion 40 years in the making?"

I motion for Dana to go first.

"Decaf if they have it," she says.

Mitchel's disappointed. "Come on. Not even a little nip of the good stuff after braving Shackleton's backyard?"

Dana shakes her head "Just decaf."

"Decaf it is." He looks at me, raising his eyebrows.

"Bulleit," I say. "Double"

"Now that, ma'am, is something I can support."

He heads to the bar to order as Dana and I spiral through smiling, breathing in, breathing out, and looking at the fake fire. We're probably both wondering if, after a 40-year hiatus, light chit chat or bone marrow extraction are our only options. I focus on the fire, imagining tonight's scenarios.

> a.   We admit we don't know what to say at precisely the same time, kick starting the Coca-Cola version of our reunion where we stay 'til closing, laughing and bonding then walk the neighborhood impervious to the cold, then finally, at dawn, we'll grab pancakes at Cobble Hill Coffeeshop.
> b.   We exchange awkward half sentences of excruciating small talk until option number three takes effect.
> c.   I drink my way into the easy-going personality that will last for a golden ten-to-fifteen minutes before I'm obnoxiously drunk and say stupid things.

Dana's looking at me, a funny little crooked smile on her face—amused, and a bit distant. "You still do that, huh?" she asks.

"Do what?" I ask, trying to match her ease, but landing on snippy. The warmth in her eyes slips behind a wall of courtesy.

wait   come back

"So Degraw?" I ask.

She nods, "Between Smith and Court."

"So weird," I say.

She nods. "And you're on?"

"Down Sackett, near Hoyt."

"I can't believe we haven't-"

"It's weird we haven't-" she says. We laugh and for a moment it seems we're both glad to be here, the Coca-Cola version of tonight almost within reach.

"So, uhm, is that your first NY place or ..." I trail off.

"Oh, no. I was in Hell's Kitchen for a few years but-"

"Oh man, Hell's Kitchen. No thanks!" I blurt. "Too crowded. And what's with them never being done working on Ninth Ave?"

She chuckles. "Yeah. That's why I left."

"The waltz of the jackhammers," I add.

"Yeah, I can't imagine you there. I actually can't believe you're here. With all the, you know, the sounds and smells and all the neon. This is the last place I ever imagined you."

I don't know what to say to that. Our Coca-Cola version stalls. I catch her checking on Mitchel's return. My guard slips back into place.

"I'm just going to help Mitch with the drinks" I say.

"Okay," she says.

She's unreadable and unfamiliar. I try to dip into my memory. Try to remember how she was, but it was so long ago. Memories of memories of what the world was like when I was nine. What Dana was like when she was nine.

fast

running   *pineoakcedarhemlock*

funny

           funnel cake   *rolypoly sparklers*

nice to me

                              the waywayback

I think   yeah she was nice to me

crunch berries

my best friend

til she wasn't

I join Mitchel.

"Hey Maggie," Drew puts our drinks on the bar.

"Hey Drew," I say, shooting my double bourbon.

aaaandawaaaayweeeego

one more or three or four

poor broken Maggie

don't let her see it

"Okay then," Mitchel says, chuckling.

"Yeah, and thanks for nothing in the cab, Sparky," I reply, motioning for Drew for another double bourbon.

"Wow. Okay, then. So, this is how you're gonna play it? If you want me gone, I'll go." He adds to Drew, "hey bud, I'll settle up."

"No. Wait. Mitch, wait. I'm just—I'm wigging right now, okay? And it's just, you guys hit it off and I was the idiot third wheel, and it's weird."

My hands are pasted together again. My doll hands.

always ready for a shelf
or a book
maybe a taco
definitely another bourbon

"Mags, hey." He pulls the second double away from me. "I'm trying to help, you know. With the stifling tension? I mean, you need to lighten up a little. Aren't you glad to see her?"

"Sure, course I am." I say, retrieving my double and downing it. I signal Drew for another pour. He obliges.

I can feel Dana's eyes on me. I don't care. I need some goddamn help right now. I down the third double and motion for Drew to pour one more. The tools and habits of consolation. We do what we can. So, what if it's not pretty or enlightened. So damn what. We grab the buoy that's closest. That's all. I down my fourth one. Motion for a fifth. This one I'll sip.

I'm not sure Mitchel has ever seen me lose my cool about anything. He's got that look you see when people drive past a terrible accident. Horrified and ravenous.

We carry our drinks back to the table, the slow warmth of four double bourbons sliding me from fifth to neutral. I can coast now. Maggie-the-Jolly will be accessible soon.

It's difficult to describe, and I don't talk about it, not even with Mitchel, but I've always felt human*ish*. Which sounds bad. But it's not. Not really. It's more a reliance on behavioral osmosis to fit in. Adderall helps, but for my easy-go-lucky Maggie coat to slide on, booze is required. It's not that my different Maggie coats are fake. They're just a series of shapes and sentences. Patterns of ease I've never inherently felt around people.

I set Dana's decaf down. "Sorry I've been so weird, it's just surreal that you're here. Cream? Sugar?"

"I'm good with black."

"It's no trouble. We practically pay rent here, right Mitch?"

"We're looking at paint swatches tomorrow." Mitchel replies.

I turn to Drew. "Hey, can I get some creamers and sugar?" Then back to Dana. "I can't believe you're here! Whenever I think of you it's always in a magical fairy forest"

I'm in the zone now. Fluid navigation.

Drew sets sugar and creamers down next to Dana.

"Thanks," she says, leaving them untouched.

"Oh, wait, wait!" I say, "Drew! We need a fork!" I can hear my voice. It's too loud. But I've found a thread. A funny moment. A way to move from adjacent to incorporated.

"And we have lift off" Mitchel says, chuckling. Dana chuckles too. They're already establishing little private 'isn't Maggie crazy' jokes.

I had plans to pierce the creamer lid foil. One of my Polaroid memories of childhood was of going to Murphy's diner with Dana and my father for waffles. He'd turned his creamer upside down over his coffee and squeezed it saying "mooooooo, mooooooo, mooooooo" to make us laugh. And we did.

She probably wouldn't remember that anyway. When Drew returns with the fork, I leave it untouched, but Dana looks at it then me. I think see her eyebrows twitch and take a sip of my bourbon.

Dana sips her decaf. Mitchel sips his Patrón Añejo.

"So," I say with my hollow too loud voice, "tell me everything! 40 years. Go! Are you working here? No. That's not—you wouldn't—but maybe you would?"

"I. Uhm. Yeah, I do work here. I'm a journalist with the—"

"I'm so confused! Tell me everything!"
slow down

"Wow. Dana. Dana Walden. How long has it been?"
slow down let her answer

"Almost 40 years," she says.

"Right. After the Firefly Festival," I say. A black hole opens in the floor. That was the night Dana's mom died. You don't forget something like that. Though I had let it drift to a valley I never visit.
stupid idiot Maggie

"Oh my God, Mitchel," I say trying to redirect, "my hometown has a festival for everything. Fireflies, fiddlin', pimento cheese."

"Cool," he says, his eyes landing on Dana.

"And the ArtDayz Festival! With a z. I come from a town that has Art Dayz with a "z"! Not d-a-z-e. D-a-y-z! Don't tell anyone. Especially Chelsea."

"Uhm. Okay," he says.

"I always loved ArtDayz," Dana says, her face unreadable.

"Right," I say, "of course. Your mom made those incredible—"

"Toboggans?" Mitchel asks. "Weathervanes? Snausages? Little saucies? Dream Catchers?"

"That would be more Ojibwe than Tsalagi," Dana says.

Mitchel's not listening anymore. He's kicked into avert-the-awkward mode and when that kicks in there's no stopping him. "Pogo sticks? Mittens? Kaleidoscopes? Hand pies? Oh man, those are good! Because it's a pie. That fits in your hand!"

"Oh, man!" I join in. "Cherry. Oh, no, wait, lemon!"

Dana smiles. We're being asses, and she's still trying. But four and a half double bourbons and happy-go-lucky Maggie is strapped to a formula one racecar with no brakes.

I continue, "And don't forget savory!" Man, I'm hungry. Who's hungry?" I'm not, but I grab the menu anyway. "Oh my God. Come on! What are the odds?" My voice echoes through the bar.

don't care   grab the buoy

"What?" Mitchel asks.

I point to the menu.

"OH MY GOD!" Mitchel yells, "Dana, you hand-pie medicine woman!" He points to the menu. *NEW* HOT POCKETS.

I cringe.

Dana's smile compresses. "She made birdhouses." Her voice is quiet, a distant rumble. I down my bourbon and wave to Drew for another.

Bronwen Carson

September 1977

if you listen, they'll tell you what they need
same for snake and bird and wolf   same for people

her dark brown eyes lookin at mine to make sure I'm listenin
I nod n sit down facin the plant she wants me to listen to she
picks up her basket n walks to the other side of the yard where
Dana's waitin by another plant Dana'll know what to do right
away cause she's good at everythin I don't mind she's funny n
she's nice n she doesn't think I'm stupid just cause I don't talk
much her voice is clear but never loud n she likes to find
stones n feathers too she waves I wave back Dana's my
second best friend after Nathy

Ohma looks at me n nods her head Dana giggles n frowns n
gives me a finger wag til Ohma turns round Dana's the only
one who can make me laugh at myself Nathy makes me laugh
all the time but with him I'm a tree too so it's different

Ohma's lookin at me n waitin so I look at my plant I look at it
for a long time til there's nothin but the plant then I look at
the spots she wants me to figure out, but I can't hear what the
plant is sayin bout the spots I try to think what Ohma would
do she'd wait til the plant was ready to talk so I wait n wait n
wait

the sun creeps from the back of my neck to the top of my head
I stand up n walk round the plant my legs feel cold n prickly
like ice tea drippin inside em cause I was sittin for too long

never said hi

momma's always tellin me starin's rude

hi sorry I should'a said hello I'm Maggie you can call me
Magpie if you want what's your name?

the plant doesn't say anythin

you don't have to tell me only if you wanna

the plant stays quiet

what's wrong? you can tell me it's okay you can tell me promise I
won't tell anyone I'll just help okay? if you want

I listen hard but only hear the trees rustlin at the edge of the
yard they sound like the river on stormy days it makes me
think of Nathy I wish I could ask him he'd know what the
spots are

I'm just gonna check your leaves okay? that okay?

I touch one of the brown spotty leaves turnin it real soft to
look under I sit back down n listen for a long time but the
plant won't tell me what's wrong I can feel Dana lookin at me
she's sendin purply silver thoughts to me I try to pull em in n
send em to the plant so it'll trust me I hear Ohma's footsteps
behind me way up inside my nose stings she sits down I can't
stop the tears from spillin n I'm mad that they keep comin

I'm sorry it won't tell me it doesn't trust me

I say it so quiet I'm not sure it made it outside me she lets me
cry doesn't try to stop me or hug me she doesn't say stuff to
make me feel different she just waits til I'm done but not like
how momma does like how momma's eyes r like burnt eggs
when I'm not smilin

Dana knows I'm cryin but she doesn't think it's a big deal or somethin to hide she even said last week her momma gets real sad sometimes n that you can't ever make sad leave cause sad stays til it has somewhere else to be that people never want sad around but that shouldn't be sad's fault I told her that made a lotta sense

Ohma waits til I'm done cryin then starts to talk quiet next to me but doesn't look at me it's my favorite way to talk n hear

> *many times looking can help but looking can make listening difficult cause eyes can be too loud not as loud as voice but almost eyes think they know and voice knows it knows plants and trees have quieter voices then ours they don't say anything they don't mean through and through take your eyes and voice away and it's easier to hear*

she never talks to me like I'm dumb like at school she just waits I can hear Nathy all the time but maybe that's different maybe he's the only one I can hear n maybe it's not even cause of me but cause of him he's real old n maybe that makes his voice clearer maybe everyone can hear him a little jolt zings through my belly I send Nathy a little thought message that I'm comin by later to see him then I try to just think bout the plant but my eyes keep lookin over at Dana she's sittin crossleg next to her plant she looks at me n smiles makes a goofy face it makes me want to cry even more so I look down at my shoes the ends of my laces have little redbrown hats on from draggin in the mud the little hats are kinda funny n they make me feel better

Ohma leans in n talks quiet to me n the plant one of the things I like bout Ohma is her voice it's never crunchy or spiky it never makes me want to back away

*their voices are part of everything else part of everything around
them that's how you'll know listen then you'll understand
how to help*

I nod but don't look at her

but don't they know what to do

Ohma has a few different smiles some are answers n some are
questions n some are bout knowin secrets she only has one big
smile when all of her is bein sent to all of you she's smilin the
big one right now it makes my throat lumpy

*yes they know it's us we forget remembering takes time listen
helps remember wake up when we don't listen we try to make
plant do what we want maybe it's okay at first but plant won't
go against its nature for long*

stuff she says always makes sense

*like when we cut 'em into shapes?
why do folks do that? don't they know it hurts the plant?*

Ohma smiles the smile I haven't figured out yet

folks sometimes have a hard time leaving things to be what they are

*I don't wanna be like that Ohma I wanna be like you how
do I know if I'm bein like the people who don't leave things
alone?*

*you just need to listen and watch my little tsi s qua learn to
understand other voices*

plant voices?

she nods n smiles

each plant has their own and also a deeper one they share
with everything else understand?

I nod

take away look take away talk just listen

I close my eyes to listen at first all I can hear is myself breathin
air whistlin in n out my nose it doesn't sound dark blue like
Nathy likes it sounds grey like used up gum I try to float
outside my used up gum breathin sound I start to hear other
sounds bright green n yellow cicadas the trees like rushin
water a cardinal peep peepin squirrels chasin each other
engines whirrin faraway but I still can't hear the plant tears r
back makin eyes blurry somethin must be missin inside me n
the plant knows it

Ohma takes my hand n puts it on the ground I usually don't
like it when someone touches me specially if my eyes r closed
just always been that way but Ohma's more like air or water
like somethin already goin its own direction n you can come
along if you want but it's also okay if you dont she starts to
talk quiet again

listen is not just sounds listen is finding what's there when look
and talk are quiet listen is good friends with smell and touch
what do you feel when you touch the leaf? when you touch the
ground? what do you smell?

I touch the ground it's pebbly n grainy like sandpaper daddy
uses on walnut branches n the ground's dry even though we
soaked it this mornin I take a deep smellin breath in the mint
plant I've been tryin to understand is there but also somethin

else somethin sort of like how our attic smells in summer I touch the leaves some are strong n firm but others are a little floppy n have dust on em I smell the dust yep like old attic I open my eyes n look at my finger it has yelloworange dust on it I hold it out for Ohma she's smilin her smile bout knowin secrets

what should we do?

I look round the yard for a minute

maybe mint shouldn't be here? but where should it live? not near the sunflowers or tomatoes n not near the black walnut tree nothin grows there cept the black walnut tree cause he laughs too loud at his own jokes

near the birdhouse Dana's momma made the one that looks like a bear there's chives n coriander over there that's where it should be I point over to the spot

there right? but

yes?

if we move mint now won't it take the yellow dust with it?

yes tsi s qua before we move mint we'll try to help get rid of the yellow dust before it turns orange then black sometimes we can help sometimes we can't mint will decide

but why do we help if the plant decides?

she smiles again

remember how I said folks like to change things?

I nod

and how sometimes those changes force things out of balance? it's our responsibility to help rebalance things

I nod again but I'm not sure exactly what she means

if you spill something at home do you clean it up or leave it?

I can feel myself gettin red cause mostly if I spill somethin momma cleans it up for me now if I make a mess I'm gonna clean it up myself

3

Clunk Foooomp
Whump......glug, glug, glug, glug, glug
Dylan's in the kitchen. Trying to be quiet.
Clenk clenk clenk
Maybe I'll take the day off from opening my eyes. Or
getting up. Maybe there's a point for some people. People who
have meaning. Like protesters.
Clenk clenk Ffffap
I'll open them after Dylan's gone. Although, when that
might be is impossible to know. Sometimes he's gone for a
week in the Maldives for a shoot, sometimes he spends entire
days at home, micro-exfoliating, and testing Pu-Erh teas.
I slept on the couch again. And, from the rows of cable knit
skin welts marching across my chest, last night's clothes are still
on. I smell like clove cigarettes. I haven't smoked a clove since
I was in Jr. High. I try to recall when cloves came into play last
night. A big swirling whirlpool of who the hell knows shrugs
back. I don't even know how I got home. Maybe the whole
thing was a dream.

click clack click clack

Dana wasn't standing in front of our building, holding a
protest sign.

hemlock groves

The three of us didn't go to the Zombie Hut and make
excruciating small talk as I drank too much. A wave of nausea
ripples through me.

not a dream

"Someone's id had fun last night," Dylan whispers from
an entirely too close a proximity.

you bet   *birdhouse*

                          water

tons   *mist*   *feather*

I keep my eyes shut, hoping he'll get the hint. He places a mug gently on the table, an 'I'm disappointed in your choices' slathered across his soft sigh, swirling with the heavenly smell of coffee.

A too bright, fuzzy living room emerges. I offer him a faded smile of gratitude while rotating myself to a half-seated position. Another wave of nausea hits. I ease back down, resting the mug on my chest, sipping with as little movement as possible. He chose my Trogdor the Burninator mug. I'm not sure if that means he gets me to a degree I never thought possible, or it's another instance of Dylan-gets-it-right without trying or knowing. Hard to say.

He pads over to the spot in the loft where a shaft of light filters through the window every morning. Despite the thin, grey morning light, a warm halo blooms around him. Even the light adores him. Not that I blame it. He's a touched by the Gods kind of beautiful. I'm neither stunning nor touched by any god. Maybe Antaeus. Or Ariadne. He begins his daily advanced Vinyasa flow, his God-like body moving with perfect form. It's deeply annoying.

cloves   *smoke*

mist

mint

call me we'll have lunch

I inch halfway into the vertical plane, releasing the trapped smell of stale Djarum, bourbon and panic sweat. A grinding throb pushes behind my eyes.

hair of the dog it is

Thirty minutes later I'm looking at my amorphous, gauzy reflection in the steamed-up bathroom sink mirror. It's just an optical illusion; the bending of light by vaporized water. But it seems my true visage is being revealed. The blur of a once-person absorbed by the air and people around her until she was almost gone. Fully gone would have been better.

Sounds begin to tumble forward. Memories too full and dams too cracked to hold them. Children laughing. Hushed voices. Something like water.

I wipe my hand across the mirror. It's what they do in movies. Wipe their hand across the mirror. My rigid, joyless face looks back.

there you are

****

I decided to go to work. Better than spending the day with a lugubrious reflection reminding me I'm barely an almost. It's now 9:30 and I'm in line for a coffee at my usual cart, reinforcing myself for a day of more intern interviews. I'm on a call with the big honcho of big oil, trying to resist rip tides.

All morning I've been trying to fill the gaps in last night's drunken debacle. Imagine a different, better me who made different, better choices. I'm not sure what choices I made, but I know they weren't good. That's a given.

After a few minutes of searching through last night, it seems The Firefly Festival moment was the turn of the tide. I keep trying to imagine scenarios where I said something kind or profound. Something that built a bridge between us. But I didn't. I went on an infodump jag about Hot Pockets. I remember Dana saying "birdhouses." After that, things get interpretive. I think I remember a conversation about dogs or maybe puppies. No idea.

The one thing I remember with any clarity is her eyes seemed to get bigger and bigger until they swallowed me, Mitch, The Zombie Hut, and all of Brooklyn whole. Then I woke up smelling like clove cigarettes, and now I'm here, getting coffee like I always do, talking to a capitalistic greed monger about how to make more money. Like I always do.

Wondering if it will now be another 40 years before I see Dana Walden again because I flushed my chance.

you could call her   or wait on her corner
act surprised to run into her
great plan   stalker

"BLAH, BLUH-BLAH, WAH-WAH!" Everything Big honcho says is underscored and capitalized. "WHA-AWU-HWAH-WAH!"

"I understand," I interject having no clue what he's said, "but-if I may——"

"WHAH-WAH, BLUH-WAH, WEEH WAH?"

I suppress a growing urge to respond as Charlie Brown's teacher. "Mr. Pittman, I'm sorry, I have Branson calling. I'll need to call you back this afternoon."

"WU-WUR-WIH-RANRUN?"

no you bloviated basilisk   not really

"WEHL WUHWEXWING WUHWOO WEWAILS-"

"And I hate to disappoint. I'll call at four with some ideas I know you'll like. Does that work for you?"

bow   kneel   scrape   vomit

He sighs dramatically, "WHYN," hanging up as if the deprivation of his voice is a punishment.

"Can't wait," I say to the boop-boop-boop.

"Uhm, *hellllloooh*," a snippy voice says. I turn to find pinch-faced lawyer from the Death Star glowering at me.

"Yeah, yeah, Hot Pockets," I say, "you're very busy and important."

I turn back to the cart to retrieve my order. Even the cart owner—despite my never conversing with beyond a coffee order, yet who has always seemed an extremely patient person—is looking at me with confused exhaustion. I hand him $5 for what will be my fourth coffee of the day and head into the building.

In the elevator, the same infotainment loop from last night plays. It doesn't seem possible. Last night's contents belong to an alternate timeline. Or Schrödinger's cat. And now we all know I'm dead because the box is open. Dana opened it. She'd asked if we could have lunch at beginning of the night. I don't remember exactly what I said. Something yes*ish*. But after things took a turn somewhere after my fourth double, she probably changed her mind.

Once I'm in my office, I pull down the shades. Despite few things making the rabble fall back into grey-green powdery lines like florescent overhead lighting, the last thing I need today is a cacophony of natural light coruscating the corners of my barren soul. I regard my wall of mirrors and windows. They're just two-dimensional reflective surfaces. No magical powers of revelation.

"I never understood why you collect those things."

Mitchel's in my office. I didn't hear him knock. Maybe he didn't. Maybe he was here when I walked in. Bumping into Dana after all these years, finding out we've been living in the same eight square blocks for five years, has uncovered a glaringly inadequate ability to notice basic atmospheric information.

"Oh, uh, hey," I say.

"I mean, how many people, you know, have looked through them or into them?" He looks at them warily. "That are probably dead now."

One of the vestiges of Mitchel's Mississippi heritage is a firm belief in hauntings. Sometimes, when we're watching *Supernatural*, he'll soberly recount experiences with the tormented ghost of a fourteen-year-old boy who drowned, or, as Mitchel believes, was murdered in a bayou near his grandfather's house. I've always thought he secretly believes his grandfather murdered the boy. A bayou baptismal gone wrong.

From what Mitchel's told me about the man, it's not exactly a stretch of the imagination.

"I never noticed it," I say.

"That's what I'm saying! Cree-py."

"They only see pieces, which is ... maybe that's why"

"Why what?"

"I collect them."

"Uh-huh. Stellar Deep Thoughts Jack Handy moment," he says, averting his eyes from the mirrors and his substantial fear that grey-green drowned boy will reach from one of them, murky green water and water moccasins spilling from his gaping mouth.

grey green drowned boy
grey green powdery line
grey green holographic Maggie
deep into that darkness peering
long I stood there wondering fearing

"This just a hangover or more fallout from little miss judge-your-life?"

I almost forgot he was here. "No-I mean, I don't think so. Maybe. I don't know-she wasn't judging me. Besides, I thought you were a huge fan. I mean, you two were practically finishing each other's sentences."

"Uh-huh. Well, that was at first. It just, I guess it seemed, I don't know, like you're some kind of huge disappointment to her, which was kind of shitty. I mean, you know, give a person a minute, right? Sure, you were a little manic after that fourth double, but I personally enjoyed your speech about life not being a box of puppies. It was an excellent point."

"I thought I'd dreamt that-"

"And your vehement rebuke over everyone wanting TP, but no-one wants to replace the roll!"

"Great."

"You really should run for office."

"Uh-huh"

"What I'm saying is, she was different in the cab. Then she just got, I don't know, it just-it seemed like the more you tried to reconnect, the more distant she got. I don't know, I just thought it was weird."

"Wait, I did?"

"Sure! You were in rare form. Funny as hell."

"Oh," I say, knowing that means I was stupid and slippery. I try to remember, but I can't see past the versions of imagining what happened.

"So, Magpie, huh?" he says, trying not to laugh.

"It's just a kid's nickname."

"Uh-huh." He's looking at me in a weirdly intent way.

"They're deeply misunderstood birds. Mythologically-"

"Mytho-oh-okay, simmer down there, sparky, I'm not-"

"Magpies are associated with divination, so..."

He flicks his eyebrows. "Uh-huh. So, I don't have to worry about you stealing my shiny things?"

"You *are* the shiny things."

I didn't mean to say that out loud. The air thickens. I'm here and he's here. So is the truth I accidentally uttered. Something flashes, bright and tumbled in his eyes, hovers between us for a moment, then recedes into the opaque clunk, clunk sound of steam through distant pipes.

"Hey, did you have cloves on you last night?" I ask with my best Katherine Hepburn lilt.

"No, that was all you." He laughs. It's forced.

"Oh, okay," I mumble.

I don't want to hear any more about my bourbon-bathed asshattery or sit in this thick, grey-green quagmire with Mitchel, so I start sorting the folios on my desk. Dead silence follows. He's more advanced in tenacity, so when I glance up after the eternity of ten seconds, his piercing green eyes tell me to snap the hell out of it. Mitchel doesn't approve of ennui.

"Look-I-it's-running into her was-"

"I get it. It was weird. But sometimes people reconnect and sometimes they don't."

"Right," I mumble.

"People change. It just happens," he says. "I don't know why everyone thinks if a connection happened once, it'll happen again. That it'll always be there."

he knows something just happened
why else would he say that?
because he's talking about Dana you idiot

"But mostly," he adds, "It was just the once."

he knows something just happened
our moment?
do you want a moment with him?
do you? do you? do you?

"Humans are situational..."

He's got his prosecutorial voice of reason in place now, and he's about to start talking about phenomenology versus ontology.

too late

Some things show up once. Even though I'd say I'm a realist, when I do think of possibility, I always imagine an ocean. But it isn't. It's in the flash of lighting. In dusks and dawns. It doesn't walk out into midday and wait for you while you sort your shit out.

nothing gold can stay

"Take any connection, no matter how intense or everlasting we think it is..."

you are what you is

"...add distance and time and poof. Gone. Like it was never there."

poof   never there
it's not wise for fleas to dream of eagles

I don't say anything. He waits, his varnished regard now fully cured. A bizarre urge to sing *The Greatest American Hero* theme song in full, off-key glory washes through me. But if I do, he'll just take me into the fiery pits of 80's pop tv theme song hell. *The Dukes of Hazzard, The Jeffersons, WKRP in Cincinnati,* and if he's really feeling vicious, he recreates the theme song to *Knight Rider.* I decide against it. Mitchel's above my pay grade. Always will be.

"Hey," he says, his voice softening. I don't want soft. I want his usual Amour-all'd voice. This one makes me want to scream. "She seemed cool at first, and I know she holds some untouchable place in your memory, but she was seriously judgmental of you for no reason. I just think sometimes a memory of something is better than the reality. You know? You can choose which one to hold onto." He leaves, flashing a smile at Chelsea who flushes.

what ifs and if onlys

I want to erase the past 36 hours. Dive deep into it didn't happen. Denial's such a reliable friend. It shows you how to fade into your surroundings. Like tofu. Until someone points it out. Then you're like, "Oh, that was *tofu?*" And then it's never not tofu again. Mitchel just pointed out the tofu.

I fish the crumpled card with Dana's number on it from my purse. It's just lunch. Maybe Mitchel's wrong. All those pretty, blunt theories of his are just armor. But that armor is nice. If I don't call today, I'll never call. That much I know.

****

I'm going to wish I'd done this differently. Going to wish I'd somehow found a way to acknowledge the shared moments still faintly legible in our eyes. Moments receding with each passing moment as we sit at this cramped table in this noisy, cramped Thai restaurant in Hell's Kitchen. But shared memories or not, she's a stranger and I'm a stranger. I'm going to wish I'd done this differently. I just don't know how.

We're supposed to be happy to see each other. Eager to share everything that's happened over the past four decades, but instead we're stuck inside an experimental film. The kind where people swallow broken glass as a metaphor for things unsaid. I just need enough conversation to last twenty more minutes. Then we can go our separate ways. And I don't have to wonder anymore about what happened. A sinkhole forms in my chest. Long-ignored truths have surprising density.

"So, you're a journalist? That's impressive," I say, trying to don my engaged and curious hat. "Do you have anything I can read?"

Dana looks up. "Sure, I mean, I could send along—"

"That'd be great," I inject, "I'd like to read your stuff."

"Okay, though, maybe not the one I'm working on right now. It's about—"

"Fracking?" I say, chuckling. I shouldn't laugh. It's not exactly SNL material. "I mean, I'd be interested in what you write about. There's a lot to-I mean it's topical now, right?"

"Sure, though I mostly try to stay off the BINGO card"

"Right, of course." I have no idea what she's talking about, and she knows it.

"It's a NAJA reference for tropes and clichés"

"Oh. Right."

"Yeah. I lean more toward material like Savanna's Act, or The Snoqualmie Tribe donating defibrillators to the King County Police Department. And political optics. Displays of contrition after truths are revealed."

"So, no MLB mascots. Or thunderbirds or-"

"Dream catchers? Yeah...no."

say something   supportive
about injustice   or alienation

"Must be frustrating," I say. "The systemic injustice and disparity that isn't being addressed in any real way beyond conversations and token…" I have absolutely no clue how to finish this sentence without it sounding like a shitty catch phrase memorized by people whose understanding of injustice doesn't reach beyond pasting a COEXIST sticker on their bumper.

Dana's brows knit into a query of did you really just say that? Yes. Yes, I did. For the head that wears the crown of privilege is gleamingly idiotic for all to see.

"Sorry—about the-the alienated comment thing," I say, "I-it's hard to know the right thing to say-"

"Yeah," she says wearily, "the great white sorrow. Not knowing what to say."

She's right, of course. I don't. All I've got is a bucket of clichés, and a growing sense of pointlessness.

"Sorry. That was harsh," she says, "It's just tiring constantly having to, and you of all—"

"Yeah," I say, not wanting her to finish that thought, "I bet it gets old."

We push our food around our plates for a few minutes. I finish my Singha and flag the waiter for another. Dana's eyes are steady on my glass. She probably thinks we're headed for a repeat of the Zombie Hut. When the waiter arrives, I clarify that no, no, not a beer. A coffee. (I'll have a scotch or three when I get back to the office.)

"Uh-huh," he says clearing my glass.

"And you're in PR?" she finally says, trying to sound tactful, "I never would have guessed you'd end up in PR."

"Yeah, well, winding roads," I say.

bob   weave   dodge   slither

"Yeah, very," she says quietly, "but you seem suited to it, I guess."

"Well, I'm not sure I'd say that, but it's a skill set. I guess." I feel myself flush.

I haven't felt anything beyond fleeting peripheral emotion for years and the first real one to get a toehold is shame. And now anger. Mitchel was right. She is judging me. I don't blame her. I'd judge me too. Still, maybe take a minute to get to know someone before lumping them into the all-is-lost category.

"Over the years, I've wondered what it'd be like to bump into you," she says. "What you'd be like."

The thought of her thinking of me during the four decades we've been apart is surreal. She's probably just saying that. Because that's what people say when they bump into someone, they left behind without a second thought when they finally do see them again. They say things like 'I always wondered.'

"Yeah? Me too," I say

"It went differently" she says. "You're different now."

"Yeah? You too."

left hand right hand do-si-do

Someone could say something honest right now. If someone did say something honest, things might change.

say something   it's still here   come on   say it
did you ever... say it

SAY IT

"Hey, so, out of curiosity, did you ever-" The words catch in my throat.

why didn't you write?
why didn't you say goodbye?
what happened?
I tried to find you
everything changed when you left

It's been a long time since I've allowed myself to think about any of this. Now it's all I can think about.

forget
drift to the back
under the noise
into the walls

"Did I ever what?" Dana asks.

"Nothing," I say, "Just, it was weird how you were there one day, then, you know."

"Yeah, it was weird for me too," she says. I wait for her to add something. She doesn't.

I suddenly have an overwhelming desire to throw my food in her face. Which is extreme. But I want to. I want to see peanut sauce covered noodles splat against her disappointed-in-me face. I'm angry. Really angry. It feels good. Uncomplicated.

I realize Dana's saying something, but I can only catch snippets because I'm having to put a surprising amount of effort into restraining myself from picking up a handful of noodles and throwing them at her.

"You —— and —— —— it —— sense —— —— represent —— —— and damaging —— —— —— problem. Are —— —— —— fracking —— —— angling for —— is —— —— only —— ——

It suddenly occurs to me that maybe she's giving me the answers I want. I kick my anger. Hard. It growls, retreating to a corner. It'll return tonight around 3 a.m. It will bring friends. But that's then and this is now.

"...complete denial of tribal lands, and I'm trying to understand how you, of all people, could be a part of that."

I'm an idiot. This lunch isn't her wanting to catch up. She's a journalist trying to get information on my client. Her non sequitur proves it.

never gave you a second thought

I need a moment to figure out what to say. I raise my hand to the waiter. He returns. "I'll have a Singha," I say. Dana's eyebrows twitch.

screw you Dana Walden screwyouscrewyou
The waiter returns with my beer. I take a sip. Cool and fizzy. Bitter. Just a little bite. It reminds me this lunch is just a moment in time. No more. No less. I take another sip. Disappointment is the norm. Exceptional and connected is rare. Was doesn't mean will be. Mitchel *was* right.
"Is this an interview?" I ask.
"No. No, It's not. Really, it isn't. I'm just trying to understand," she says, then pauses. She's being careful again.
"How you're-it's just you're nothing like I remember you," she adds. "You were so different. Really different."
Another feeling is surfacing. I'm not sure what it is so I look out the window to give myself a minute to figure it out. A woman is intently scrolling on her phone as her dog pees on a small tree. Next to the tree a hand-painted sign reads:
Please don't pee on me, I'm trying to grow!
EXACTLY
shitty things happen all the time
choices are made   we live with them
Mitchel was right
"Well, I hope I've changed," I say with all the nonchalance I've been trying to achieve for the past half hour. "Being the same person at 49 as you were at nine would mean something was clinically wrong with you." The cold heat building in my chest feels good. She doesn't know anything about me. "As far as my client," I continue, "it's a complex issue, and as a reporter, I'd think you'd know that. We're all part of a capitalistic system facing a fossil fuel crisis with few viable solutions"
BOOM   there's your sound bite
lady who used to be my best friend
"A viable—do you actually believe that?"
"I believe people vilify others rather than admitting their own complicity. That sometimes people break things because

they don't care enough not to. And no amount of glue will ever fix it" The question tumbles out before I can stop it. "Why didn't you ever write to me? I thought you were-you know I thought you were-but I tried to find you. You just disappeared. Do you have any idea what that was like?" The words are out there now, and I can't take them back.

She's very still. After a few moments she says, "It wasn't my choice. I was a kid too. They decided everything. Do you think I had any say?"

"Who? Who decided?"

"Don't you remember?"

"Remember what?" I ask. "I mean I know it was because of your mom and all, I guess, but you just left without saying goodbye."

"No-one told you why?"

"Well, I mean-wait, what do you mean?"

The problem is I've lost the thread of what exactly we're talking about in the rat's nest in my Adderall deprived head. I'm trying to make a point. It's in there but I can't find it.

"You don't know?" She asks.

I try to think back. It was so long ago. I know memories change every time we remember them, but since I don't remember how I remembered it before, it's impossible to know how it's changed. Is it just an 'it was a red sweater not a purple one' type deal, or more an 'I wasn't there at all but just think I was because I was told the story so many times' situation? An argument could be made that I'm not here right now. For instance.

"Not really," I say.

She's looking at me strangely.

"Look, forget it-it's okay, really," I add. "It doesn't matter. It was almost 40 years ago, so-"

The curtain that's been over her eyes for the past 30 minutes lifts. "You should talk to Ohma."

Ohma?

"Wait. The lady with the—with the gardens? What does she have to do with this?" I ask.

I remember the woman Dana's talking about, but only atmospherically. I scour my mind for memories of her and I come up with a few. Always outside, in her gardens, which were sort of half-wild. She didn't talk much. She had a nice laugh. And knew a lot about the forest. We hung out at her farmhouse after school, and in the summer. And that her farm belongs to the time I was happy. Before everything that came after that. But why Dana's telling me to talk to her makes no sense.

"I don't understand," I say. "Wait, was she the reason you left? That can't—that doesn't make any sense."

"She's not. Not really," she says, "but there are parts about what happened that she-they'd be better coming from her."

"So, tell me the parts that you can tell," I say.

"I'm not ready to do that," she replies quietly.

I try to stop a spiky exhale of frustration, but it escapes anyway, tangling itself in the net of unspoken words and disappointment between us. I wish she would just spit it out. Maybe it has something to do with who I am now. Or maybe it's just time. Winding paths. This ocean of nets between us. Whatever the reason, I'm tired.

"I'm sorry. I'm not trying to be cryptic," she says.

I chuff. Cryptic is exactly what she's trying to be.

She starts again, "I'm just not sure you'd be—"

"Look, it's okay," I say. "You don't have to dredge all that up again. I was just wondering why you left so suddenly but we don't have to talk about it. Everyone has to move on at some point."

"I thought you'd know at least some of it," she says.

Something in her voice makes me unsure I want to know. I've got enough on my plate as it is with the apathy and the Adderall and the Mitchel and the Owsley and the loathsome Big Oil client and the Dylan. I carve a check sign into the air for the waiter.

"I should probably get back to the office," I say, "and I don't want to press whatever it is you don't want to talk about, and I mean, we had fun times as kids and sometimes the good memory of something is—"

"Maggie..."

She sounds genuine but I don't care. I should. I know I should.

"I'll tell you," she says, "I will. There's just a lot to it and I need you to hear some of it from Ohma first. Then what I have to say will make more sense. I just need some time. I didn't expect to bump into you, and I just need some time."

"Yeah, okay. Though it's been 40 years, so I wouldn't know how to get in touch with her anyway"

"She's still there," she says.

"Really? Wow. Okay, I'll think about it. Do you have her number?"

Dana shakes her head. "No phone"

"Really? Who doesn't have a phone?"

Dana nods but doesn't say anything. She's not going to. I'm starting to learn the patterns that belong to this grown-up Dana. The things I remember of the Dana from my childhood is she was fearless, was my best friend, knew the best spots for finding cool rocks and her mother made birdhouses. This judgmental, evasive person bears little resemblance. I'm not the only one who's changed.

runninglaughing

mist   *stones*

sparklers

The waiter brings the check, I insist on paying because millimeters of control count at times like these. Once the bill's paid I'm out of my seat. I don't want to get caught up in the possibility of a goodbye hug so once we've made it to the sidewalk, I pull my phone out and use it as the collectively accepted shield that it is.

She understands. Doesn't try to force it or pretend I'm not doing it. It's such a departure from the #amazing, #blessed bullshit of my regular life I almost stop. Can almost feel the air outside the soldered seams of my armor. Almost. It's a running theme in my life.

"We'll talk again soon," she says. She seems to mean it. "Once Ohma-"

"Sure." I hear in my voice the distance reserved for interns we don't hire. I try again. "Might be a while though. Work's pretty demanding right now."

She nods. Her eyes look sad. As weary as mine. I should tell her how sorry I am about her mother and thank her for giving me a chance to find out what happened. I turn and walk the other way instead. I'll look back on this and wish I would have done it differently.

The rest of the day was obscured by work, meetings, phone calls. I was going to take my usual train but waiting in a too crowded York Street station for a too cramped F train seemed, after the few days I've had, a bit like tempting fate.

I decided to walk, the metronomic fall of my shoes blunted the need to hurl things at passing cars and yell SHUT UP to the cacophony.

A hard, frozen thirty minutes later, I'm at my street. Turning left will take me home. Where it's warm. Where there's wine. But the thought of having to see Dylan or talk about alignment or eat any more damn Vindaloo is exhausting. I'm too tired to talk. Too tired to rest. Too tired for wine.

I turn right, towards Red Hook. Towards a viciously magenta sunset. Maybe if I ask nicely, it will swallow all these questions and doubts. Maybe the edge of water and light will take the me I've become, so I can see if there's anything left from before.

Magenta turns plum, then indigo. I'm still here. No magical stripping of scale and stone. No revelation of the real me because this *is* the real me.

****

I've traveled beyond ground-into-paste to the bardo of functional weariness. Sleep tonight will be perforated. Since moving here, I've often walked the neighborhood between 3 and 4 a.m., trying to absorb the rest of others—sitting on stilled stoops, leaning on hushed façades. The partitions of sleeper and non-sleeper blur enough for me to feel the serenity of others. But I won't be doing that tonight. Or anytime soon. Now I know Dana lives within these same blocks. Not that I think I'd end up on her corner trying to figure out which windows are hers (which is of course what I'd do), it's more now I know she's here the time of my wandering solitude is over. My sanctuary has been invaded by finite magnifications of ifs and thens. I'll need an extra dose of chemical sanctuary tonight.

I haven't slept without what my mother would call a 'little helper' in over a decade. Everyone here has one. Alcohol, weed, diphenhydramine. Something stronger. It's the only way to loosen the death grip of shoulds.

Unfortunately, due to the empty pill bottle in my purse, this means traversing the gauntlet of Designer Imposters perfumes, armpits, and bleach that is my local Rite Aid before heading home to Dylan. I power through gag reflexes, and speed through the doors, up the coffee and tea aisle. It's the best shot at an unimpeded corridor because the families that used to live in these ten square blocks south of Brooklyn Heights, northeast of Red Hook, and sliced off from Park Slope by the eternally viscous Gowanus Canal, used to get their Folgers or Chock Full o'Nuts here, but that was a long time ago. Gears of gentrification that began in 1980 started churning in earnest around 2003, and along with the elevated coffee expectations new money brings, came the slowly gathering silt of obsoletism to dull their once shiny rubber lids.

Five minutes later, obsolete lids and the fickle whims of temporal priorities slide beneath the soft rattle of my full bottle of helpers. My very own James Taylors humming maple-y notes of "You've Got a Friend". I pop one, chasing it with a Nutter Butter, feeling a renewed hope of reclaiming my life.

I reach the stoop of the once-church-now-co-op lofts where I live, as Mrs. Costa, the last-standing wolf of original families from this block, shambles up from her basement apartment with a large garbage bag in tow.

Mrs. Costa is in her late eighties. Wiry and shaky. Untethered. I wouldn't be surprised to find her caught in a nearby tree like a deflated mylar balloon.

It's a bit of a neighborhood mystery what fills her almost daily five-gallon trash bag. Slowly irradiating the artifacts of an abusive husband? Or an all the missing neighborhood cats scenario? I'm a firm believer in you never know about people. Now, more than ever.

"Oh, oh, hello my dear!" Mrs. Costa exclaims, surprised at our auspicious timing—that happens every day.

"Mrs. Costa, is this a dead drop for your drug empire?"

"It *was* a beautiful sunset, wasn't it?" she says, her orphaned baby otter eyes swimming with joy.

I decide not to tell her of my unrealized hope of floating away on its last fragments of indigo. Instead, I lug her mysteriously heavy trash to the dented metal cans she insists on keeping instead of getting rubber ones like the rest of us. During Nor'-easters you can hear Mrs. Costa's trash cans clambering down the block, ricocheting off cars, prying howls from the neighborhood dogs.

I replace the lid and bolt up my stoop, turning to wave as I open the foyer door, but she's already shuffling to her own door, bright smile now deep, downward trenches. Glaciers of disappointment etch across us all in the end.

Mrs. Costa represents the type of older years I'm determined to avoid. If I work my ass off for ten more years, I'll be set. Just ten more years.

I unlock our mailbox. It's jammed full. I grab the crumpled mail, tearing a few envelopes in the process. Once I make it to my floor, I leave the four delivery boxes waiting for me outside. No clue what's inside. Things I bought at 2 a.m. Furniture sliders. Spiralizers.

****

There's not much evidence of me in my loft. Dylan's esthetic, predominantly Tibetan art has seeped into every nook and cranny of my once wonderfully sparse loft. A few islands of me remain—my *Big Trouble in Little China* poster, a framed David Bowie See|Hear|Speak No Evil T-shirt, my music collection, my coffee mugs.

Dylan strolls in from the kitchen area wearing harem pants dyed a cacophony of red. No shirt. His golden skin gleaming as if airbrushed.

I replace his healing drums CD with Charlie Parker and pour myself a healthy glass of Pinot.

"My flower," Dylan says slowly (he'd call it mindfully). Sometimes I want to reach down his throat and rip the words out. He kisses me, my lack of reciprocity entirely unnoticed. I hand him the mail.

"I made Vindaloo" he says, placing the mail on the entry table, padding like a sleepy panther back to the kitchen.

I've decided tonight's the night Dylan gets mad about something. There's something wrong with people who are always placid. This would be a classic pot-kettle moment, but my placidity is neither calm nor mindful. Gertrude Stein would say my there isn't there. Dana would no doubt agree. But my there is somewhere. It has to be. But Dylan's calmness, his slow and mindful choice of words, his openness—just once I'd like to see him react badly to something. Anything.

"I think we should say something, *Dyl*." He dislikes being called Dyl. "What if," I continue sharply, "one of those was a legal document or a letter a friend sent right before they died?"

"Our true self has no beginning or end." He pauses for the precise amount of time compassion requires. "Who journeyed on?"

me
can't journey on from somewhere you've never been
of course you can idiot
shut up
you shut up

"My flower?" His query floats through the air. How easy it is for beautiful people to be transcendent.

"I'm saying hypothetically, *Dyl*"

He leans back, his amber eyes contemplating. "Pieces of paper, butterfly. Define our existence if we let them."

"Yes. Absolutely. Paper flies. Fly-paper," I mumble.

If I sat down right now, it's possible I'd never move again. Maybe that's what happened to those trees in Arizona. No reason to stay alive-so they just slowly turned to stone.

wonder if it hurt
probably not

"The point is," I say, "our mailman is incompetent. Either that or it's some hazing for being evil gentrifiers. Like those old families didn't make a killing." My mind drifts to Mrs. Costa and her dented trash cans.

maybe not all of them

Dylan approaches me with a velvet smile, placing his hands on my collarbone. My brain tells me they're soft and warm, but they feel like wet dough. I peel out of his grasp, finish my glass, and pour another. He takes it all in stride. To him, we're all imperfect, all trying.

"Don't stress, my dove. Come get some spicy-spicy, and let's see if we can channel discord into alignment."
He means sex. I'm not certain it's humanly possible to be less interested. But the wine will help me go through the motions, and I don't want to think anymore.

****

The tree outside my loft window looks like a charcoal sketch. The memory of something beautiful. I've never seen a single leaf on it. I asked the Parks and Rec Department if it was dead, shouldn't it be pulled? A guy came out to look, then said,

"It's not dead, it's dormant."

Dormant tree knows more about me than anyone. It never expects improvements—in me, or its own circumstances. Because of this, I trust it completely. It holds my secrets. Every inch given and hope relinquished, strewn like tiny lights across its branches. I look at the smooth bark and spindled boughs.

do you know you're dormant?
free of complications
obligations
expectations that you be something beautiful or wondrous
just stillness   and remembrances
was and nevermore was and nevermore was and nevermore
not dead
dormant

Dormant tree doesn't move. Just waits patiently. But I don't want to tell it anything tonight. Don't want to let the thoughts in. My shortcomings. Dana's weary eyes.

Dormant tree already knows everything anyway. Normally I'd find a small patch of solace in those branches, but tonight, its stripped, brittle fingers are more like splinters in my bones. I opt to study the dark walnut buttresses of my ceiling instead. Dormant tree understands.

A few inches to my right, Dylan's sleeping the sleep of the unencumbered, the soft rise and fall of his chest a counterpoint to my clenched one. I'm not a tense or anxious person. Breathing is just something I forget to do sometimes. I come closest to remembering at 3 a.m. This is because 3 a.m. is more a place than a time. A place between yesterday and tomorrow where I almost remember how to breathe.

Unfortunately, liminal spaces don't screen occupants. Truths slip in through unsealed cracks. Like roaches. Tiptoeing close, little voices whispering, *Dana knows*, and *something's wrong*, and *nothing from nothing leaves nothing*. Maybe roaches are divine messengers. It's entirely possible.

I tip toe to the couch and open my computer for some input exhaustion. Etsy and The Joy of Painting. Yellow Ochre, Alizarin Crimson, Phthalo Blue. Somewhere between the happy little clouds and the peaceful rolling hilltop I fall asleep. My alarm goes off at seven, interrupting a dream about running up slick stairs wearing oversized shoes. My subconscious is not particularly subtle.

May 1978

on two   ready steady go   one TWO

jump skip skip hoptwothreefour down the stairs out the door
like air like wind like dandelion seeds it's Dana's birthday
today daddy helped me make a ka-lie-dough-scohpe outta a
walnut branch he found n some glass beads that look like
smushed jellybeans we got at the Hobby Lobby daddy let me
pick the colors from the big bowls I got dark blue purple dark
green n yellow ones I liked puttin my hand into the smushed
jellybean glass beads cause they're smooth n cool n they
pressed against my hand in a friendly way I don't really like the
Hobby Lobby though too big n full of stuff but empty too
the glass smushed jellybeans were just right though n I can hear
em soft clickclick when I turn the scope it makes me feel
fuzzy n sleepy I hope Dana likes it

over the metal strip tween inside n outside skip to daddy's
shed   tap-tap-tap knock on the side of the door it's open but
I don't like to just walk in when he's workin on somethin
daddy looks round smilin eyes sparkly he's always happy in
his shed

off to Dana's?

yyyyyyeeeeep

got the ka-lie-dough-scohpe?

yyyyyyeeeeep

I show him I wrapped it in sparkly tissue paper momma gave
me

here   take this too

he puts a small wooden bird in my hand

you give her mamma this

OOHMMM a humminbird

he smiles n nods it's perfect n I know Dana's momma is
gonna love it

how'd you know it's her birthday too?

did you know she loves birds n makes birdhouses

how'd you know that daddy?

daddy winks n laughs his peanut butter laugh

everybody knows that

4

It's been seven days since running into Dana. For the past three I've been telling myself *if I run into Dana today, it'll be a sign. A sign to contact Ohma.* When I went to Rite-Aid. Or Union Market. Or Stinky Brooklyn. Or the subway. Or Smith and Vine. Everywhere I went, I thought *if I run into Dana, it'll be a sign.* I lost track of how many times I thought it. Of how many times I looked for her along the cramped sidewalks of Smith Street or across the subway platform. I thought I saw her many times. I came closest to running into her last night when she walked by my corner bodega while I was picking up Mallomars. By the time I went outside to see if it was her, she was gone. I don't think that counts.

So, after a week of not running into Dana in the five square blocks we both occupy, I've decided that is my sign. I'm not going to contact Ohma. What would I say anyway? How exactly does one start a letter to someone they only knew as a child? There's no way to write that letter without sounding like a selfish ass who's only writing after almost four decades of silence because she wants something.

It was good to see Dana again. Good to see she's fine and none of the things I'd imagined had happened. I can let it all go now. Let her go. Leave the past where it belongs.

sure   that's exactly what you're gonna do

Maybe this stuff—all this time wondering, then forgetting I was wondering but never truly stopping—maybe that's what's been wrong with me. This could be a good thing. Isn't that what self-help books say? This could be a good thing.

****

"Hey, Dyl? Dylan!" No response. He's in the bathroom doing something he calls deep flushing. I have no idea what it is. I never could bring myself to ask.

Having spent the past week obsessed with Dana, trying to run into her again, and trying not to run into her again, then trying to run into her but look effortlessly self-possessed, I've fallen behind on ideas for the pitch to Big Oil. It's due tomorrow. I've been working on it all morning. So far, I have **'Time to give the f-word a try'** and **'We all win when we play the frackpot'**.

Eight more days til I can have Adderall again. Yesterday I asked my doc to reconsider the length of time til I can refill my prescription. She did. She added five days. If I was smart, I'd reschedule the meeting. Every neuron in my brain has been stretched to its snapping point. Spaghettified. That's what Stephen Hawking called it. Spaghettified.

"DYL!" I shout as loudly as I can.
He pops his head through the doorway, his face flushed.

"What is it, dove?"

I resist the urge to coo sarcastically because it would be lost on Dylan. He's too well-intended.

He sits, kisses my hands, then smiles at me like a child throwing a tantrum who deep down just wants to be held. I pull my hands away. I've always wanted to be the person who doesn't pull her hands away. But I always do.

"Can you give the music a rest? I'm on a deadline."

He's been playing his healing drums and pan flute compilation for the past hour and a half. He chuckles. "Oh, crabby dove"

more commonly known as a pigeon

His amber eyes are waiting for a connection I've never been capable of providing. Maybe that's the sum of my allure. Emotional neuropathy parading as enigmatic depth.

I get up to turn the music off, but he of the wouldn't-recognize-a-clue-if-it-were-duct-taped-to-his-overly-earnest-abs, shimmies in front of me and starts sexy dancing. To the pan flute. It's strangely off-putting. And a little boring. It shouldn't be. He's kind and sensitive and gorgeous. I'm the husk here. That much is clear. I look at dormant tree.

"Is there something wrong with me?" I ask, mostly to her. Her agreement that there is something wrong with me takes the form of rain dribbling off her drooping branches. Meanwhile, Dylan's focused on unbuttoning my blouse.

"Hmm? Uhmm-hmmm." he says, circling behind me.

"So, you think so?"

He slips my blouse from my shoulders. The buttons at the wrists transform silky Hollywood descent into limp straight jacket. Seems appropriate, so I leave it. I look at dormant tree again because she'll get the joke. She does. In the meantime, Dylan has started to kiss the back of my neck. My body couldn't care less. And neither could I.

"Maybe there's something off. *Fundamentally* wrong with me."

"No baby. You're perfect. Beautiful. Volcanic."

volcanic?

He gently bites the back of my neck, but all I feel are the wet spots his mouth is leaving behind. The urge to wipe them away is overwhelming. A pinpoint of rage pricks the center of my chest.

"I'm not-I'm-can you just-I'm trying to ask you something."

His response comes in the form of trying to unzip my jeans from behind which brings me light years past crabby dove. I just want one Goddamn moment of communication that isn't about his version of it. I square off to him, my blouse fluttering behind me.

"Seriously?" I demand. "Aren't you supposed to be a listener? Isn't that what your religion teaches?" I try to pull my hands free because it's hard to be taken seriously with a silk straight jacket hanging from one's wrists. But the more I pull the more it resists. The pinpoint of rage floods my bloodstream. I'm yanking my arms to try to get free of this hell spawn blouse.

"Get off. GET OFF! FUCKING GET FUCKING FUCK OFF ME!" I finally rip one hand free, sending the buttons skittering across the floor. Dylan's now backed up a few feet and is looking at me with that look males seem to be taught somewhere between high school and their first real job they roll out anytime a female's actions are beyond their comprehension.

I rip my other hand free and stand, daring him to say something. "What, Dylan? What? Something you want to say?"

Red patches march across his cheeks. He returns to the bathroom. "Well, Maggie, maybe, you are. Meditate on it."

"Yeah, I'll do that," I say loudly to the bathroom door. "Thanks for the insight, DYL." I button my blouse, glaring at dormant tree. Water steadily drips from her branches.

"Shut up."

Freezing rain dribbles down her trunk. She's stuck here forever, carrying thoughts too heavy for me to hold. No leaves or flowers or birds to make her laugh. I feel like crying. I don't.

****

After the Dylan/blouse debacle, the walls of my loft began to resemble that trash compactor Leia, Han, Luke, and Chewie got trapped in with the Dianoga.

It finally occurred to me I have a choice in all this. I can resist or succumb to the riptide of what was. It's too easy to drown in a teaspoon of known quantities. To just swallow life wrong.

not dead
dormant

Newton wasn't pleased, but because I'd buffed my mediocre ideas to a high shine for Big Honcho of Big Oil ahead of schedule, this is my reward. Ten days of PTO.

I almost invited Mitchel because he needs a break too, but if he came along, he'd make everything frothy and funny-ha-ha and we'd drink too much. Plus, there hasn't been enough distance from the weird moment between us in my office and he might think I'm inviting him for some kind of romantic thing.

I need to reset. Stop avoiding all the crud bubbling up since running into Dana and a break from the stress of potentially running into her. It's always there now. The will I or won't I run into her-ness. So, I'm going to sit on a cliff overlooking the ocean somewhere warm and try to shake this tsunami of inevitability. Try to find something about myself I don't hate. Something I can defend. Or at least claim.

It's begun to occur to me I have no idea who I am. Which is, I think maybe, a problem. I feel like an amalgam of patterns. Cliff notes and catch phrases. Storage lockers all over Manhattan of opinions and quippy retorts I pull out whenever I need to sound more interesting or more not gone. Maybe the cliff overlooking the sea somewhere warm will let me know if there's any authentic part of me that's still here.

When I left for the airport this morning, Dylan gave me a hug and said this journey would change my life if I let it. And I'm going to. I'll let in the big magic. The great mysteries of existence will surreptitiously unlock while learning how to make authentic ceviche from an elderly local. Eight full days to put the dragon back to sleep and kick start my next chapter having finally released my past.

sprinklers   *smoke*
birdhouse
  stop   *garden*   *Ohma*
          oak tree
STOP IT   *garden*
Firefly Festival   *sparklers*
    be where you are be where you are be where you are
Firefly Festival   *sparklers*
    five four three two one be where you are be where you are

When I deplane, heat and brightness push through me, separating the me from the plane and the me now walking the tarmac to the covered walkway. It will burn away the debris if I let it. I'm going to try.

I stride in and out of the throngs, a clear and unquestioning path. I'm an ancient river. Air moves freely through my lungs, into my bloodstream, connecting me to my atrophied higher self, unrestrained by the clogged filters of past choices. Everyone I pass can sense my transcendence. They part gently for me and smile. *She is an ancient river* they think, "her path is clear" they whisper. This was absolutely the right choice. No past or future. Only now.

My bags are the first to emerge. It's a sign. I pick them up and glide like a water spirit to the hotel phones.

****

This is bullshit. I'm here. I showed up. I let go and let God for three days straight. I've eaten (a lot). I've prayed (sort of). The love thing isn't really a demand/receive situation at the best of times so I'm not going to make a thing out of that one. Especially now.

I've taken the walks. I've floated in the volcanic mud. I even tried Salsa dancing. That alone should count for something because rhythm isn't exactly a birthright. But nothing. No signs. No epiphanies. And the closest I've come to making authentic ceviche is eating a flight of it at La Cevicheria. All this trip has given me is a soulburn. I should be grateful. But I'm not. All signs pointing to the increasing likelihood I'm unsalvageable.

> *dead little magpies live in charcoal trees*
> *everybody knows that*

I'm right back to where I started. Just in Cartagena where remaining excursions to surreptitiously rediscover my heart are now pointless, so instead of viewing Getsemani street art, I've spent the day on my computer, ordering room service and retyping versions of "something is wrong with me." It's staggering how much pops up when you type that in, only overshadowed by the hundreds of variations on a theme of "Top 10 ways to jumpstart your best self."

I even typed in "childhood memory loss" but that's a PTSD wiki-wormhole nightmare that doesn't really apply. I don't have unresolved trauma. I'm not missing time. I remember Ohma, though she's receded into a Yoda-like Cherokee grandmother with a relationship with nature beyond my reach. Beyond that image of her, I simply remember spending time on her farm, that Dana was my best friend until her mom died, and how after she died Dana didn't live there anymore. The only stuff I don't remember is, according to Dana, what actually happened that summer.

I just opened the bottle of Amarillo Aguardiente I'd planned to bring back for Mitchel. The heavy licorice already snuffing my thoughts. I pour four more fingers into a glass. Then another.

> *clickclack*   *clickclack clickclack*
>   *silver yarn*   *blue trees*
> *Tap-tap-tat-tat-tat-tat-tatpthwwwwwwwwwwrrrrrrrrrr*
>   *clickclack*   *clickclack clickclack*

Tap-tap-tap

pthwwwwwwwwwwwwrrrrrrrl tat-tat-tat-tat-tat

Tap-tap-tap

Tap-tap-tap

I peek through the swath of hair pasted to the side of my face. And, it seems, sometime in the night, sucked into my mouth. My eyes leak watery protestations against the sunlight cutting slats through the air. I prop myself up and wipe the hair out of my mouth with a hand that has so little circulation from my drunken body origami, it feels like it belongs to someone else.

The indigo moleskin journal I bought to jot down the numerous epiphanies I'd have on this trip, slides off my chest, flopping face down onto the floor. I look at the table and see the empty Amarillo Aguardiente bottle.

Another tap-tap-tap is followed by a young, full of life and promise voice.

"Breakfast for Ms. Morris."

"Come in!" I yell, the sound scythes I've just driven through my skull oddly satisfying.

The room service attendant enters, assessing the tableau of empty bottle of Aguardiente and violently disheveled tourist. A small grin emerges as she sets my breakfast tray on the table. She's seen this before. Many times. I sign the tab and watch the door quietly click behind her. Something about her grin is familiar.

I catch a glimpse of myself in the mirror. A fresh field of mini corduroy has been welted across my cheek by the hair now dementedly sculpted by Aguardiente and drool. Perhaps a few tears from the quickly drying well of my future. Though it's not likely I cried. I wonder if it's possible for tear ducts to forget. Deflate into desiccated grapes staring into the world, waiting for something to remind them why they're there. I peer through the wood slats to another perfect, clear blue-sky day.

yonder see the morning blink
the sun is up, and up must I
to wash and dress and eat and drink
and look at things and talk and think

rummmmmmhummmm

seven   poppopcrrrrrrrunchpop

I pour some coffee. Despite its promising glossy mahogany gravity, it's just hot. Tasteless. I can't get the room attendant's small, almost smile out of my head. I've seen it before. It itches at my memory like a phantom limb. I scour my life for the person it belongs to.

Dylan?   no

He can do a small smile, but it's always part of his 'hey baby, you thinkin' what I'm thinkin' vibe.

Mitchel?

I try to picture a small almost smile. Maybe.

Dana?   no   well maybe   no

Dana's mom

I haven't let my mind linger on her, even after my lunch with Dana. Too tragic. No-one wants to rehash tragic shit. Best not to dwell. Still. The smile was her mom's. Definitely. Like she had a secret. A Mona Lisa smile.

I'm too tired to stop my mind from wandering back to what I can remember of Dana's mom. Her smile, the birdhouses she made, how she liked to dance. At least, I think she liked to dance. I'm pretty sure she was dancing at the Firefly Festival. But maybe not. I can't tell what I'm remembering and what I'm making up to fill holes. I try to extract more, but her birdhouses and maybe dancing the night she died is it for now.

I look around at my beautiful resort room. Four walls, windows, a bed, coffee, arepa and eggs, things I bought over the past three days, and an empty bottle of Amarillo Aguardiente. The familiarity is already stifling.

to wash and dress and eat and drink
and look at things and talk and think

If I can't find a way back to who I was a very long time ago, or forward to something other than these echo patterns, each day from here to my grave will be filled with things to pass time and make enough money so I can someday move my things, patterns, and memory particles somewhere like where I am right now.

this is all her fault

This vacation was supposed to be a whole David Foster Wallace the truth sets you free deal. But he also killed himself, so there's that. Maybe he couldn't get past the not til it's finished with you part. I used to think he was weak. A genius snowflake who folded in the face of the harsh realities of life. But now I get it. He got caught in the stare of the abyss.

There's mounting evidence the truth is just getting started with me, and all the ceviche in Cartagena isn't going to change that. So, it's stare into the abyss or stare into the truth.

On the plane home I open my notebook. I stared at a blank page for an hour.

5

It smells like snow tonight. It won't be the soft flurries of romantic comedies that float atop eyelashes as one's soulmate suddenly appears to offer warm hands that fit perfectly in yours. It will be the grey, spiteful, snow of New York in late February. Tiny grey ice daggers with a penchant for eyeballs and ears. If one's soulmate did appear, their red-rimmed eyes would barely glimpse your leaky nose as you plowed past one another on the way to a bar.

I really should just go home. Showing up like this is a bad idea. But it's too late. I've heard the distant strains of the life I haven't lived. The echoes of sounds not known to me because they belong to a life not lived by me because I took other roads. The sounds of that other life are getting louder, echoing across the roads that brought me to this moment. If I listen closely, I hear...*maybe, maybe, maybe.* So, I'm here, doing this. Because maybe.

I am prepared, though. Just because I can hear the chords of another life doesn't mean I can't salvage this one. So, I've practiced my how-weird-to-bump-into-you-again, my it-must-be-fate, and my you-must-be Dana's...", making sure I practice not adding "sea cucumber."

On my way back to Carroll Gardens from the airport, I decided to stay in a hotel on Schermerhorn St instead of going home. I didn't want to deal with Dylan or his quasi-spiritual inquiry into why I cut my trip short. I didn't want to talk at all. I especially didn't want to bump into anymore childhood best friends. Of course, I did see her the very next day. She didn't see me. At least I think she didn't. She was walking up Baltic with the sea cucumber. Too tired to resist the rip tide, my feet followed them.

The three of us scurried in our isosceles for several blocks, while I mentally rehearsed a stop-and-look-at-very-interesting-thing-in-shop-window act in case they saw me. But I couldn't stop following. Couldn't break the tether pulling me through Dana's wake.

They disappeared into a building on Court Street. I pulled my phone out and pretended to be on a call as I slowly walked past the door she entered. It turned out to be one of the last functional churches in the neighborhood that hasn't been commandeered by gentrifiers and real estate flippers. It's clear why they've left it alone. A squat, single-story rectangle with a flat brick façade and a dented metal door with a mint green laminated flyer taped to it.

World Too *LOUD*?

Too much *NOISE*?

Start with *YOURSELF*!

Over-talkers Anonymous. Wednesdays, 8PM.

ALL ARE WELCOME!

It was a Wednesday. And it was 7:52 pm. At first, I couldn't wrap my head around why Dana would be going to that kind of meeting. She's not an over-talker. If anything, she's taciturn. The only two reasons I could come up with is she's here to support the sea cucumber who has a verbosity problem or it's research for something she's writing. I'd read that article. People that talk constantly just to remind themselves they aren't dissolving into particulates. For example.

I didn't go in that night. I went into the Chocolate Room, which happens to be next door. Two mugs of hot chocolate, three glasses of cabernet later, I realized an over-talkers meeting might be a six-hour event. So, I went back to the hotel.

It's now a week later. A week of quasi-spiritual inquiries from Dylan, avoiding Mitchel, and ignoring Chelsea, Newton, and all things Big Oil. I've fixated on tonight—the night I'm going back to that building to see if Dana's there so I can give her the speech I've prepared. "I can't imagine what losing your mom was like. I am so sorry you had to go through that. I wish I had the chance to talk with you that summer. I tried. I really did. Can we maybe try this reunion again? I promise to not be such an ass. You can trust me. You can tell me whatever it is about that summer. I'd like to be friends again."

I worked on my little speech all week. I even did research online about how to talk to someone who is closed off to you. You're supposed to say lots of "I" statements. You're not supposed to bring accusations or demands. You're supposed to nod and raise your eyebrows and lean in. Create a welcoming and emotionally safe environment. Since I don't trust my ability to do that, I ended up cutting and pasting a bunch of example conversations I found on YouTube and adding my own specifics. Like Mad Libs.

So here I am, waiting for Dana and an epiphany in a basement meeting room where the tangy mustiness emanating from a huge swath of green and black mold swirling across ceiling tiles welcomes me with thick arms.

desperate times makes believers of turnips
everybody knows that

"Beautiful, aren't they?"

I turn to find a young woman with silver hair and otherworldly, pale blue eyes looking up at the mold.

"First time?" she asks. Her voice is lyrical and soft.

"Oh, Hi. Yah. Just, checking it out, you know" I say.

She cocks her head slowly to one side then the other as she regards me. She must be medicated. "Welcome to OTA. I'm Seidr."

"Hi. Maggie."

"And this is Calvin."

For a moment I'm wondering if she's referring to a giant invisible rabbit when a man with rumpled auburn hair and a shy smile emerges from behind her, carrying a large, pink bakery box. Part of her druid magic act, no doubt. Seidr smiles warmly at Calvin then turns back to me, waiting. I offer my best 'we're all fine here' gaze.

"Hi, I'm Maggie. Nice to meet you."

Calvin's eyes widen. Almost as if he's looking through me. "Heart strings, missing chord," he says, almost in a trance, "The song, lost, but not yet lost." He snaps out of it and looks me intently in the eyes. "Wrong section, wrong part."

I feel my face getting hot and my throat tightens.

defend the castle
defend the castle

"Well, maybe, but don't we all?" I say with gentle admonition hoping that's the right response. I have no idea if it is, but cryptic chastisement works nine out of ten times when you want someone to back off.

Seidr nods solemnly at Calvin then turns her eyes to me.

"Yes, you're right. I see it too."

Calvin gives her a sheepish grin as he says, "Eyes through death see all. Before, after, now and then. Hidden not from you."

"Wise-cracker," she says laughing. Even her laughter is melodic. She ruffles Calvin's hair like a dog. He chuckles, ambling away to a rickety table along the wall where a huge coffee urn teeters precariously. I resume looking around. No Dana. No Sea Cucumber. No epiphany. I reposition myself so I have a good view of the exit. I spot a message board with flyers on it next to the door. If I read a few I could slip out before this thing starts.

Seidr tilts her head gently, assessing me.

"Well, I'm just gonna...It's nice to meet you," I say.

"Don't mind Calvin, he was hit by a car on Atlantic last year," she replies, placing her hand on my arm. It stays there for a few moments before slowly slipping off like warm honey. I loathe it when strangers touch me.

"When he woke up," she continues, "he could only talk in haikus. And Billy Joel lyrics."

"Cool. Greatest hits or the whole anthology?"

"I'm not sure, Maggie," she says, smiling serenely. Whatever her prescription is, I want it.

"Communication is a tree with many branches, some invisible," she says.

"I guess," I respond, my mind flicking back to dormant tree and her sad, thin branches.

And Seidr's back to tilting. I look at the clock. 8:02. Dana's not coming. I can tell. I don't think she's someone who would be late. This was a stupid idea.

"Hey, I think I'll grab a doughnut before they're all gone," I say, backing up. I immediately stumble into a gangly teenager with a formidable ridge of cystic acne running across his cheek.

"Oh, yah, definitely? I mean, definitely?" he ask-states.

I hear Seidr's voice again "Hello Timothy, this is Maggie."

I've been trying to put my finger on what her voice sounds like and now I know. It's exactly like one of those creepy, overly serene computer voices that count down self-destruct sequences in sci-fi movies.

"Hello, Timothy."

10 … 9 … 8

Timothy and his unfortunate skin lean closer. I avert my eyes to the more infinitely appealing swirls of green-black mold.

"Historically?" he ask-states loudly, "Baked goods have been called upon to solve problems?"

"It's okay, Timothy."

7 … 6 …

"Maggie understands, don't you Maggie?"

yes, Maggie does

Maggie would like to go now

"… like my cousin? She ate a prune danish once and threw up for, like, three days?"

Out of the corner of my eye I see a man approaching us. Everything about him screams cult leader. Charismatic, weirdly serene, bloated air of ownership, underfed shark. He fits perfectly in this moldy swirls, elf-girl, baked goods, Billy Joel deep cuts experience. I'm starting to wonder if this whole thing is some immersive avant-garde theatre of the people off-off-off Broadway play I accidentally stumbled into.

"And-and now?" Timothy continues, "she can't even look at danishes? Like any danishes? Not even cinnamon? I don't know?"

At least Timothy's a purist in the over-talking arts. I can appreciate his commitment.

"I hear that," the creepy cult leader says too loudly. Everyone within earshot chuckles. Seidr smiles luminously at him.

"Sorry. Just a bit of O.T.A humor." His voice is oily.

"I'm Bartholomeu, but everyone here calls me Tholo"

I offer him my I'm-not-susceptible smile and its accompanying voice. "Hi. Maggie."

"So, Maggie, what brings you to us?"

"Curiosity, I suppose," I say. I see Calvin edging closer. After Seidr's creepy countdown, Timothy's panicked stammer and Tholo's viscosity, I'm ready for a haiku.

"Disciples lead on!" Calvin announces, "Treats will group meet then to seats! Chocolate is few!"

Tholo lays a hand on Calvin's shoulder. He flinches. Good to see I'm not the only one creeped out by ol' Barty Tholo.

"Thank you, Calvin," he says with saccharine'd approval. He turns and announces, "Doughnuts and coffee are ready!"

yeah Lo-Lo Calvin already said that

I look at Calvin, attempting one of Mitchel's eyebrow waggles. Calvin flushes. I hang back as all rush the table, their sounds of smacking and slurping making my skin crawl.

aaaaaand time to go

I edge slowly, so as not to alert the hyenas, searching the crowd to get a bead on Tholo and for one last scan of the group to make sure I haven't missed Dana or her friend, but my eyes find Calvin approaching me with a chocolate old fashioned on a napkin.

He offers me the doughnut, whispering "Absurd but more still. Stay to first endure, then amuse. Soon the big ending." Hands down Calvin's the best of the bunch.

Five minutes later we're all seated in a circle of shiny taupe-painted folding chairs. I've often wondered what the inventors of taupe were thinking. Did they say, "Hey, what's the color of despondent resignation? Let's make that!"

Tholo stands. "Acknowledgement! Acceptance! Support!"

The group parrots in shades of vehemence. "Acknowledgement! Acceptance! Support!"

Tholo nods "Yeeeees. Finding neeeeew tools. Uuuuuusing new tools"

A thinner number repeats this mantra, but they more than compensate with fervor. "FINDING NEW TOOLS. USING NEW TOOLS!"

Tholo is pleased. "Yes! Good! Now, everyone, we have a new friend with us tonight."

Everyone looks at me. I attempt a breezy wave but put a bit too much running English on it.

Tholo is waiting. Tholo is smiling and waiting. I've met people like him. In one way or another, everyone is consumable to him. Feeds whatever he decides needs feeding in him. I've always hated bullies, but none more than his breed. Arsenic-laced caramel.

"Maggie, welcome. Whenever someone new joins, we start with a basic question. When did you last communicate non-verbally?"

"But isn't that why language exists? A clear and direct means of communication?" I ask.

"Ah," he says happy I've landed in the snare, "but is it? If all you have is a hammer…"

The believers jump in. "Everything is a nail!"

Tholo smiles, his eyes predatory. "Would you be willing to try something?"

try? silly mortal
I am the great Queen Apathonia
of the realms beyond the petrified forests of Burnis Outus
challenges are but meat for my ennui HAHA
you're losing it Maggie
losing what?

"I just came to listen," I say, "Unless listening is something OTA doesn't encourage?"

Patches of red bloom across his neck and cheeks.

"Gotcha," I mutter.

I'm starting to understand why Dana might come here. New twist on old white male pseudo cult leader complete with wacky band of misfit followers, toxic mold, haikus. And doughnuts. It would make a good piece of journalism. I decide to stick it out. Add it to the things Dana and I can discuss. Put it in our re-connect-as-friends column.

but you followed her here   it doesn't count

shut up   it counts

"I understand. We all do. Don't we?" Tholo sits back with a woeful shrug.

The minions murmur.

"Yet, to build trust, we must share our challenges. Sharing begets trust. Trust begets possibility. Possibility begets transformation."

His logic is sound. Which is what makes him all the more awful. I'm about to respond when an eruption of voices floods the circle.

"We all share here!"

"Great, another Karen, just what we need!"

"Can't shirk the work, lady."

"I don't feel safe, Tholo," a moue-mouthed girl whines.

"She don't wanna talk. Leave her alone," a mammoth, purple-haired guy covered in tattoos says.

Calvin joins with "Hold the future now. The then, now cannot see. The door is closing!" His eyes are squeezed shut.

"She-she doesn't even like doughnuts?!" Timothy adds.

"It's pointless. It's got no point," a businessman to my right says over and over.

"What's shared here stays here," Seidr says.

"I want her to go, Tholo," the moue-mouthed girl says. This must be how those giant velcro walls at fun parks feel.

"Stop pushing her," a new voice says.

"No one's pushing anyone, idiot," another replies.

"Names are not part of our lexicon," the first lobs.

"I hate you," the other replies.

"And I'd hate you if I cared that much," the first says.

"Now, now, friends! Let's—"Tholo says, arms raised.

A very pregnant woman teeters to her feet, her voice piercing the din. "People who are mute, have it made!"

I should've listened to the mold. It told me to run.

note to self   always listen to mold

Tholo attempts to regain control. "Eva, That-okay, first, thank you for sharing your truth. Mike, Cori, remember, finding new tools, using new tools."

But the pregnant woman's floodgates are blown. "I'm tired of talking, tired of listening, tired of people and their crap. What's the point of saying anything? No one can hear anyone over the sound of their own screaming."

A man wearing a 'Demons, Devils and Democrats' shirt chimes in "What? You gonna V.O.S? That's jacked up."

I tap Seidr on the arm. She turns her Siberian Husky eyes to me.

"What's a V.O.S.?" I whisper.

"Vow of Silence," she whispers back.

"Oh, okay. Thanks. So, what? No talking? At all?" She nods, her glacial eyes returning to Tholo.

"Have you ever done one?" I ask.

She nods. "Once. For a year. After my incident."

"Oh, okay. Thanks," I say, receding into my chair, wondering what the incident was and if running into Dana was maybe mine.

"A silent retreat is a good way to try it out. Depends on what you're seeking."

Well, if Cartagena taught me anything it's that I have no idea what I'm seeking other than a general not this.

A voice next to me softly says, "Sometimes hearing my own voice is the only way I know I still exist."

I look to my right to find a pair of soulful brown eyes next to me. He must be one of those people who are camouflaged until you look right at them. His eyes are searching mine for answers. I want to tell him people shouldn't come to me for help. I shrug, trying not to seem like the cold lost in space bitch that I am, then search for somewhere else to put my eyes.

Calvin. He's staring at the floor. I follow his gaze to a stain where something brown-ish happened. A Rorschach of all the dead hopes and dreams of each person who has sat in this dingy, putty colored, mold encrusted basement.

yellow dust   *dirt*

fireworks

this land is my land

this land's not your land

clickclack clickclack

"Shut UP! JUST SHUT UP! ALL OF YOU!" a woman's voice booms. God bless pregnant women. They suffer no damn fools. The man next to me covers his ears and begins to rock and hum.

Tholo shouts, "New tools! NEW TOOLS!"

Seidr leans in. "Come on, this'll last a while."

She walks toward the stairs. I grab my purse and follow. As the door closes behind me, I hear Devils and Democrats guy's voice booming. "Shit's Darwinian! Always has been. Always will be!"

The cold air feels incredible. Inches of fluffy snow have fallen over the past hour, softening the edges of buildings and cocooning street signs. It's still. And blissfully quiet.

Seidr leans against the building, lighting a joint. Her elf-girl persona evaporated once the door closed behind us.

"Hey, so," I say," I was wondering if maybe-do you remember, from last week, an enigmatic Cherokee woman with a tall woman wearing a green coat and hat?"

"Oh, yeah. Dana and Patricia," she says. "Yeah, they're cool. Tricia comes all the time, but last week was the first for Dana."

"Oh, right. Right. Okay. Cool" I say.

"Yeah, Dana's cool," Seidr continues. "She's writing something about the colonization of language and white power structures. Something like that. They're a great couple."

waitwhat?
no way Dana could be with a green beanie wearing Tricia
who probably only ever talks about recycling
OVERtalks about recycling

It's disorienting to be told something so intimate about a person who used to hold a huge place in my life, from another stranger who just met her. But the Dana and I that were best friends who told each other everything there was to tell were from before all this after. Before puberty and sexuality and green beanie wearing partners who overtalk about recycling and carry protest signs and glare at former best friends.

why didn't she tell you?
she thinks you're a bigot

"You should come to a Language of the Body class," Seidr says, offering me the joint. I take it. This night couldn't get any weirder anyway.

"Yeah?" I ask, passing the joint back to her.

"Sometimes the body can unlock what the mind won't. Already halfway down the rabbit hole anyway, right?"

"Yeah, you could say that." I answer. She passes it back to me. I take a long pull and hand it back.

"Keep it. I have to get back in to help Tholo."

"Oh, okay. Thanks."

Before the door closes, her creepy countdown voice returns. "It's every Monday at 6:30. SyntheDance Studios on 3rd."

The snow will turn to yellow dotted brown-grey slush by morning, but for now it's soft and untouched, drifting so slowly it's almost suspended.

September 1978

Ohma?

yes?

*can I-I mean would you could I become a-a if I tried real hard n
can I be maybe if I tried real hard n learned lots more first*

she sets her basket down it's my favorite of all her baskets
long n curved n it's got seven stripes of dark blue woven in like
ripples it's also stained purplely-red cause she uses it for
elderberries a lot we've been harvestin em mostly from her
property but also from the woods like today Ohma says you
haveta leave most of it for the ones who live in the woods
bears specially love em she says if people take all of bear's
elderberries they shouldn't be surprised when bear comes
lookin for food in their kitchen everythin she says makes sense

what do you want to know tsi s qua?

she gave me that nickname and I love it love it love it cause it
feels like it always belonged to me but no one noticed til Ohma
said it out loud she says it's really a-s-da-ya usdi tsi s qua but
she mostly calls me tsi s qua she says the whole of it means
loud little bird   she thought it was funny n I did too n Dana
laughed n laughed cause I go hours n hours without sayin
anything most days then sometimes the words come bubblin
up n out all of a sudden like a rainstorm   Ohma likes jokes like
that sortof jokes like sayin one word when it's really another
one or like my nickname being a talky bird but also really
mostly bout the other side of bein talky Ohma's real real funny
but she never smiles when she tells a joke

if I can   maybe someday if I work really hard if I can be saa laa gee too?

the second I say it my stomach squeezes n pulls like the taffy machine at the boardwalk

Ohma doesn't say anything she just looks at me n smiles a small smile it makes me feel like smoke floatin from a fire

you see that cardinal over there?   next to the crabapple?

I nod

and the robin there?   in the birch?

I nod again

they're both birds but cardinal doesn't try to be robin and robin doesn't try to be cardinal

my face is gettin prickly even though I'm tellin it to stop

wishing to be other than what you have been born to be brings only sadness and a bitter taste inside it never brings the wish

I watch the cardinal n the robin fly away

wishing does not see anything but the wish, understand?

I try to nod but my neck doesn't want to she takes my hands and closes them round each other leavin a small tunnel she puts it up to my left eye n puts her hand over my other eye

what do you see?

I can only see part of the birch tree where the robin was   I can't see anythin else

where the robin was

when there is only a wish or want there's nothing else
no tree no field no earth no sky nothing else

she takes her hand away from my eye

only branch   understand?

the wind is swishin the trees like an ocean far away   everythin inside me seems like grey paint spilled over it n it'll never be bright again cause I don't ever get to be saa laa gee   I want to crumble into the ground   hide there til forever

come...

she touches my shoulder   I never feel like I have to get smaller when Ohma touches me n how she knew my nickname before anyone else   she just knows things

let's make elderberry tonic and you can tell me how many rosehips to add

she hands me a few elderberries to eat n starts walking back to the path that leads to her farm

6

"Enough." Mitchel's in my doorway. "Ever since you bumped into Dana, you've been acting like a crazy person." The glare on the building across the street begins oozing across my window. It's almost here. Mitchel's timing is terrible.

"Maggie. Hey, Mags?"

"There you are," I whisper to the light.

In the light, there's only the light. There's no me. No now me to compare to a before me. No forgotten shards scratching their way to the surface. No things I'll wish I left alone. Things that will change other things.

"You're losing it. You know that, right?"

I don't know what to tell him. I'm not sure he'd understand even if I could explain it. The light careens in. Around me and through me. Mitchel is saying something but I'm not listening. I'm not here now. I close my eyes. The tintype outline of windows burned into my retina dissolves into a wall of red, black, and white sparks.

sparks sparks sparklers

The room darkens. I open my eyes. He closed the shades.

"Don't make me use the Tiger." he says. He means singing the entire four-minute version of "Eye of the Tiger." We've binge watched every one of the first 250 episodes of *Supernatural* least four times and watching the outtake of Jensen Ackles singing "Eye of the Tiger" is a top ten favorite moment. "I'm not kidding. I'll do it."

He's not kidding. He will. I decide to be honest about something. Just for a minute. "I followed her."

"You, wait, you what?"

"I followed her, okay? I didn't plan it. I saw her on Smith and Atlantic and just, you know, walked in the same direction, until she went inside a building. And then last night I went back. I was curious."

"Uhhhhhh-huh."

"It was a meeting she was reporting on, and she was with the sea cucumber from the protest-"

"The sea cucumber?"

"Her girlfriend, apparently"

"Uh-huh. The sea cucumber. Her girlfriend. Right. Interesting. Kinda naughty too."

"Mitch ..."

"Come on, you walked into that one."

"That's not, just-her name is Patricia. Tri*cia*? No. I mean, I guess it's fine as far as names go but it's just, Dana with a Tricia? No. A Tahlia or maybe a Serrat, yes. But a Tricia? I mean, come on."

"Have you messed with your Ambien dose again?"

"What? No. I'm-no. I'm saying I just happened to see Dana."

"Just happened?"

"And I was curious, so I sort of followed-"

"*Stalked.*"

"*Stalked* her for a few blocks and it was weird."

"Yeah, I'd say that was weird."

"No, that's not. Okay fine. I'm a crazy stalker. What I mean is where she went"

"Uh-huh. And that was...?"

"I wasn't really sure. It was it was that, you know, the church near the Chocolate Room?"

"She was going to church? Huh. She didn't seem like a churchy person."

"No, it's-it was a meeting, you know like, how those places rent out space for meetings? So, I went back to the same building last night to, you know-"

"Dig inappropriately into her life uninvited?"

"Potato, potaaahto, po-toe-toe," I say, hoping levity will divert him.

"Right. So?" he asks, ignoring my joke.

I shrug hoping detachment will divert him.

"What was it?" He's not going to let it go.

"A meeting. An Overtalkers Anonymous meeting."

"A what of who?"

"Over Talkers Anonymous."

He starts to laugh. "Okay. So, you're following Dana and her 'friend' to a meeting for people who talk too much."

"Well, yeah."

"Then you went back last night to check it out?"

"Yeah."

"And?"

"Nothing. That's it." I say, pushing papers into piles on my desk.

"Okay, well ethics of stalking aside, I have an important question."

I'm tired of this conversation. I expected him to get it and the fact that he doesn't makes everything worse.

"How many Chee-tos were there?" he asks. "It must have been full of wack-a-doos."

"Mitchel ..."

"What? Jesus, you've entirely lost your sense of humor."

"Not everything's a joke," I say. "I mean, haven't you ever thought you might have taken a wrong turn somewhere, but it's so far back and you're who you are now because of it so there's no way you could find that turning point again even if you tried because it belonged to the *you* you were, not the *you* you are?"

"Hey, Sylvia Plath, whatcha doin?"

"What?"

"The existential spelunking? This spin out? It won't help. She's playing games. I can tell."

"I don't think she is."

"Okay, fine. Then it's worse. She's a yellow light."

"What are you even talking about?"

"I've known a few Danas."

"I doubt that."

"People who act so enlightened, like they have shit all figured out and it's always the other person who is blowing it? And heaven fucking forbid you call out someone indigenous on their shitty behavior. Noooo. Can't do that. It's all eggshells."

"Mitch, calm down."

He ignores me. He's on a roll. It's rare for him to get this charged up and I have no idea where it's coming from. "It's on you to speed through or slam the brakes." he says. "Any damage is on you, cause it's always on you. They're forever exempt from being called out because of the injustices, right? Well, join the world, folks. Plenty of injustice for all."

"Okay, okay. Good sermon. Thanks." I immediately wish I could shove the words back down my throat.

Mitchel's grandfather was one of those traveling salvation show types. He thought he could faith heal his grandson's CP, but when he couldn't, to save face—and no doubt his movable feast upon the fearful and desperate—he spent the remaining years of his life condemning Mitchel to hell because "the devil has dominion in your bones, boy". Pretty sure Mitchel is in the clear on that count, but for damn sure his grandfather's paying dues in the fourth and eighth of Dante's nine.

round about the cauldron go
in the poison'd entrails throw
you're losing your mind little bird
losing?
shut up

"Meaning," Mitch continues, needles in his eyes, "is a manmade concept. We put it where we put it. That's all. Regrets are for suckers. Or have you forgotten?"

"I remember. And you've been a sucker too."

"I don't do regret."

"Not even Amanda?" I ask.

Below the belt punch number two. Amanda was a cellist with the Met who Mitchel fell for a few years ago. She grew tired of his defenses and moved on to a soulful Flamenco dancer just as Mitchel was about to ask her to move in with him. He never talks about her. She and his grandfather's 'faith' are no fly zones.

"Look, I'm sorry," I say, "I'm being. I'm just saying-"

"Yeah, I know what you're saying," he replies flatly. "Want my unsolicited advice?"

"May I please?" I don't know why I'm trying to pick a fight with him.

"Treat this little existential crisis of yours like a kidney stone. Ride it out and let it pass." He slaps on a frigid grin for good measure then leaves, singing "Eye of the Tiger" at top volume, saluting Chelsea as he passes.

The Amanda thing was too far. I have a gift for stupidity at the precise moment it will do the most damage. But his weird lash out at Dana is baffling.

Chelsea's eyes hover on him. Admiration. Then back to me. Bland reproach. I ignore her. Despite my irritation and his resentment, his advice has merit. Ride it out, let it pass.

****

8:15
email   computer to sleep   desk lamp

I don't want to think about how many times I've done this. The accrual of these seconds into minutes into days of doing the same three things. Time I'll never get back.

The floor is dark save my office, and Newton's. I have no idea if she's still here or if she just leaves her light on in an Eye-of-Sauron way. Doesn't matter.

I shut my office door, sink back into my chair, and close my eyes, listening to the muffled whir of floors being buffed somewhere in the building. The radiator in the corner clacks and hisses. I feel myself begin to drift between sleep and wake, and even though I know it's the precise place where truths wait for defenses to slip, I let the currents pull me anyway. bus engine huuummm sun's low still hot though I'm doodling a feather on my backpack between my keep on truckin' n Calvin n Hobbs patches something's wrong with the pen though because every time I'm done with the doodle it fades til it's gone again fth-th-th-th-th-thrump fth-th-th-th-th-thrump fth-th-th-th-th-thrump runnin the side of my sneaker along the ridged rubber floor hard black spots that used to be gum like the polka dot scarf mom likes she's gonna be mad I don't wanna think bout that sad eyes floatin in the air where faces should be bus door closes **fump** driver lookin into his mirror at me puffy face n tiny eyes like beads I scooch down in my seat a motorcycle rumbles past my window

wait, that's not right

My office is dark. The whole floor is dark. I grab my purse and head to the elevator. The muzak version of *Send in the Clowns* flows from the speakers. Some perfect moments have claws.

It's bitterly cold out. I pull my collar up, hat down, and focus on avoiding the lily pads of black ice that formed after a wheezing sun slid into night at 4 p.m. As I round the corner all I see is metal and wheels. I skid and slip on a patch of ice, catching hold of a scaffolding bar.

The coffee cart owner's soft, weary eyes hold mine. Six years of twice daily coffee at his cart. He's smaller than I thought. Older. We peer at one other through billows of startled breath.

After a few moments he nods, places his shoulder against the cart, and resumes his Sisyphean journey. I watch him maneuver his cart into the street, and slowly out of sight.

I don't feel cold anymore. Probably just the adrenaline. I walk past the concrete buildings, the bagel place, the bespoke clothing stores, the tequila bar. Down the same uneven sidewalks and cobblestones, to the York Street F train station, stopping at the top of the first flight of jaundiced stairs, letting the acrid, warm cauldron of hipsters, roaches, corporate lawyers, trendy parents, rats, urine, models, and mole people surge around me.

round about the cauldron go
in the poison'd entrails throw

I turn and climb the stairs back out to the sidewalk and frigid air eager to gouge my lungs. Uneven sidewalks become wide and flat, then narrow and cracked, and eventually the steady, side by side squares of neighborhoods here before Bloomberg or Dinkins or Koch. Neighborhoods that used to overflow with life and laughter and block parties. Where people looked out for one another. Helped raise each other's kids. No one does that now. Gentrification brings the opaque isolation of self-sufficiency. Cups of flour aren't shared here anymore.

Maybe that's why dormant tree is dormant. Maybe watching the tethers between each home wither away and drop, replaced with moats of autonomy, broke her heart beyond repair. A heart can break beyond repair and keep beating out of habit.

I drift past Mrs. Costa's house, half hoping to see her, but her windows are dark. I even glance up at the tree in front of her brownstone to see if she might have accidentally drifted into its branches.

I continue up my stoop, past glutted mailboxes, up narrow curved stairs, past the old wedding photo on the second-floor landing with a hole through the bride's heart where the nail pierced through during someone or other's move. Once inside, I'm welcomed by stillness. Dylan's not home, and I don't want to think about how grateful I am for that.

I set my things down and push off my shoes. The pale, yellowed streetlamps of Sackett Street project dormant tree's frail arms across the walls. She gently twists and reaches as if she's been inside all this time, restlessly waiting.

I breathe for what feels like the first time today and open a Montrachet. I remember the first time I could afford it. It's flinty and creamy. A bit salty. I had no idea wine could be like that. Growing up in rural western North Carolina, teenage elegance maxed out at Bartles and Jaymes Wine Coolers. The second bottle of Montrachet I bought was also incredible. The third was good. Now it's just the wine I drink.

I pour a generous glass for dormant tree and set it on the window ledge for her, letting the undulation of her shadow on my walls smudge my heavier thoughts.

****

It's still dark, but paler. Almost morning. I shift onto my side and look at dormant tree. The glass of wine I left for her on the windowsill is empty. Maybe she drank it while I was sleeping.

yeah Maggie   the tree drank it

I listen for sounds of Dylan, but all I hear is the radiators thunking and someone downstairs listening to R.E.O. Speedwagon. My battle of ice darts with Mitchel resurfaces.

I roll the couch pillows I used as a blanket back into place, and shuffle over to start the process of coffee. I don't want to think about the damage I did to my friendship with him. Or Dana waiting for me to contact Ohma. Or bumping into her at any moment in what used to be my neighborhood but is now *our* neighborhood. Or anything else for that matter. I'm tired of thinking. Thinking, thinking, thinking.

blah blah blah

I stare at my mug collection. Choice seems significant today. *Surely Not Everybody Was Kung-Fu Fighting* has been a recent favorite, but it's not right. *My Spoon is Too Big*, always true on a metaphorical level, isn't right either. I grab *The Sleeper Must Awaken.* On the nose it is.

walnut eyes

coffee cart

"Butterfly? You here?" Dylan's voice asks.

One of the more bizarre of Dylan's attributes is he often doesn't notice when I'm the only other person in the room. Once he does, a tepid smile is all I can muster.

"I just had the most affirming practice!" he says, flushed with excitement, "Shay finally joined us!" He leaps across the room and grasps my hands. "I think she's finding her mind-spirit connection! It was incredible to watch! Such an honor." I maneuver away. His brow furrows.

"You okay?" he asks.

I'm not prepared to answer that on a micro or meta level. I just need one day. One day of not having to talk to him, or anyone else for that matter. One day without explanations. Maybe the sea cucumber and I have something in common. Maybe she's not so much an over talker but more someone who finds navigating all the noise and the blah, blah, blah here exhausting.

world too loud?

start with yourself

"Yeah," I say, trying to balance world-weary with soul-searchy. "I'm-I just-I think I might try a vow of silence for a day. I have a lot of noise in my head lately and-" It occurs to me I never told Dylan about running into Dana.

"VOS, huh? Alright! Pure lotus flower, babe. Pure lotus. Big time!"

He gives me a supportive thumbs up. I volley back a flaccid one and head to the bathroom with my *The Sleeper Must Awaken* mug.

"Super mindful action, babe! I'm proud of you! Really proud!" he says.

"Uh, huh," I say quietly as I close the door. It's the last thing I'm going to say for 24 hours. I already feel better.

****

let go of the sink
it's just one day
My hands relax a bit.
don't limit your challenges   challenge your limits
A sneer flicks through my eyes.
working depth of a postcard
but you already knew that
Dylan's voice filters through the door. "Nudity's fine if it celebrates the body electric." He's using the voice he reserves for children, dogs, and me when he thinks I need guidance. "Listening is a verb we practice together to build trust. Let's build that trust right now." He pauses, then says, "Let's say it together. "Holy vessel. Holy...we're a team, right?"

I can get behind Body Electric because Whitman. But forcing someone to say Holy Vessel? Eesh. The sooner rather than later of our ending takes a leap forward. It won't be today, but sooner is almost here.

I return to the mirror and focus on perfecting a subtle wing of charcoal liner.
yes you crap friend stalker master of avoidance
at least get your eyeliner right

Make-up really should have names for what they really
are. Ashes of Your Hopes and Dreams. The Black Hole of
Your Heart. Unmet Expectations.

My eyes gaze at me dismally.

shut up

"It's about preserving the sacred self," Dylan's voice says.
I look at my impeccable eyeliner.

yeah

Ten minutes later, I'm heading for the door while Dylan
continues to work on to whoever he's attempting to
indoctrinate. He's like the Colorado river—relentlessly carving
his preferred shape of you. He sends out a you're-a-champ-in-
my-eyes soccer dad point as I close the door.

you bet

champ

I hate that he says it without saying it. He thinks it. Somehow
that's worse.

****

The ever-shifting corridor between things is important
here. Negative space has walls—partitions between self and the
noise. The smells, edges, and movements of millions of people.
This negative space is my home. But today, the corridor eludes
me. My Teflon coating is gone. I'm looking right at people.
Running into them. Their sweat, unwashed hair, freshly
shampoo'd hair. Their cologne, and halitosis. Their coffee, and
everything bagels with lox, and the grind of their teeth
chewing. The click-click-click of their texting, the shaking
impatience of their knees waiting for a train. All of it is sticking
to me.

They flick their eyes and edge away from the nut job
standing on the platform thinking thoughts and looking at
them and unable to Teflon.

that's right folks

it's the crazy sticky lady who looks

Someone brushes past me and settles a few yards away, peering around the platform in that pursuing-a-dream way young hopefuls do when they first arrive.

this is no place for little bunnies

The bunny flinches. She's looking right at me, eyes huge and dejected. As if she heard every word I was thinking. I decide to thought-wave her some advice.

you need to toughen up
learn to fit in
build a shell
it's easy
can't be a bunny anymore

She collapses into soft, wounded earnestness, and drifts like lint behind a group of hipsters. It occurs to me Mitchel's going to have a field day with this. I'll try not to be weird, which will be weird on top of the already weird between us, and then he'll say, 'What's up with the weird?' and I'll just stand there, silently being weird.

summation of insights since commencement of VOS
working depth of postcard
crappy friend
stalker
master of avoidance
Teflon
possibly able to transmit thoughts to strangers
probably crazy
definitely self-absorbed asshat
silently weird

Stale, sooty air stirs as a train careens into the station. I scan for vacancies, disregarding suspiciously open cars. Only tourists fall for those. The same way they fall prey to an empty seat in a packed train oblivious to the Russian Roulette with mystery fluids they're about to play.

A crammed car comes to a halt in front of me and twenty of us push into a space made for five. Fump-fump. Fump-fump. The doors are trying to close. The conductor's voice booms ominously from the speakers. "Let go of the doors or I'll take this train out of service."

New Yorkers follow a set of unspoken rules. The main one being do not be an idiot. Jerk is okay. Idiot is not. Delaying a train because your bag or body parts are in the way of the doors is squarely in the latter category. After the doors have finally closed, I settle into my usual spot leaning next to them.

We creep past an elderly woman with a granny cart. She was probably the reason the doors couldn't close. She makes weary, confused eye contact with me.

shit-we—I-I—we-shitsorrydammit

I look to see if anyone else noticed her but mine are the only eyes raised above 60 degrees.

****

Having already blown through my 34oz *The Sleeper Must Awaken* travel mug while trying to give myself something to do other than stare at people, concoct casual ways to ask Dana and the sea cucumber to dinner, or wonder if Ohma looks as frail and old as the lady on the subway platform, I'm now waiting in a line at the coffee cart, contemplating the progression of minutes from the Firefly Festival moment last night to this one.

a progression of minutes
the title of Maggie Morris' autobiography
also Maggie's speaking in the third person now
good times

I try to focus on things outside myself. I opt for observing the people in line with me. A woman with a deep

Louisiana patois chatting on her phone while eating a huge apple fritter.

"MmmmmHmmm, that's what I'm telling you," she says, "He got that gamblin' problem. And don't get me started on that man's elbow. It don't know straight."
Behind her are a trio of suits, scrolling, typing, and talking in each other's general direction.

"So," Suit One asks, looking at his phone, "how's the Amber thing?"

"The Amber thing's done," Suit Two says, his eyes also latched to his phone.

"I told him," the woman continues, "I said, it's simple. Just don't put the money on the wood. That's all. Mmn. MmnMmn. But you know, no telling the man cause the man's gonna do what the man's gonna do. Mmmmhmmmm. Man never gonna change."
She talks as if there'll never, ever be enough words.

maybe that's how you sound Mags

no way

you sure Magpie?

"What's up with that?" Suit One asks Suit Two.

"What?" asks Suit Two.

"The Amber thing"

"Level 10 crazy"

"Chicks"

"Women are like bacon," Suit Three says. "Once you understand that, life falls into place, kemosabee."

kemosabee? asshole

and why the HELL is everyone yelling?

Suits One, Two and Three walk away. It's just me and the coffee cart owner now. A tiny smile tugs a corner of his mouth as he hands me a large coffee and a twist doughnut. Borders of a large, pink scar peek out from the frayed cuff of his sleeve like a timid bird.

I've ordered a large coffee and a twist doughnut every morning for ten years, but I don't know anything about him. What gave him that scar. When it happened. If it happened during the decade I've been coming to his coffee cart. This is the first time, the second if I count last night, that I've truly looked at him. If the peaks and valleys of our face are a map showing the life we've led, I'm not sure I want to see mine. But his is softly creased with lines born of a lifetime spent smiling. At least that's what I want to think. People like to think things like that about people who serve them coffee from a tiny metal cart in the middle of February.

I make a point of looking him in the eye. It feels forced but we bonded in an inexplicable way last night so reverting to avoidance would mean things about me. Irreparable things.

I put a $100 bill on the ledge and gesture for him to keep the change. Suddenly, holding his gaze is harder. A $96 tip seems a drop in the very large bucket of apology I owe this man, but it also feels like I'm doing that *money* thing. It's not as if I think money is an actual apology for ten years of disregarding his basic humanity, but it's a start.

October 1978

Dana's the funniest person I ever met but she doesn't tell jokes
more like she notices stuff

that's weird or doesn't belong n then she nudges me n points it
out then we laugh n laugh n laugh til my throat is thick n my
sides r too tight she notices all the stuff I don't see people
stuff funny stuff grown-ups do sometimes kids too we meet
at Nathy almost every day after school n she acts out funny
stuff she saw people do I never notice funny people stuff like
she does only how smelly or loud or crunchy-too close or talk-
talky they always r I see funny stuff like how robins look like
they're always late for somethin or how cute spiders r when
they take naps n how I'm pretty sure they make teeny meep
meep meep sounds when they snore or how rivers love stories
bout how things start or where they end up Dana hears n sees
non people stuff too but in a different way   she can tell stuff
like how cold it's gonna get in winter by how many acorns
Nathy makes

Dana knows how to be Dana all the time but I'm more floaty n
wobbly round people stuff sometimes I lose track of myself I
try to be more like em but I always feel like I'm pretendin or
wearin clothes that don't fit right only time I am who I am is
when I'm watchin orb weavers make webs or when Jake is
purrin or watchin the river n always always always with Nathy
the only people I don't feel floaty-wobbly or itchy around r
Dana n Ohma n daddy most of the time though sometimes
he gets the itchiest of everyone

we're gonna have lunch today daddy's takin us he said we
could choose n we decided on Murphy's cause they make
breakfast all day we're almost there just one more block past

the Hallmark n the Radio Shack people on the sidewalk r
lookin at us Dana holds my hand n it keeps me from gettin
floaty again she walks with her chin up lookin right back at
people she's amazin I don't like lookin right back at people
they look at me like there's somthin wrong with me

Dana squeezes my hand n whispers *what're you gonna have?*

I pick up a small stiff black n white woodpecker feather in the
gutter

dunno what bout you?

maybe banana pancakes? she says *or waffles*

*waffles! yeah, waffles! n sccccrrrrrrrrrrrrrrrrrrrrrrrrraaaaaaple! n maybe
a cone at Libby's if daddy lets us*

what flavor you gonna get?

hmmmm I say *chocolate marshmallow swirl what bout you?*

hmmmm she says *think I'll get sidewalk grease*

BLECH I say wrigglin

old shoes? she asks

belly button lint I say

EW EW EW moldy bread n bologna she says

EWWBLEEEEEHHHKKEEEBLUUUUUH

we're laughin so hard

you know, laughin's a serious crime daddy says peanut butter chuckling *n the punishment for such a terrible crime is...*

Dana squeezes my hand n looks at me her eyes real wide

I squeeze her hand n whisper *he's just jokin*

waffles n scccrrrrrrraaaaaaaple! daddy's laughin soft n round so, *Dana, do you like waffles n scccrrrrrrraaaaaaapppple?*

he's laughin but it sounds like it's far away

Dana nods but doesn't say anythin her hand is sweaty now n I wanna take my hand outta hers so I can wipe it on my shorts but I don't cause it would hurt her feelins daddy smiles at her then me then her then me

rummmmblllleeebuuummmbleeebummmble an old truck rumblin by real loud faded red n it says Chevy on the front the truck slows way down prolly lookin for a place to park daddy looks at it funny

Dana nudges me n whispers *look*

I whisper back *what?*

Emilynn she whispers

Emilynn Martin the meanest girl in all of North Carolina is peekin out at us her eyes r so small n hard they look like her face is swallowin em

the truck driver man looks right at us daddy waves at him the driver man waves back but his face looks like the river after it rains too much the truck **rummbleebummbles** away daddy opens the door for us   *ladies? after you*

it's busy n loud n clanky inside Murphy's but Dana n daddy don't seem to notice so I stay close hopin they'll make some walls between me n the noises it smells like eggs n waffles n bacon n coffee n bleach I hatehatehate bleach the lady at the counter is starin at us smilin but the smile isn't inside her eyes she's prolly been smellin the bleach too long

> *okay ladies this way* daddy leads us to a table at the big front window

Dana n I sit on one side n daddy on the other Freddy comes over with coffee for daddy Freddy's nice n quiet with short red hair n real long legs n arms he's wearin green n black striped socks like a shy spider who knows maple-y knockknock jokes

> *thanks Freddy we'll have three waffle breakfasts with scrapple n...*

daddy looks at us

> *scrambled* I say
> *yeah uhm scrambled* Dana says

> *three scrambled it is Freddy make sure they're cooked okay? we don't like runny eggs do we?*

Freddy nods n shuffles away daddy takes his fork n pops it through a creamer he turns it upside down over his coffee n squeezes it

> *moooo, moooo, moooo*

I giggle so does Dana   daddy smiles it's a nice smile but kinda wobbly too

115

7

"This more of that over-talkers crap?" Mitchel whispers. He's been trying to get me to talk for the past hour of yet another meeting where Newton pees on our shoes. His cologne is at my favorite stage. A faint cinnamon, nutmeg, bourbon, and oak moss mix that's only detectable if he's a few inches away. My thoughts jumble.

"This is weird. Even for you," he whispers next to my ear. Warm spiced oak floats across me.

it's not him   it's the smell

I shrug, maintaining my poker face.

"Seriously? You're not talking at all now?" he asks.

I look at him with exaggerated surprise and mouth out 'Daaaaaaaamn, nuthin' gets past you!'

"You're losing it," he says, sitting back into his chair. His backing off helps, but I can still hear my pulse in my ears.

just another bizarre VOS side effect

and his green eyes

stop

It's just sensory amplification syndrome. I read about it when I got to work. The amplification of familiar surroundings when we alter an entrenched pattern or system. Up is down. I write on a notepad "Just something I'm trying. I'm not losing it. Yet." He reads it, eyebrows lifting.

"You'll break," he whispers in my ear. It sends a tiny electric jolt down my spine. "They all break."

what the hell?

whatthehellwhatthehell

calm down   it's just sensory amplification syndrome

"People!" Newton's voice booms across the table. Everyone hushes. Her eyes land on me.

"One more thing. I'd like you to take a page from Mag Morris. She practiced active listening today. No explanations. No apologies. She listened. Take a page, people."

She exits, leaving a wake of disgruntled eyes on me.

"You've got to be kidding me" Mitchel says, loud enough for all to hear. "Don't let this teacher's pet thing go to your head Ms. Speak No Evil," he says, watching me carefully.

jealous?

"No, Taciturn-a-potomus" he says, "I'm not jealous."

he can read your thoughts
leave the room
NOW

I give him a 'hey, it's not my fault' shrug

"Whatever you don't say Charlie Chaplin," he volleys.

I'm never going to win a battle of wits with Mitchel, so I toss him a royal wave as I walk out. I hear him chuckle behind me. It's low and warm and unfiltered. It sends a thrum through my chest.

up is down
today doesn't count

Three hours later I'm looking at a stack of finished work that's been hanging around my desk for over a week. Seems implausible to have been this productive just by not talking, but I reclaimed three hours of my usual workday because I didn't have to hand hold clients over the phone. Chelsea, no doubt, is concocting an intricate payback over the number of messages she's taken.

As if on cue, she strides into my office carrying a large stack of messages. She places them on my desk with searing precision, blinking her disappointment before curtly leaving. I leaf through the slips. The usual needy client suspects. The last one catches my eye. A message that says FROM: Dana Walden. There's nothing in the message body. Just Dana's name and "please call back." Maybe she saw me the night I followed her and she's finally calling to confront me about it. Or she wants to know if I've contacted Ohma.

red dust

station wagon

the way way back

tangy sweet spicy earthy salty

I sweep the messages into the top drawer of my desk and head to the elevator. Less than a minute later, Mitchel joins me, doing his best to appear indifferent. I take a page from Chelsea's book and blink at him.

He grimaces. "My morse code skills are rusty, so …" I burst out in silent mock laughter. He keeps looking at me. I feel myself getting twitchy for something else to look at. His eyebrows lift a fraction. I concentrate on the digital screen telegraphing which floor the elevator is on.

14 … 13 … 12 … 12 … 12 … 12

come on   12 … 12 …

"So, Sir Mutes-a-lot, off to a wild night of karaoke?" I try a goofy laugh, but it ends up more like a donkey. "I see," he says, "Sounds allowed? Don't know, seems to denote a lack of commitment to your non-verbal life choices."

you're being disproportionately lame

"Whelp," he announces, "I'm off to Chelsea Piers for some parallel bars action. Since it's national DO CRAZY THINGS Day."

"Finally," he says under his breath when the elevator arrives.

I guess our friendship is based on a much narrower bandwidth than I thought. We ride down with the muzak version of "Space Age Love Song" accompanying the videotainment screen's coverage of some politician's sex scandal and fires raging in rain forests. The video seems slow. And the colors are oversaturated. I can hear my heart. Air entering and leaving my lungs. My feet sinking into the floor.

I turn towards him with an exaggerated grumpy face. He glances at me, then turns his eyes back to the screen.

"You're unstable," he says, reining in a smile. The doors open and he dashes out with formidable speed. "Okay, crazy person, have a fun night with swami-Bob. He'll love the mute thing. It's always better when you chicks don't talk, anyway."

I stick out my tongue, letting out a long "pppppppptttt hhhhhhwwwwwwwwwwrrrrrrrttttttttttttttt!"

excellent comeback, Maggie

crap

I'm supposed to meet my professional women's group at Zaytoons for our bi-monthly winning at life-a-thon. One of us, I can't remember who, nicknamed us The Powerheels. Should have never returned after that. I could make tonight the night of not returning. Though I am curious what my silence will do to the dynamic.

By the time I arrive conversation is already in full, overlapping swing. Not sure how I've managed to do this every Tuesday without an epi pen. I try to picture how this might go:

a.   They all talk over and around me as if I'm invisible.

b.   Inspired by my silence, they join me in non-verbality, and true friendship begins.

c.   Numerous Queen Maggie's finally lost it looks are not too subtly exchanged followed by their excuses for an early night.

Doesn't take an astrophysicist to know how this is going to go. But I should try. I might be wrong. I'm starting to sense wrong might be my default mode. My mind starts to cross the street, but my feet won't budge.

listen to your feet
like the mold
listen to the molds of your feats

I pull out my phone to text Zoey, an ex-model turned mega-influencer who's gained two million followers through her eviscerating commentaries on other people's beauty misfortunes. She calls it honesty in a dishonest world.

I type "hey, girl no go 2night - deadlines - drink 4 me" and hit send. Zoey, whose phone is never beyond her impeccably manicured reach, checks it right away. Triumph creeps across her face. We all promised to keep this night sacrosanct even if it meant having to go back to work afterwards. My breaking it means I'm a welsher. Welshers aren't competition.

Zoey drinks the rest of her wine and holds her phone up for the others, who lean in greedily. Maire, a VP at Sur la Table shakes her head in disapproval, popping an olive in her mouth. Odelia, a contemporary choreographer on the verge of becoming Broadway's next genius after her breakout work on a carnival-themed musical based on Dostoyevsky's *The Idiot*, offers a gesture of disbelief. Kenia, a rising star in Buyout & Growth at Merrill stonewalls.

This is it. My chance to slip through the floorboards under their designer shoes. Never again be expected to compare notes on the incompetence of others or toast our willingness to shoulder the burden of exceptionality. It'd be a relief to escape the choke hold. No-one would miss me. We're just a collective of accomplishment. Seeing Dana again reminded me what friendship can be. There's no friendship here. Nothing to mourn.

I feel like a picture left to fade in the sun. The image of a once but now indeterminate someone. Someone once there.

text her

red dirt this land

text her

this land faded red blood red

text her

I pull my phone back out. "hi got ur message no chance to contact Ohma yet deadlines but soon promise -M" I press send. She replies right away.

"That's okay. Let me know when you talk to her." Jumping dots. Jumping dots. Then she adds, "I know it was kind of weird and we sort of mis-fired, but it really was good to see you."

I try to think of something to say.

it was great to see you too
it was!
it was...
you should give up on me I'm not worth it

I choose a blue cartoon thumb up. Not even thumbs. Just thumb. In essence, I've conveyed 'I'm indifferent about all of this. I can't even be bothered to write that so I, a grown-ass woman, shall give you a blue cartoon thumb up instead.' I use the thumb up frequently.

On the way home I grab a small Bulleit and drink it on a stranger's stoop watching the dried silver leaves on a nearby birch rustle, clinging to the tree that created them. Papery ghosts unable to move on.

Around eleven I creep in, trying not to wake Dylan. It's quiet and dark. Only dormant tree's backlit branches to greet me. I've come to realize I prefer the lights off. Otherwise, my loft with all of Dylan's Dylan-ness is too colorful. Like living inside dyed carnations.

I kill the bottle of Bulleit, splitting it between two glasses. One for me and one for dormant tree. Her naked arms are still tonight.

were you a person once, tree?
a nun?
or a parishioner?
when people still visited this building with hope?
when it was a church?

Bronwen Carson

were you someone no-one ever noticed?
or wanted
or missed
so you slowly turned into a tree

****

I can hear her running from a hiding spot I was about to find
the sun's so bright coming from everywhere the blades of grass
and the wings of birds and the roots of trees the air is hundreds
of tiny rainbows suspended in air they taste like plums it's hard
to see through them but I run into them anyway because I'm
not scared some of the rainbows move as I pass some stick to
my eyelashes and my hair I'm covered in tiny, sticky rainbows
bolting across the lawn around the corner the edge of her
yellow t-shirt disappears round the side of the house isn't a
house at all it's filled with birdhouses tat-tat-tat-tat-tat-tat-tat-
tat-pthwwwwwwwwwwwrrrrt a lawn sprinkler followed me
inside but the rainbows didn't she giggles bubbly and tinkly the
sound of pink and yellow the birdhouses fall through the
ceiling and the ceiling is an old attic with a tarp covering
something big in the corner something big trying to be invisible
but I can see it breathing it's too big to be her so I want to run
but my feet are too heavy someone taps me on the shoulder I
look around catching her shadow running down the stairs
laughing you're still iiiiiiit I run to the stairs but she's gone the
stairs go up now I follow them to a room with wooden tables
and huge windows covered in red dust and green pollen
making a sortof color that doesn't have a name everything in
the room is the sort-of color sortof colored jars filled with
sortof colored old keys and sortof colored tiny plastic words
sortof colored window frames stacked against the walls and
empty sortof colored cereal boxes everywhere I'm not scared
It's interesting I think I might be dreaming but it's nice here

122

even if it is sortof colored I want to stay so I do everything turns to face me like eyes in a painting that follow you around the room arrows and u-turn shapes are filling all in the in-between spaces where everything else isn't on the floor the walls and even the ceiling all the arrows point in different directions dead plants start falling from the ceiling I don't like the dead flowers I don't want to be in this sortof place anymore but broken birdhouses are piled up in front of the door I don't want to be here anymore I want to move the birdhouses but they're all stuck together like barrel monkeys something that sounds like rushing water starts to move the arrows til they all point to the thing in the corner under the tarp the room gets dark and I'm falling I'm awake now but not entirely. I usually like the ether but

wake up **WAKE UP**

I open my eyes. I'm on the couch. I can't remember what I was dreaming. Something about a room. I look at dormant tree. Her glass of bourbon is still full.

I get up and tip toe past the bed to the bathroom. Dylan's still asleep. He looks like a mannequin.

must be nice

I whisper it out loud as an official end to my 24-hour VOS. "Must be nice." My voice sounds hollow and captured, like it's inside the walls.

****

I avoided the coffee cart today. It was surrounded by a moat of awkwardness so I pretended I was on a work call, ignoring the coffee cart owner's eyes, but I could feel them as I walked past. Maybe that huge tip I gave him yesterday was a jerk move. I don't know anymore. It's so damn hard to know what the right thing to do is anymore. Unintended consequences always follow.

poor Maggie doesn't know what to say
shut up
you shut up

Mitchel joins me as I wait on the elevator. Without looking at him I utter, "Asshat."

He chuckles. "Queen Crazypants." The elevator arrives and we get in. "Glad it was just *temporary* insanity," he adds. Mitchel can't leave well enough alone. Sometimes I admire it. Sometimes it's exhausting.

"Why did it bug you so much?" I ask. "It was one day. Why were you so-so…so?" I can't quite find the word I want so I just gesture like someone tripping out.

"Aaannnnd, Harpo returns," he deadpans.

He must be wearing a different cologne today. Synthetic pineapple and lavender pine-sol. So dense I can taste it. I inch away, trying to find a pocket of air.

"Look," he continues, "it just-it seems like you're-I don't know, I guess I don't get why you're unravelling over a random path cross with someone you knew as a kid."

"I'm not unravelling," I say.

He shoots me a look that seems to say that if I'm not unravelling, I've lost a substantial amount of IQ points.

"I wouldn't mind figuring out why I'm so-"

"What? So *what?*"

"I don't know. Something's off. Maybe I'm trying to open my mind or, I don't know, figure out why I don't-"

"Don't *what?*"

"Jesus, Mitch, you're the one always talking about keeping an open mind."

"I was talking about work. Keeping in the game. And you know that," he says. "If you want to open your mind, take some Ayahuasca. I know a guy who could get you some-oh, wait, no, no, no! Peyote!"

"I'm not doing Peyote," I say.

Maaaaaaggiiiiieeeewaaaaaannnnnaaaaabeeeeeeaaaaaaa
 maybe you should

 iiiiinnnn-diiiiiiiiaaaaaannn

 mud

 it won't help

 click clack click clack click
clack

The stupid elevator is more glacial than usual. I consider the stairs knowing Mitchel wouldn't be able to follow. I don't do it. Too much of a jerk move. Even for me.

"Okay, fine, don't. Though you know, peyote."

"What?"

"Might help you reconnect with Dana," he says.

"Tsalagi aren't known for their peyote use," I say, injecting as much rebuke as I can into it, though not actually knowing if it's true or not.

"Point is a day of not talking isn't gonna change squat." We remain silent for the remainder of the ride.

"You're right," I say as the elevator doors finally open.

"Thank you!" he says.

"One day wasn't long enough," I add.

"That's not what I meant, and you know it," he replies.

What he meant doesn't matter. I stride towards my office with renewed purpose.

"Seriously?" he demands.

"We'll see who's prepared to do enough," I say much to Chelsea's bland disinterest. I set my things down and draw a large VOS over the entire month of March on my calendar with a red wax pencil. As I do it, I feel stronger. Well, not exactly stronger. Something.

impervious unreachable

"30 days," I say out loud. "Then we'll see whose mind is open. 30 days and we'll see who is reconnected. We'll see."

Observe and be silent. My new creed. Tenets of my new religion. Even lost things require oaths. Maybe especially lost things. But even as I begin, I know it's not going to help. It's just a new place to be invisible.

knowing is half the battle

The knowing starts to slip. Like a word I knew a second ago.

something important
you know what you need to do
talk to Ohma
not yet
you're starting to remember
feel
think
be
30 days
you might be her again the old you
master of avoidance
but what if
no
this is different
this is the way back
the invisible way back

I look at my calendar and the giant red VOS drawn across March.

this is the invisible way back

My eyes refocus. Something's written today at 6 p.m. The Language of the Body class Seidr mentioned at the Over-talkers Anonymous meeting.

if you want something you've never had
you must do something you've never done

****

I've been here for thirty-three minutes. I had no idea how long it would take to get myself stuffed into the tights and leotard I bought at the SyntheDancewear shop (both of which are now securely hidden beneath my oversized *What Would Noam Chomsky Do?* t-shirt). I figured a buffer of time was in order. Plus, Seidr knows Dana so it's not too much of a stretch to think she might be here too.

haha stretch

anyway

I have my Mad Libs prepped speech still ready to go. The VOS thing doesn't matter. I'll drop it if she shows because if she shows it'll be a sign a karmic watchdog is guarding our reconnection.

this crazy class is exactly what we need
we'll start to laugh
but in a nice way
she'll tell me everything over dinner
or she and Pa-cucumber will come over
for Vindaloo
we'll have wine we'll talk and laugh and share
it'll be like that summer never happened
but it did

I look down the hallway of cacophonous emo conversations and limbs splayed across the floor as if discarded by a sadistic child, willing myself to imagine Seidr and Pa-tricia heavy in conversation. Dana strolling toward me, waving. But they're not there.

just go home

I start to gather my things when a torrent of energy erupts down the hall. Seidr emerging from a swath of admirers. She spots me, waves, and glides over. My heart starts to thump. I scan the crowd behind her for Dana. She's not there.

"I'm so glad you decided to come!" Seidr exclaims.
I try to smile.

She cocks her head. "You took a VOS."
I nod.

"Interesting, isn't it?"

uuuuuuuh yeah

"The lies we tell get harder to believe when it's quiet."

yeah it's super neat

I skate my eyes down the hallway again. Seidr looks intently at me and cocks her head again. A wolf listening to sounds us normal humans can't hear.

"She's not here," she says. "Not her thing."

I try to give the illusion of confusion. She smiles serenely. The glaring downside of a VOS dawns on me as the studio door opens. I need to have a few options beyond charades to communicate. A note pad at least. There must be an app I can use. One of those translation apps. Something. I'm not going to last more than a few days if I can't communicate beyond 'Maggie is smiling' or 'Maggie is frowning'.

why are you doing this?

we covered this

it's just a means to the end

a burial for this Maggie

A few dozen sweat-drenched dancers spill out of the studio releasing warm, damp air. Crotches, feet, Tiger Balm. I back up.

no air   need air   nope nope

There are fans in the room, but they're only pushing around the thickened air. I can almost see it swirling.

"Here we go!" Seidr exclaims, waving me over.

I reluctantly weave through the crowd and take the spot next to her, embarking upon the only warm up moves I know (Olivia Newton John's *Let's Get Physical* video), trying to not watch Seidr because even warming up she looks like a goddess.

go ahead Maggie look in the mirror

dare ya

128

A hush spreads as a spry man pauses in the doorway. He's wearing a flowing tunic. His braided goatee is tied with a leather cord and a lotus seed. Puck stripped of jocularity. He enters, two musicians trailing behind him. They set up drums, a Tibetan singing bowl, a rain stick, and a few other small mystery items in a corner. A little ball of panic starts to bounce in my chest.

remember the mold?

GO NOW

I'm about to apologize to Seidr and slip out when the spry man glides to the center of the room, dancers parting like the Red Sea. His eyes drift to Seidr. He bows slightly. She returns the bow. Then his eyes pause on me.

oh shit shitshit bow

no don't bow

Before I can figure out how to acknowledge him without bowing, his eyes glide away.

Seidr leans in and whispers, "That's Endymion. Your life's about to change."

Endymion lifts his arms as he says, "Journeyers."

A slow, deep drumming begins from the musicians in the corner. Then a whistling sound from one of the mystery objects. A small "pft" of laughter leaks from me.

"Connectivity," Endymion says, "flow... release... restore. CFFFFRRRRRRRRR. Again. Breathe. CFFFFRRRRRRRRR. Again. Breathe. CFFFFRRRRRRRRR"

Everyone's eyes are closed. Seider's eyes are closed. All CFFFFRRRRRRRRRing.

insight's a bitch

the way way back's a bitch

I close my eyes, try to breathe with the others, and the drums, and the CFFFFRRRRRRRRR, but my balance isn't what it once was. I peek to get my bearings. Endymion is directly in front of me. A hiccup of air escapes before I can stop it.

"Truuuuuust," he says. He places a hand on my forehead, another on my solar plexus.

heyhey NO

I pull away and shake my head. I'm not about to play the 'you can put your hands where you want because you're the guru' game.

"Why do you fight?" he asks beginning to weave like a cobra.

oh you're legit crazy
that's manageable

"Release-ah. Release-ah. Releeeeeaaaase-aaaaaaaah!"
I am pulling every shred of restraint to not laugh or run.

"Close," Endymion says.

uhm no

"Cloooooooose," Endymion says.

uhm nooooooo

"Truuust-aaah. Releeease-aaah. Liiisten-aaah," Endymion says. I try to sway, and bend my legs, and move my arms like a tree in the wind. I keep my eyes open. "Do you think what you see is what is there?" he asks.

uhm yes?

He starts to circle me like a shark. "There is *no* there, there," Endymion whispers.

if there's no there there is the there here?
somewhere has to be somewhere buddy

"There is only the ALL," Endymion says.

come on Morris   try
sway bend   release the there there
CFFFFRRRRRR   CFFFFRRRRRR   CFFFFRRRRRR

And just like that, he's gone. The brilliant surgeon who did everything possible to save the patient, to no avail.

he's wrong don't worry he's wrong

doors that open are the way way back
all doors?
the tide unto another brought
nothing lost
that may be found
if sought

The dancers are all moving in unison now.

"Yes. Yes. The journey," Endymion says, raising his hand. The musicians stop. "Let us begin."

BEGIN?!

April 1979

did you bring em?

she's crouchin down to pick up a blue jay feather n a small
piece of quartz under a holly bush

uh-huh I say *you?*

she stands up nods n slips the feather n piece of quartz into the
pocket of her faded green cords she always wears cords I wish
so bad I had some too they make the best sound when you
run **zwipzwipzwipzwip**

RACE YA Dana says boltin into the field

she's the fastest person I ever saw but I don't mind cause I'm
lots faster now after tryin to catch up to her all the time

thwushthwushthwushthwush dried grass n wild carrots
brush against my legs I catch up to her halfway across the field
n we keep runnin til we reach Nathy n old barn

TIE she says laughin n fallin to the ground

I skip round Nathy runnin my hand along his rough bark til my
hand starts buzzin

did you see that Nathy? a TIE first time EVER

I finish my circle round Nathy but Dana's face looks real
different now so I stop laughin

what's wrong? I ask just as somethin wet falls on my head

I look up just as a dribble of spit falls on my cheekE milynn Martin her brother Pete n Penny Becker r up in Nathy spittin down at me

STOP IT Dana shouts at em

I back away next to Dana n old barn Emilynn Martin can spit a real long way she hurls another thick foamy spit bomb it lands next to my shoe

I said STOP IT Dana yells louder

MAKE ME WAGON BURNER Emilynn yells back

Penny n Pete join in *wagon burner wagon burner*

Dana gets real still like someone sucked all the air outta her somethin spiky starts growin in my chest

SHUT UP YOUR STUPIDSTUPID FACE I yell

my voice doesn't sound like me

Emilynn starts laughin

Maaaaaaggiiiiieeeee waaaaaannnnnaaaaa beeeeeee aaaaaaaa

iiiiinnnn-diiiiiiiii-aaaaaannn Maaaaaaggiiiiieeeee

waaaaannnnnaaaaabeeeeeeeaaaaaaiiiiinnnn-diiiiiiiiiaaaaaannn

Pete n Penny join in gettin louder n louder

Maaaaaaggiiiiieeeeewaaaaaannnnnaaaaabeeeaaeeeeaaaaaaaaaa

iiiiiiinnnn-diiiiiiiiii-aaaaaaaaaannn

Maaaaaaggiiiiieeeeewaaaaaannnnnaaaaabeeeaaeeeeaaaaaaaaaa

iiiiiiiinnnn-diiiiiiiiiii-aaaaaaaaaannn

Maaaaaaggiiiiieeeeewaaaaaannnnnaaaaabeeeaaeeeeaaaaaaaaaa

iiiiiiiinnnn-diiiiiiiiiii-aaaaaaaaaannn

my stomach feels flippy maybe they know maybe they know
I've been fishin momma's iced tea bags outta the trash n
rubbin em on my arms n legs so they're not so bright white or
when I'm with Nathy all by myself whenever the ground's
mushy from a storm I take my shoes off n push my feet as far
as they'll go into the earth so I can be part of the earth like
Ohma maybe they've seen me maybe they know I'm tryin but
that I can't get it right

**so what if they know so what they're stupid they always
wear shoes n their hair never moves**

> *so? SO? It-it's better'n bein a-a-a stupid statue with with-with
> SHOES* I yell

they start laughin so hard they almost fall out of Nathy

> *don't listen to em* Dana whispers, takin my hand n leadin
> me back to the field

I don't understand why she wants us to go n why she's lettin
em have Nathy

> *NO* I pull my hand outta hers *they think they can have
> Nathy n it's not fair*

Emilynn Pete n Penny keep laughin n hittin their mouths sayin
oooo-oooo-oooo oooo-ooo-oooo n pullin Nathy's leaves out

STOP IT he don't like that I yell

I'm tryin to make my voice big but it sounds real small

stoooooop iiiiiit he dooooon't liiiiiiike thaaaaaat Emilynn
copycats me then she starts singin *this land is my land, this
land's not your land I got a shotgun n you don't got one*
she's twistin one of Nathy's smaller branches

STOP IT that hurts him STOPITSTOPITSTOPIT
I yell as loud as I can but she keeps twistin n twistin til it snaps
I feel the snap in my chest it hurt him I can tell cause he got
real still when she did it

poor widdle Maggie the weirdo gonna cry?

she throws Nathy's branch she just snapped off him at me it
was a part of him a minute ago n now it's not sharp hot rocks
start growin inside me

I hate her hate her hate her

I wanna hit her n break off every one of her stupid fat fingers
see how she likes it

my foot feels somethin hard a rock now it's in my hand not
sure how it got there I'm gonna throw it at her make her fall
break her arm then she'll be sorry my insides feel mean n
prickly but I kinda like it

*EEEEEEOOOOOOOEEEEEEOOOOOOOOOOO
EEEEEEOOOOOWWWWWHHH*

that was Dana   she's not yellin but her voice sounds so big it
could cover the whole world

WOOOOO WOOOOOOWOOOOOOAAAAHHH

WOOOOO WOOOOOOWOOOOOOAAAAHHH

she starts doin a dance I never seen before   she's pickin up
dirt n tossin it in the air   then she points at em

WOOOOO WOOOOOOWOOOOOOAAAAHHH

WOOOOO WOOOOOOWOOOOOOAAAAHHH

she picks up the small branch Emilynn broke off Nathy n
starts movin round with it stompin her feet on the ground n
swingin it round then she yells at em again with more sounds I
don't recognize they sound like words but I don't know em

stop it Emilynn yells but her voice sounds like Jell-O

SHE GONNA CURSE US Pete screams

YEAH I yell back *she'll turn you into a slug n then we'll step on
you n you'll be SLUG GUTS*

Dana yells louder n starts dancin n jumpin round Nathy
pointin at em as they jump down n start runnin cross the field

STOP IT I'm tellin Pete screams he starts runnin with
Penny n Penny starts cryin

Emilynn follows em but she's a lot slower cause she's too
rolypoly then she turns around n her mean face is so pink n fat
it makes me wanna laugh then I do start laughin

I'M GONNA TELL MY DADDY ON YOU she yells

GO AHEAD Dana yells back

*YEAH, GO AHEAD I yell SHE'LL TURN HIM
INTO A SLUG TOO*

we look at each other n start laughin so hard I start dancin the
way Dana was she laughs but then she stops her face looks
funny I musta done somethin wrong n now she's upset

what's wrong? I ask

nothin she says

she takes Nathy's branch n puts it next to him then she puts
her hand on him n whispers something I go stand next to her
she doesn't say anythin so we just stand there she's been quiet
before but not like this usually when she gets quiet it's cause
she's bout to tell me a secret or a joke

r you okay? I try to be quiet cause she seems sad

yeah she says *it's just that's not how it really goes I made some
stuff up*

yeah I say *they were so mean you had to make up some new stuff*

she looks at me a small smile on her face it reminds me of the
little waves on the lake she keeps lookin cross the field but I
don't know why they won't come back now

bet they never ever come back I say tryin to sound sure

yeah she says

she's still lookin cross the field n kinda not here anymore I pull the crinkly plastic bag outta my backpack

> *we should plant these n then maybe you can teach me a plant growin dance?*

she looks at me n smiles then says *maybe*

> *yeah* I say jumpin n twirlin *the crunch berry swirly whirly*

Dana laughs n we start lookin for the best place to plant em

> *it's gonna be the best bush EVER* I say

we decide halfway between old barn n Nathy is the best spot cause it gets sun n shade there's only seven left in the bag cause we ate all the rest while we were lookin for the right spot once they're all buried we mark it with the quartz rock n blue jay feather Dana found earlier then we skip round the spot makin up a plant growin dance together swirlin n twirlin

suddenly Dana stops n takes my hand real tight n starts runnin but she's runnin too fast n I keep almost fallin

> *WAIT Dana wait I can't run like you*

But she doesn't say anything she just keeps runnin I look back cross the field way at the other end Emilynn is comin back with a grownup

> *WE HAVE TO HIDE* Dana says

her eyes look weird n scared but Dana's not scared of anythin

8

People can change. People change all the time. They evolve. Annie Besant, Grandma Moses, Matthew Perry. And Maggie Morris.

It's been ten days. Ten days of silence. But other than the realization that people talk constantly for no reason, no other insight has arrived to save the day. Or the Maggie.

Worst of all, I've only seen Dana once. She was walking towards me on Court. She was with Patricia. Instead of dropping my silence and rolling out my Mad Libs speech on friendship and safe spaces, I pretended to get a very important call. I waved at them, rolling my eyes dramatically at the non-existent voice on the other end of my very important call. Dana smiled. Patricia sort of smiled. We passed each other and continued our separate ways. Them holding hands, me holding my home screen to my ear. Dana looked back and so did I.

It's kind of a bummer realizing you're a coward. That your ability to recognize important moments is pulverized by your incomprehensible devotion to doing nothing about them.

Each day I wake up and ask myself why I'm continuing this VOS charade. I don't know. Other than the buffer it provides me, which is certainly welcome, it's probably just some unconscious culmination of years of utterly describable moments followed by three indescribably disorienting ones.

Maybe a shift is happening even if I don't feel it or even know what it is yet. I keep hoping something just beyond my understanding is happening. Like opening a window in the middle of the night when nameless, ancient things can enter undetected. Shifting the interiors slowly. Invisibly. It'd be nice to think windows I thought were cemented shut with the stale, encrusted seemingness of my life are opening again. And despite having no damn clue what to do with fresh air or how to entertain nameless ancient truths, I don't want to go back to the way I was. That much I know.

I thought my silence would be something Dylan would admire. That he'd be happy about my attempt to change. To become more aware. But after the first few days of soccer dad, you're a champ support, he's gotten increasingly grumpy. The only one enjoying it is Mitchel. My not talking is a constant source of amusement for him. After a few days of being pissy about it, he began leaving little surprises for me almost daily. A picture of Harpo Marx, a Sorry for Your Loss card, a poker chip with 72 hours written on one side and Talk-a-holics R Us on the other, a Sign Language for Dummies book, a Taciturn-o-pottomus coffee mug. Today's gift is an artist sketchpad with *MAGGIE SAYS...* scrawled on the cover. Each one has a cartoon emoji face with a corresponding caption: Maggie is GRUMPY, Maggie won't tolerate SHENANIGANS, Maggie needs MORE coffee, Maggie believes Mitchel is PERFECT in every way.

As if on cue, he peeks around the doorframe, smiling impishly. I flip to an empty page and draw a concerned face with the caption: **Maggie thinks you need medication**. I hold it up for him to see.

He nods mournfully. "I agree. You drive people to drug use. It's tragic."

ha-ha

We enter a stare contest, but complexity arises again so I continue to flip through the pages until I find an imperious emoji with a crown declaring "PISS OFF, for Maggie is VERY busy and important!" I hold it up. Mitchel bows slightly, locking eyes on me one last time with the slight eyebrow raise he's been overindulging in lately, then departs, just as Newton enters.

She closes my door behind her and approaches my desk, inspecting my new system for clients and their campaigns:

NEUTRAL, SUSPECT, and KAISER SÖZE. The Söze pile is huge, and the neutral pile has zero. I blame Dana. And the damn nameless, ancient things.

A grim smile cracks Newton's face, but she doesn't look at me. "I thought we might have a chat." She flips through each mockup and folio. "I've seen it all, and then some. Your work is good. One could even say you're a valuable part of the agency."

but

"But," she continues, taking my pad of sticky notes and a pen, writing a word on one, peeling it away and sticking it to my desk, then repeating the same with a second, "your, what would you call it? Absence of speech? Is upsetting the tank."

the tank

a show about a bullshit pr firm

Her voice continues, "Whatever triggered it—finding yourself or maybe a resetting the hard drive power play …"

Fig Newton   shark

Chelsea   swordfish

Mitchel? hmmm tricky

"It doesn't matter why. I've been more than patient because of your track record…"

he's sort of all the fish and none of the fish

The background noise has stopped. I refocus. Newton's waiting, her eyes finally on me.

"If you're physically capable of speaking, I expect you to do so. You understand? Clients aren't happy."

can't have that

"By the end of the week," she says, then exits, closing my door behind her. I inspect her handy work on my filing system. Two piles with a single sticky note on each marked "Done" and "To Be Done." She's placed the piles on either side of Mitchel's **MAGGIE SAYS...** sketchpad.

"Ha, not this time! Nice try, my friend." Mitchel's still outside my office, no doubt he and Chelsea tag-team guessing this entire time what Newton had to say. He's using his non-stick voice. I hear Chelsea giggling melodically.

what the hell?

Even though Mitchel is jaw-droppingly handsome and puckish, I'd never pegged Chelsea as the type whose IQ would drop 30 points when she's flirting. The thought of her being interested in anyone at all is unsettling—she's so bony and severe, sex would be dangerous.

bet she's a dom

STOPSTOPSTOP

Mitchel laughs. It's low. Throaty.

WHAT THE HELL

My blood now battery acid, I stride to my door and open it wide. Mitchel's leaning onto Chelsea's desk where she seems amid a futile attempt to manifest cleavage. I glare witheringly at Mitchel, then condescendingly at Chelsea.

everyone standing right here can go to hell

Mitchel's smile dissolves. He stares back stonily. It's the same look he had staring at the infotainment screen the night I saw Dana again. He looks at Chelsea, a secret understanding passing between them. I hate them both. I slam my door just as my eyes start to sting. My 37 mirrors and windows shutter from the force, my splotchy, angry self-wobbling within them. When I leave for the day, I take the stairs.

****

I was too tired to walk so I waited on the too narrow, too crowded platform for the F train trying to ignore the cauldron of B.O. and carbon dioxide posing as oxygen. When a C train came, I got on. I'd walk from Hoyt/Schermerhorn or wait for the F train there.

As I settled against the door, I took in the car's occupants. I've been doing it ever since I stopped talking. A strange sort of side effect. My eyes land on an unusually tall man wearing a long red satin cape, three neckties, a President's Spreadable Butter lid pinned to his lapel, and a large black rubber boot as a hat standing next to a young priest who appeared to be quite drunk, and quite happy about it. They were chatting about the pros and cons of self-imposed exiles and the scarcity of establishments where one can procure a bona-fide cape nowadays as a Paul Bunyan sized man next to them absentmindedly touched a pink ribbon pinned over the chest pocket of his mustard colored Carhartt overalls. Something about the whole thing made me feel deeply lonely. For the first time in as long as I can remember, I feel profoundly out of place. Like I'm supposed to be somewhere else. Somewhere that's waiting for me to get there.

****

Someone's making marinara. I know it's not Dylan because he says tomatoes are too acidic for his Dosha. I have a sudden urge to curl up with the garlic and oregano inside the walls. Never come back out.

where'd Maggie go?
oh she's with the oregano in the walls
oh okay   well tell her hi for me

I look at my mailbox. Edges of magazines and envelopes sticking through the small vents and the sides. Daring me to refute the overwhelming evidence of my pointless life. I refuse to accept the judgement of a receptacle. There's no coming back from that.

One pull and it all breaks free. I Humpty Dumpty backwards, landing with godlike precision on the two-quart container of Greek yogurt. A rush of heat floods my eyes.

poor weirdo Maggie gonna cry?

Maaaaaaaggggiiiiieeee waaaaaaaaaannnnnnaaaaa beeeeeeeeeeeaaaaaaaaaaaaaa iiiiiinnnnnddiiiiiaaaaannnn

I take the oversized Bed Bath and Beyond 20% coupon postcard from my stack of mail and scoop the yogurt as best as I can off the floor and into the little trash can in the corner, then gather the rest of my gloppy mail and shove it into the grocery bag.

As I approach my door I'm hit with a cloud of Dylan's sickly-sweet incense. At least the smell of heavily garlic'd marinara comes by its potency honestly. Even the sweaty feet and Tiger Balm at SyntheDance is better than this.

I just want something real
just til I remember how to be real too

I used to think Dylan was real. That he could make me real again. Like a spiritual Geppetto. I don't even want to think about the jacked-up sexism hiding in *that* decision.

He's been increasingly irritable over my extended silence I'm starting to think he's just like me. A pop-up book of behaviors and phrases masquerading as identity.

ROSE

He's burning rose incense. I hate any kind of rose anything. Fresh roses in an actual garden are fine, but any kind rose fragrance makes queasy. He knows that. So, it seems we've moved on to the passive aggressive phase of Dylan's reaction to my silence. Part of me is impressed. It shows unexpected vitriol. Which I think is great. I just wish he'd expressed in some way other than filling my loft with the smell of charred plastic flowers. I try mouth breathing. Now I can taste it.

rushing water   *blueblacktreefeather*
                         silver buttons
                                              scrapple bologna old fries
waffles mooo mooooo mooo

I unlock the door and swing it wide, hoping some oxygen will enter with me. Shay, Dylan's model friend, is draped across my couch. The incense smoke undulates around her as if her bidding is for it to amplify her already Lauren Bacall-meets-praying mantis vibe.

She appraises me with bored disdain—my rapidly aging, yogurt-dipped self-confirming she is undeniably the winner. I kick my yogurt-ed shoes onto her Alexander Wang boots. A sneer flickers momentarily across her flawless skin.

there you are you vacuous pile of string

Shay smiles viciously. "Well, hey there Maggie-may. You look teeeeerrible. Rough day?"

don't play with toys you don't understand little girl

Ice picks form in her eyes.

something you'd like to say?

Dylan strolls in from the kitchen with a platter of raw vegetables, and loose tea steeping in a French press.

Shay morphs into the embodiment of concern. "Lando, don't you think Maggie looks exhausted?"

Lando?

"Hey, babe," he says smiling at me. Only in the company of Shay does Dylan call me babe. Still, it's better than champ.

He sets the platter down, oblivious to the thicket of loathing that's sprung up in his absence. I ignore him and head to the kitchen to dump the grocery bag into the sink.

DO NOT follow me

"Rough day, babe?" he asks, following me. "You should join us. We've got some amazing Menghai Pu-Erh steeping. Shay brought it."

I bet she did

Dylan continues, "Cultivated organically on the summit of Bulang Mountain."

I slam the grocery bag into the sink. All I've wanted for months is to end things, but now, on the cusp of it, I'm being petulant and jealous.

"Hey," he says projecting his voice like Muad'Dib addressing the Fremen, "Let me help. We could do a guided meditation or let Shay know we need some 'us' time."

He sweeps my hair off my neck and kisses it. I step away from him, wiping where his lips touched me.

that was mean don't be a bitch just be clear
The desire to be a bitch is overwhelming.

Dylan glances at Shay, who moues sympathetically. He looks back at me, wounded.

oh stop it
a damn paper cut hurts your feelings

"Lando, the Pu-Erh is over-steeping. It'll be bitterrrrr."

Dylan's attention whipsaws over to her and the tea as if it, and Shay-shay, are on fire. He looks back and forth between us, flummoxed, hoping he can somehow secure both our good graces.

He dramatically whispers his case, "Please don't be mad, babe, it's just-it's-Beau's been acting from his lower frequencies again, and you know the kind of discord that creates for Shay. She's a sensitive. She needed a friend and ..."

uh-huh

I'm the callous one. His hands are tied. I return to my task of slimy mail pulled out of gooey bag, separating it into piles of His and Hers.

like an autopsy
in a Witkacy play
a dormant tree
thick ropy veins of cigarette smoke suspended
the broken strata of wasted years
a lone table a cold bleak room
Maggie the coroner pulling Alexander Wang ankle boots

pucks of Pu-Erh tea
and incense out of Dylan's chest
as he repeatedly says 'babe' with different inflections
baaaaaahhhhhhe   bAYbe   babEH   babeeeeeeeeeee

There's always a moment that becomes the last moment. The last grain of before as after takes over. This is that moment. I look at Shay, who's looking at Dylan, who can't decide who to look at. Without fanfare, our before is gone. I go back to sorting the mail, allowing the familiar anesthesia of endings to do its work.

"You're so angry lately," he says.

I can hear the sadness in his voice. I should be kind. I want to want to be kind, but his feelings, and his constant need to talk about them, flicks at something sharp inside me. He's not going to get it until I spell it out. I resent the hell out of that. The sharp thing starts to flick back.

I take each envelope addressed to him and drag it carefully through the lake of yogurt at the bottom of the bag. He looks at me, a perplexed baby bear. For a moment I feel myself soften. The undertow of our before reminding me how his skin feels like warm silk, how his amber eyes spark when he laughs.

"Maggie, breathe. This isn't healthy. You're embracing discord."

just can't leave the tender moment alone can you buddy?
for the best anyway

I pat the yogurt dipped mail into perfect stack, walk serenely over to him, and slap the whole gloppy pile onto his perfectly defined abs.

"What the...?"

I look him square in the eye.

stop it   just stop
we're done
you know that right? you must know that

I walk past him, grab a bottle of bourbon from the bar cart, toss a Cheshire-Cat smile at Shay, shove my feet into sneakers and slam the front door behind me, pounding down the stairs.

"Hey!" Dylan's voice cascades down the stairwell, "This is my Fashion Week check! Aaawwwcomeon! Not cool!"
As I reach the marinara'd sanctity of the foyer, Shay's laughter tinkles down the stairs. Stillness washes over me.

no   this is my home

I walk back upstairs opening the door to a Shay-consoles-Dylan tableau. He jumps off the couch. For a moment I regret what I'm about to do. But this is my chance. I hold the door wide, gazing unflinchingly at Shay.

run along now

Shay looks to Dylan, but he's looking at me. She performs a dramatic pout, grabs her perfectly distressed hobo fringe bag, her yogurt speckled ankle boots, and tosses a highly rehearsed "whatever" at the air behind her as she leaves.

Dylan resumes his baby bear act. "My fern…"

no   no more foliage

"That wasn't what it-it's-I've never-you've just been—your vibration—it's so-and we're all beings of clay and fire."

absolutely

I'm still holding the door open. I'm being a jerk, but I just want it done already. I'm so tired. I just want it to be done. He's confused. This may be the first time anyone has ever ended something with him. But we choose what we choose. He chose to be with someone who was always ambivalent about him. No one outsmarts their baggage.

"Seriously!? Over one moment of human frailty?"

no I didn't mind that   which is kind of the point

Finally, some genuine anger surfaces out of his sea of calm. "FINE! You know what Maggie, FINE! This just saved me having to hurt you while you're amid a personal struggle."

He ricochets around the apartment, grabbing clothes and cork yoga mats, and the still full French press of Pu-erh tea. "Since this is it, and in the spirit of the universal flow of love and energy that transcends this temporal manifestation..."

CFFFFRRRRRR

"I'm going to tell you the truth."

all ears my palm frond

stop being such a bitch Maggie

sorry the OS upgrade to the better person functionality is unavailable until further notice

"I think you might be mentally unstable right now..."

you say it like it's a bad thing

"Which can be integral to a true shift in consciousness..."

I look out at dormant tree. Today's snow rests in perfect lines atop every branch. She's very still. Listening.

"... but upon reflection in this endlessly unfolding moment, I realize," Dylan drones on. I feel my eyes soften and fix on the fragile lines of silver snow balanced on her branches.

up, and up, and up

silver buttons

if sought   *don't blink don't blink*

"There is a vortex of darkness you're creating around you and although vital to your growth, it's unhealthy for me."

vortex of darkness?

I can see it now. A giant pitch-black vortex behind him, dragging him spinning into its tarry depths as he screams 'Noooooooooooo!' followed by a voiceover, 'Vortex of Darkness. It came and it **sucked**. In theaters soon'. I can't help but chuckle. Dylan looks at me like I might be dangerously nuts. He grabs a bag of nutritional yeast and his gloppy mail.

"I will mourn us. I have loved you with my very soul, and always will, but this has become a toxic environment, and I have done too much work to backslide into that mind space."

He approaches me, pauses, then crosses the threshold, turning back to look at me.

Then I catch up. I've wanted this for so long—fixated on it for so long—that I'd forgotten there'd been some good moments. Before I completely turned to ash. I look at him with as much gentleness as I can muster. I should break my silence, just for this moment. It would be the right thing to do. But the pocket of air between me and other people has become a demilitarized zone, and I like it. I try to focus my thoughts so he can at least feel them.

you were sweet you tried you're a good person don't date Shay

He looks so puzzled and hurt, It occurs to me this is a person who tried to believe in me. I decide to allow one moment of pure giving on my part—possibly the first in our entire relationship. "Bye, Dylan" I say softly. Then I quietly close the door.

He deserved a momentary lapse in my silence. Much more, really, but that's all I have for him.

The next day we texted to arrange a time for him to get the rest of his things. Last night was the excavation and removal. I hung out at the Zombie Hut for three hours playing Parcheesi with a regular named Garv who spent the entire time chronicling the many ways his parents doomed him to a life of mediocrity by naming him Garvin. A hell of a Parcheesi player though.

When I got home Dylan's keys were staring up at me from the entry table. Two years reduced to two keys, lain side by side.

awaiting a proper burial

Maybe I will bury them.

here lie the keys of Dylan Chester Montgomery
stray dog and believer in lost causes
may his after-Maggie life be filled with happiness

July 1979

daddy n momma think I'm in my room readin but I'm not
I'm sneakin out for the first time ever

daddy said to come straight home after school I asked him
why but he just said *cause I said* so daddy never ever said that n
his voice sounded wobbly again like when we went to
Murphy's then he tried to tickle me he knows I don't like
tickles but I laughed for him anyway cause it seemed like he
needed me to I did come straight home after school but he
never said I couldn't go over to Ohma's after dinner I know
he prolly meant that part but he didn't say it

I never snuck out before but stayin in my room when I know
Ohma n Dana r prolly laughin n drinkin sunset lemonade n
listenin to crickets n frogs makes me feel like peanut shells r
stuck in my teeth I'm pretty sure the peanut feelin'll go away if
I can just go over there for a little bit

gotta be careful cause the wood in the stairs belonged to a tree
who loved to laugh specially when the wind ticked him then
when some stupid person cut him down n made stairs outta
him he had to tell himself jokes so he didn't haveta think bout
his roots or his leaves or the other trees he used to know

his favorite joke is to squeak when people try to be quiet he
thinks it's pretty funny I usually like to make squeaks so he can
laugh but right now I'm gonna ask him if he'll let me stay
invisible just this once cause when stairs that were once a big
tree that told funny jokes agrees with you it means what your
doin is okay n even maybe a good idea too I make it
downstairs without a single squeak

Bronwen Carson

almost there momma went to her book club so I just havta
sneak past daddy he's usually in his chair readin the paper but
he's not there that means he could be anywhere gotta be extra
quiet once I'm outside I can make myself invisible real easy
I'll be over at Ohma's real fast if I go the river path   maybe
when I get there she'll show me how to make sunset lemonade
she uses bunches of little red berries that look like tiny like red
grapes

out the kitchen screen door sideways so it doesn't creak it's
colder than I thought n I forgot my jeans jacket it's okay I'll
just run n then I'll be plenty warm

somethin smells weird n ugly like that sticky tar stuff they put
in cracks in the road

> *Den you don't need to do that I'm-it's not*

daddy's outside standin next to a faded red truck I don't
recognize I duck behind the rain barrel next to the screen door

> *I'm just sayin* someone daddy calls den is talkin

> *I know what you're sayin buddy* daddy says *I do and you're a
> good friend to care I'm just sayin it's not gonna be a problem*

I peek round the rainwater barrel I can't tell who daddy's
talkin to all I can see is the man is smokin I hate hate hate
cigarette smoke It's like sticky floors I try not to think about it
instead I close my eyes so I can hear what daddy n the man r
sayin

> *nah you don't see what's gonna happen man* the man says his
> voice is scratchy

it's not a problem den come on daddy's voice says

you don't see it Mary only cares bout Mary man you don't see it but I do the scratchy man says

that's not true hey where's all this comin from? daddy asks

I'm tellin you it's a bad idea to let Maggie spend so much time with em with Dana n the old lady

WHAT? WHY? NO STUPID SCRATCHY MAN

DON'T LISTEN TO HIM DADDY

I open my eyes I wanna see daddy send my thoughts right to him

DON'T LISTEN TO HIM DADDY

that's not-how do you-? daddy asks he looks sad

Emilynn told me the man says

STUPID ROLY POLY SPITBALL EMILYNN

I'm tellin you she sees em together all the time n she says Maggie's actin different now

that's just kids bein kids daddy says *you're makin somethin outta nothin*

no you can't see it but I do the man says

see what? daddy's voice is wobbly again

I'm just sayin things go south I have your six Ben you know that

I don't know what six means Ohma talks bout four a lot n
seven too but I never yet heard her talk bout six I'll ask her
what it means when I get there

*I don't need-look Den buddy they're just friends they help Ohma
with her garden that's all you're readin too much into this*

the man throws his smoke on the ground the end is glowin red
daddy steps on it

*this whole thing's gonna get away from you you got a real good life
no idea how good*

I do Den I do

*nah man you don't you're gonna screw up your whole life Helen's
pregnant right? you're being stupid*

I feel like I'm dreamin I gotta be cause the man's mouth is
always filled with smoke n momma's gonna have a baby n the
man keeps tellin daddy not to let me go over to Ohma's farm
or be friends with Dana

I pinch myself hard so I wake up but I don't I look at my arm
where I pinched it n a red mark is there I pinch it again
enough to make it hurt but I still don't wake up I'm awake but
I don't understand what's happenin

*hey I do Denny come on I do I wouldn't do anything to lookokay
you're right okay? I hear ya buddy I do*

the man doesn't say anything he just smokes   maybe he's
stupid roly poly spitball Emilynn's dad

hey come on come inside Ellie made a pie

smoke puffs out of the man's nose n the sides of his mouth
he looks like a dragon

a peach pie come on Den

daddy sounds like a balloon tryin to float but only half fulla air

the scratchy dragon man nods n they both start walkin to the
door I think maybe daddy saw me I sneak quick as I can inside
n up the stairs **squeaksqueaksqueaksqueaksqueaksqueak**

*shhhhh pleaseplease it's not funny right now okay sorry okay
please?* I whisper to the stairs

I close my door almost all the way n jump into bed with my
clothes n shoes still on I hear daddy's feet **fump sqeeeaaak
fump fump fump squeeeeeak fump squeeeeeak fump**

I pretend I'm asleep but the bees in my tummy n my head r so
loud I know daddy can hear em too   but he lets me pretend n
he pretends too he closes my door I wait a little bit before I
take my shoes off then I lie down on the floor n put my ear
against it but their voices r too low all I hear is forks clinkin
on plates n voices sayin *huffle muffle muhm muhm huhff*

I get back into bed but I can't sleep the bees r still in my ears
I know I'm in trouble cause of what I said to Emilynn bout
Dana turnin her into a slug   but she deserved it

I look at the shadows my trees n birds nightlight r makin on
my walls try to figure out what to say so I'm not in trouble but
I can't come up with anythin n my eyes feel like the bees'r
stingin em I'll just close em for a second   inside my eyes I still
see the tree shadows n the bird shadows   then they start
dancin n the bees r laughin cause Dana's momma is tellin a

funny joke bout how she left a part of herself somewhere else but she can't find it on the map cause the map's lost Ohma's laughin n Dana's laughin n the bees r laughin I'm laughin too but only cause everyone else is I don't get the joke n I feel stupid Dana's momma always keeps jokes inside her eyes she has some in there now n her eyes r twinkly she's a feathery indigo flute speakin in feathers n invisible jokes she's tellin nother one now bout the time a bird stepped in red paint n Dana's laughin n Ohma's laughin n all the birds r laughin n I'm tryin to laugh but I can't remember how their laughs turn into rain n it fills the room n everyone's ridin big waves out the windows I'm alone n the waves r gone everythin is dry again so I start walkin home but when I get there it's a birdhouse with curvy windows n doors in the floors n tunnels to cubbies where I can read all the books I want n never have to do homework or eat cantaloupe

ruuuuumbuuuummmbuuuuummmbuuuuummm

bees r playin drums in my birdhouse

no that's not right

buuuuummmmmbuuuluuuhbuuuuhluuuummmbuuuuuu muuuummm

I open my eyes the trees n birds shadows r still on my wall

buuuuummmmmbuuuluuuhbuuuuhluuuummmbuuuuuu muuuummm

I creep to my window n peak out the moon's out now n everythin looks greyblue daddy's standin next to the driver's side I can only see the dragon man's hands on the wheel n also the back of his stupid dragon head looks like it's on fire cause

smoke's all round it again his truck says CHEVY   the back
fender has a big dent in it n there's a sticker on the back
window that says A-R-M-Y   momma's green machine is
parked next to it daddy n the man r talkin but I can't hear
what they're sayin over the **ruuuummbuuuuuumuuuummm**
of the man's truck daddy pats the roof of the truck the sad-
mean dragon man drives away daddy watches him leave then
he looks at our house

he stays outside with the grey blue moon I listen to the moon
n so does daddy the moon whispers but never lies n it'll tell
you your own secrets the moon's tellin me to make sure I
don't stop goin to Ohmas n that Dana's my true n true best
friend but that Nathy's something even bigger than that

I listen n watch for a long time   so does daddy

9

"Do you need something, Ms. Morris?"
I whirl around to find our new intern, Donovan, leaning towards me, sweating earnestly. I back up.

Mitchel and I dubbed him Lemurnturn due to his twitchy boy-man limp ravioli'd handshake and his unfortunate propensity for scurrying. If sunlight hit Donovan Kenyon in a certain way, he'd disintegrate into a million floating specks of dust, fated to hover for eternity, watching life being lived by others. Over the past few days, for reasons entirely unknown, he has attached himself to me, his waxy skin perpetually glazed in a film of oily, musty sweat.

"C-coffee? Black, right? With th-three sugars?"
I've been hovering outside the break room eavesdropping on Chelsea and Mitchel, and whatever form of mating ritual they seem to be engaging in. Now lemernturn has outed me. Mitchel and Chelsea abruptly stop talking.

shit   shitshit   shitshitshit
just be cool   be cool

I grab my phone, typing intently as I enter the break room. Lemurntern follows me in. I barely acknowledge Mitchel and Chelsea as I make a beeline for the Keurig, choose a pod, and drop it into the machine.

turn around
CASUALLY

I turn around as casually as possible. I find Mitchel staring at me. Tepid eyes. Monochrome smile.

"Okay, so send me a text about the place," Chelsea's voice declares, "and I'll meet you there. Can't wait!" Her words stick to the wall like throwing stars.

yeeees   I get it   he's yours   no need to spray darling

Mitchel salutes her. This is not the response she wanted. Her smile dissolves. She turns to me. "Choosing to withhold your voice when men have been gagging us for centuries isn't particularly admirable. You know that?" She departs without awaiting a reply from anyone, Mitchel's eyes watching her with admiration and shock.

"Bye, Chelsea!" Lemurntern waves, opening his Scooby Doo lunch pail looking back and forth between myself and Mitchel.

"So, Mr——," Lemurntern blurts.

"I told you to call me Mitchel, Donovan."

"R-right right, sorry, uh, Mitchel. So, I-I got that box set you said—you know, the one you said."

"Uh-huh," Mitchel mumbles, staring at me acridly, "Good."

My blood feels like battery acid again. I never noticed Mitchel's eyes are more swamp green than forest hued.

Donovan continues, "and it-it's really like-I mean, those guys can wail."

Mitchel shifts his gaze to Donovan, the veil across his eyes lifting to reveal the spark and good humor I was once granted. "Ever hear of Little Feat?" He asks Donovan.

"Little feet, like …" Donovan points to his foot.

I can't help but smile. Neither can Mitchel. We catch each other's eyes. We're being given a chance to climb out of the pit. I do nothing. Mitchel does nothing. The Keurig beeps. I turn to retrieve my now full Taciturnopotomus mug and by the time I turn back around the moment is gone. Despite this, I try. I'm quite gifted at trying *just* after a door has closed.

I look at Mitchel and raise my eyebrows. Mitchel returns his attention to the Zagat's. Lemurnturn looks back and forth between us, crunching Cheetos.

I type into the translator app I installed on my phone yesterday and choose a female voice with a Scottish accent. I press play.

"Maggie says plain or peanut?" it asks. It's a private joke. M&Ms. Maggie and Mitchel. It's not funny-funny, more of a you had to be there kind of moment that involved a lot of tequila and a weekend long binge of Supernatural.

"Oh, I get it! M," Lemurnturn points to Mitchel, "and M" he points to me. Then he laughs. It's a nice laugh. Warm and rounded—utterly incongruent with the rest of him and this whole scenario. Also, it's interesting that he did, in fact, get it. I smile at him and nod. A mottling of purpley-red ripples across his face and neck.

"None for me thanks" Mitchel says robotically, "I'm trying to cut back."

It's my turn to be mottled and red. I wish I knew what to say. Glue words together in just the right order, say them just the right way to fix this. But words and their right order when it comes to real human interaction aren't my strong suit. Marketing and perspective manipulation I can do and because of that, I stopped trusting words a long time ago. Saying something doesn't make it real or true. It just makes it said. But say a thing enough times in just the right order and it becomes real. I'm so tired of doing that. I've done it so long I can't tell the difference between the things I've told myself are true and actual truth, whatever that is. Life's little more than a giant mobius of collective agreements and catch phrases anyway.

"You look terrible by the way," Mitchel adds. "Like you're disappearing or…". He trails off.

I type "or what?" removing the Scottish accent before I hit play. A genderless robo-voice says, "or what?" I max out the volume and press play again "OR WHAT?" Unfortunately, I've inadvertently placed "OR WHAT?" on a loop and I can't stop it. Mitchel starts to chuckle. It's a cold chuckle.

"OR WHAT?"

"OR WHAT?" my phone and Mitchel ask perfectly synchronized.

"OR WHAT?" my phone, Mitchel, and Lemurnturn ask, perfectly synchronized.

I turn my phone off.

"awwwwwww boooooooooooo!" Mitchel says.

"Yeah, awwww, booo!" Lemurnturn parrots. Mitchel is his guru after all.

"Looks like Mags here has lost a little more than her voice, Donny."

"Oh, hahuhha, yeah," Donovan Keyon says. He looks at me and stops laughing. His brow furrows, his fingers crinkling his bag of Cheetos.

Maybe Mitchel and Chelsea make sense after all. The lump in my throat travels to my eyes. I wish my reacquaintance with emotion didn't include this moment. No way I'm letting Mitchel have the satisfaction of knowing he got to me. I stare at him as an earthquake of fury builds in my chest.

don't stop now   finish it
finish it or I will

My endings don't shatter or explode. They're an evaporation. Pure emptiness.

Something flickers in his eyes. Something else. Loss or regret? I don't know. He looks away before I can interpret it. There are moments a person can slip between your fingers. Even someone irreplaceable. I'm not sure who just slipped through whose fingers, but someone just did.

He starts leafing through the Zagat's again as Donovan peels open his pudding cup. Crrrrrriiiiiiip. The smell of artificial butterscotch coats the now burnt bridge between me and Mitchel. The earthquake in my chest collapses into a wobbly tremor. Time to go. I seem to be collecting endings.

****

I've been wandering the aisles of my corner bodega for 20 minutes and am now trying to decide between chicken noodle or clam chowder. I quit my job yesterday.

It'd been snowing steadily for two days. Late season nor'easters are always depressing. Even though spring always emerges—if only for the three precious NYC weeks that hover between winter and summer—late April snowstorms seem to bring the thought that maybe this is the year spring won't arrive.

The streets had the muffled tones of desertion and, due to a citywide transportation shut down, Newton was forced to allow everyone to go home early yesterday. The entire building was dark and quiet. Nothing but the soft knock-clack-hiss of radiators. Initially it was nice. A relief to be alone. I ordered in enough food for a small country and hunkered down to catch up on work in peace. I've always preferred solitude. Not because I enjoy my own company, but because I can dissolve into my surroundings when I'm by myself. I only recently remembered that because of this, the surroundings matter.

I hadn't planned on quitting. It just happened. I'd had a nice dinner of warm rosemary olives, Branzino, and fried cauliflower with tahini and sumac from Celestine, one of my favorite restaurants in the area. Wind and soft pelting snow on my windows. Soul-sucking overhead fluorescents off. Just my two desk lamps transforming my wall of mirrors and old windows into suspended flecks of gold.

Then something changed. Nothing in particular triggered it. I was staring at a mock-up for the luxury skincare line pitch I'd rejected a few weeks ago. They'd changed the model in response to my note that she should be an older woman. The new one looked 20 instead of 12. I tossed it into the trash. Just a simple act. But it was after that I started hearing people. Not really hearing them. More remembering what they'd said.

It started with Dana. What she'd said the day of that abysmal lunch. "I wondered where you were, what you were doing. I never imagined this". Then Mitchel. "You're disappearing". Then Dylan "You're mentally unstable." It was Mitchel's *you're disappearing* that landed the most. Because he's right. Parts of me are. I'm just not sure that's a bad thing. That's when I decided to let fate choose. I always saw it as a lazy person's camouflage for inaction. A state of mind dependent phenomenon to point to if things went wrong after the fact. But not at that moment. At that moment it seemed like the only way. I closed my eyes, pulled a random mock-up from the pile, and thought 'if this one isn't KAISER SÖZE, that will be a sign to ride it out and let it pass'. I'd forget all about Dana and Ohma and the summer I turned nine. Forget that life was magical and beautiful once. That once I was more than just a husk. If the gods of fate asked, I'd find a way forward without myself.

I opened my eyes and looked down. Palm oil. Everything pretty much snowballed from there. I remember trying to pull it together. But the only images that my mind would latch onto were of a focus group watching slides of deforestation, starving elephants, toxic runoff, the Great Barrier Reef dying, and finally a devoid-of-life, ball-of-dust planet once called Earth.

That's when I caught my reflection in my wall of mirrors. Me. A pale, sunken ball of dust.

That was it. I took my red wax pencil, wrote "Due to unexpected evidence of a conscience, I QUIT. All the best, Maggie Morris" across the palm oil pitch, grabbed a small, wood framed mirror off the wall and left.

They say don't make life-altering decisions amid a meltdown, but what if that's exactly when we should? What if it's the only time the threshold to something else is visible? And if we don't take our chance, the threshold disappears forever.

So, I'm taking my chance. Here, in a corner bodega. My choice of soup will determine my course of action. It's as good a dousing rod as any. So, chicken Noodle? Or Clam Chowder? Chicken Noodle? Clam Chowder? Chicken noodle might be about home. Returning to where it began. Or is it more bok-bok, you're a coward? And what about clam chowder? Is it embracing the great deep mystery of life by leaving familiar shores—or maybe that clamming up is the path I need to stay on? I grab both cans and throw them in my basket. I'll ask dormant tree what she thinks.

"You Should be Dancin'" by the Bee Gees starts playing through crackly speakers. I realize I'm laughing. I can't stop. I try. This makes me start to hiccup. I throw two bags of Mallomars in my basket and laugh-hiccup to the register.

The cashier rings me up. "$29.27," he says slowly. I'm a rabid wolf he doesn't want to spook. I could copy his tone. Make him relax. It would be so much easier. But I don't want to. I'm tired. I'm very tired now. No one seems to ever talk about how heavy easier is. So, I just keep laugh-hiccupping and push my card into the chip reader. My blurry laugh-hiccup eyes make it impossible to see which buttons to push.

A little more loudly he says, "Pin. You have to enter your PIN. Pin. Lady? Pin? Okay? Lady?"

I yank my card back, fish out $30, slap it on the counter, and grab my bags, smashing my hand across my eyes so I can at least see the door. Behind me I hear "Crazy lady!"

Smith Finest Deli is on the corner opposite Zaytoons. Through the window I see my power group. Which means today's Tuesday. I've stopped noticing those kinds of details. I'm more just awake or asleep. At work or at home. Or now just home or at the bodega. I'm not sure I'd even notice Dana now. In a protest line or on the sidewalk next to me. Everything's congealed.

As I walk along Sackett toward my stoop, a nor'-east gust sends
Mrs. Costa's dented metal trash can rolling down the street.
Fumpfump fapityfapity fumpfumpfumpfump fapityfapity
clackclack click-clack click-clack

                                  Maaaaaaagggggiiiiieeee

waaaaaaaaaannnnnaaaa   *this land is*

                        beeeeeeeeeee   *my land*

       aaaaaaaaaaaaaaa

                                       this land's not

iiiiiinnnnnddiiiiiaaaaannnn   *funnel cake*

       sparklers   *Dana*

Ohma   *birdhouses*

                    dormant tree

     tree *tree tree tree*   *hide and seek*

                  abandoned barn

day after day

                           charred plastic roses

         bus exhaust   *old fries*

            Pu-Erh tea

                      Shay's boots

Dylan

          Vortex of darkness

                    the keys of Dylan Chester Montgomery

day after day

                  up and up and up

                       don't bl   *don't blink*

By the time I reach my stairs, reassuring numbness has
returned. I pass the bride without a heart, the boxes of
something or other I bought online, and Dylan's keys awaiting
final rites. I pour myself and dormant tree a glass of Oban and
wait for her input on my fate.

                  ****

If I'm going to go talk to Ohma, I'll need an excuse. One solid enough to avoid the messiness of why I'm there. I don't have the energy to deal with family crap and its crushing whirlpool of whys and why nots. I don't want to lie about why I'm there but dredging up old ghosts is no one's idea of a good time. I could go and not tell them. Just go to Ohma's. Force myself to talk again. I'm supposed to be finished with this whole silence thing by now anyway. But the truth is I like it. It makes me feel like wallpaper.

Of course, if I go without telling them I'll immediately run into Mom at Harris Teeter. Then there'll be the suffocating guilt trip, disappointed expectations, Dad's retreat to his woodshed, and Angie's reproachful glare. No idea what Peter will be like. Last time I saw him he was still a kid. Point is, I'd rather eat a bowl of Carolina Reapers.

I need a good excuse. Seidr told me about a few retreats in the mountains after that awful Language of the Body class. I open my computer and after a few minutes of searching, find one near Blowing Rock.

it's a sign
you don't believe in signs

I pull up the website. The next retreat is in two weeks.

fortune favors the flying squirrels

I add the retreat to my cart and buy it. With the why, when and where set, all I need to arrange is the how.

to: morris_mountainmamma@gmail
Hi Mom,
Sorry it's been so long. I swear time runs at a different speed in New York. I've owed you all a visit for a while and I was thinking it would be great to swing through for a few days on my way to a retreat in Blowing Rock.
I'll be heading down this weekend if you're up for it. The retreat starts the following Thursday.

I pause. It's imperative to word this next part right or I'll trigger her emergency alert system.

> The retreat is actually a *silent* retreat. It's something I found out about from a friend who said it did wonders for her, so I thought "why not?" I'll be practicing not talking during the leading up to it so I'm more prepared. Should be fascinating! So, does next week work for you guys? - M

I proofread it five times, then click send.

Four days later I'm in my Range Rover climbing to the top of the Verrazzano, an anemic sunrise trying to awaken the island of Manhattan. In this light the city seems more like a village of petrified giants forever reaching toward untouchable heavens.

I turn on the radio. "Fried Shadows" by Zack Orion is playing. I've heard him busking in Union Square and once in my Carroll St subway stop. The melody always stopped me. It's so filled with hope and longing. This city has held so much of me and my life. So many years. I'll be back in a couple of weeks, but I feel like something is ending. The undertow of it pulls at me. One me back into the limbo of what was, circling the apex of cement and steel 228 feet above The Narrows, and the me other me heading towards a time I vowed never to revisit.

"In 1/10th of a mile keep left to stay on I-278 West"

August 1979

my tummy feels weird like it's a weasel tryin to climb out my
throat maybe I had too much funnel cake I can't remember
only that I had fun cause Dana was there I didn't even mind
the lights n all the noise the rides make cause she was there
she makes everythin less big n loud even the sparklers   I
usually hate em cause they're too bright n they burn the inside
of my nose but they were pretty like fireflies we drew spirals n
squiggles in the air with em all night cause for the first time
ever momma n daddy let me stay up til 9:00 but it's almost
midnight now I can't sleep my belly is twisty n my head is
filled with mosquitoes n rocks n every time I close my eyes I
hear footsteps in my ears

someone's here limestone crunchin n quartz poppin in the
driveway an engine too the weasel in my belly jumps into my
throat again bringin funnel cake with him I swallow hard n go
to the window can't see the car only two beams of light cuttin
the air swirlin through itself n onto the ground makin weird
little shadow shapes my heart thumpsthumps I know I'm
seein stuff I'm supposed to sleep through

the beams of light go away the car door creaks as it's openin

why's Ohma here?

maybe I'm dreamin I squeeze my eyes shut real hard n hold
my breath til I can't anymore I open my eyes everythin looks
the same I don't think I'm dreamin but it's hard to tell
sometimes I know I'm dreamin but I stay inside the dream
anyway

I tiptoe to my door n open it a crack close my eyes so I can
hear better I can hear voices inside big bales of hay

wuuuble whau wwah? that was daddy

wuh wuh whap that was Ohma

maaup ma mu? that was momma

wuh wuh whap Ohma

it gets quiet if they're still talkin I can't tell cause the footsteps in my ears r too loud I push my door just wide enough to slip out n creep to the top of the stairs the kitchen light's the only one on I can't tell if the shadows r people or chairs it looks like the world from the headlights came inside with Ohma somethin I'm not supposed to see but I'm here now n I do see it I lie down on the top stair so I can see better I can see momma's peach slippers the ones with the three little green n white daisies stitched on top n daddy's feet in grey-green socks I've never seen his feet in grey-green socks before they look like flippers n it's kind of scary but also kinda funny a shadow moves n I hear a chair scrape the floor Ohma's boots n momma's daisies n daddy's flippers under the table her boots'r a little muddy the weasel in my belly jumps again I slide down two more stairs so I can see em better

I can't see momma's face she's facin away from me n her head is makin funny movements n her hand is coverin her mouth daddy's starin at somethin on the wall he doesn't look like daddy he looks like the hollow chocolate bunny I get in my Easter basket Ohma's face is the one I see best

her face looks like it's slidin into her neck she's talkin softly to the table

I creep back to the top of the stairs n lie down try to be real quiet like wallpaper no-one says anythin for a long time I wanna peek again but I don't momma n daddy wouldn't notice me but Ohma'll see me right away so I wait n listen I can hear all kinds of small sounds the wind outside rustlin the hemlocks at the end of the drive the house creakin under the carpet n inside the walls crickets n katydids playin outside I close my eyes n ask the other sounds to be quieter

her uncle took her to the koala Ohma says

I thought koalas only lived in Stralia n zoos

oh that poor little thing I can't imagine momma says

her voice sounds funny tight also like puddin

somethinhappened somethinhappened

good daddy says *good she should—*

yes Ohma says real quiet

then it's real still again I slide back down the stairs like a water moc just halfway so I can see em they look like dolls like someone posed em at a tea party

what will you tell her? Ohma asks quietly

we should-I don't know-honey? sweetheart? ben? what should we tell her?

that Mary-that-that-Mary that Dana moved away that-

she-she won't understand how could this happen? who would do such a thing? how did this happen? we just they just–are you sure? momma's cryin

momma does lots of stuff but she doesn't cry much it makes
my heart thumpthump thumthump harder then there's a
chuffin sound like how Jake sounded under the house like all
the pain can't fit inside I think it's daddy Ohma's eyes look
right at me n my throat feels too small the weasel in my belly is
climbin out again I can't stop him I try to catch the funnel
cake n cheer wine in my hands but it goes all over my jammies
n the carpet too the air is ringin n the footsteps in my ears
sound like the ocean now big waves crashin in my ears

up n up n up n up
if you can't hear me you can't see me

momma's puttin a cold washcloth on my face n I can't stop
cryin but I don't know why now she's holdin me n rockin me
but she's holdin me too tight n I can't breathe she always
holds me too tight I can't breathe I push her away Ohma's
eyes r at the foot of the stairs now like dried leaves floatin n
floatin something gone from the leaf that used to be there she
knows I know but I don't know what I know she holds me
with her eyes I can smell my throw up tangy too sweet like
rotten peaches

Ohma waited there while momma wiped all the throw up off
me n put me in a new nighty but I can still smell it n I know I'll
smell like rotten peaches forever the waves in my ears aren't
big anymore but they're still there **whoosh whoosh whoosh**
whoosh whoosh whoosh

momma put me back in bed maybe daddy helped I don't
remember it didn't feel like he did but maybe he did maybe I
couldn't tell cause he was a hollow chocolate bunny I
pretended to fall asleep so momma would stop strokin my hair

she kept sayin *my poor Maggie poor Dana poor Mary*

every time she did I wanted to scream n scream n scream but I just kept thinkin

if you can't hear me you can't see me
if you can't hear me you can't see me

momma finally left a few minutes ago time feels funny like yesterday wasn't yesterday still dark outside my strawberry shortcake clock says 3:07 I peek out my window Ohma's wagon is gone n it's so quiet no wind or creakin or crickets maybe it was a dream I sniff my hair it smells like rotten peaches I tip toe to the bathroom n try to wash the rotten peach smell outta my hair with momma's roses soap then I go back to bed but my eyes won't close so I look up at the ceilin at the glow in the dark stars daddy stuck up there on my birthday the waves in my ears r gone now   the only sound I hear is Jake the Fireball cryin in the dark under the house by himself I think it's Jake but I can't tell cause he died last year I guess he still cries sometimes

10

I'd forgotten how it is here. Green and green and more green, divided by brush strokes of bark and earth until it all juts upwards thousands of feet, casting shadows of bears and craggy grandfathers reaching for gentler territories to the east.

Where I grew up was, and still is, a place of wildness. A place I left at eighteen with a vehement need to escape ghosts I'd tried unsuccessfully to ignore. Ghosts that found me again, 586.5 miles and four decades later.

It's no surprise the Scots settled here. The low, briny flatness of the tidal marshes, and soft rolling wideness of the Piedmont weren't right. Too open. Too accommodating. So, they kept moving, pulled like dousing rods, back to the mountains. Back to where one's place must be earned daily through holding a line nature effortlessly erases each night.

I roll the window down. It's cool now, almost night, but it was warm today. The air is still rich and malty. The smell of growing things. Wild things. Of places people haven't spat concrete over.

I take a deep breath. Little stars explode across my eyes, and I start to get lightheaded. I pull to the shoulder. My brain is confused about what to do with this much oxygen.

Cars speed past at 75mph to somewhere other than here. But in-between the steel and rubber, there's nothing but trees rustling with wishes whispered, thoughts thought, hopes hoped. Losses lost. If I could scoop this smell into the palm of my hand and embed it there, I would. Make my skin forever smell like this moment.

home

I take another deep breath. I feel a bit nauseated. I guess too much beauty can make you sick if you haven't been around it in a while.

up and up and up

don't blink   don't blink   *stay with us*

   no

sparkers

   not yet

****

Loosely packed dirt pops and crunches under my tires as I slow to turn onto the narrow lane of my parent's driveway.

   quartz pops limestone crunches

It looks brighter and smaller than last time. I catch a whiff of fresh paint. Pale yellow, clean white trim. Dad must have done it over the past week. Since my email. The thought punches a tiny hole in my chest, just large enough for the calcified pebble passing for a heart to fall out and roll under the driver's seat. Guess it's as good a place as any for it. I ease into the space between Dad's blue truck and Mom's faded sea foam green Subaru.

   the green machine

I lost my virginity in the green machine to Nate Pearson. Nate had thick, smooth dark auburn hair and pale green eyes. He was the first boy whose shoulders widened between 7th and 8th grade. I sat behind him in Geometry. He was an enigma. Just out of reach. I adored that about him.

Hugging the farthest edge of the drive next to the barn as if the other cars have consumption is a slick, gunmetal grey next-gen Honda Civic.

   Angie

My sister could give a master class in how to be extra. I have no idea where she gets it. Dad is all subtext and Mom is all earnest heart to heart. I cut my lights and look past Angie's car to the barn. I spent years in there. Burrowing into hay, watching the orb weavers create perfect circles, feeding...

Jake the Fireball

Jake was a feral orange tabby who liked to sleep in our barn. I was the only one he'd let pet him. He crawled under our house one day. I heard him yowling after everyone had gone to sleep. I remember tiptoeing outside, lying down on the ground next to the house, calling to him. But he wouldn't come. I think I stayed there all night, talking to him, but I never saw him again. He's probably still there. A perfect, curled up skeleton.

"Well, who do we have here?"

My father is a bear of a man. Not so much in height and weight as in heart and density. He pulls me into one of his famous hugs. Equal parts joy and admonition. After years of watery hugs and air kisses in the PR industry, I don't know how to manage this real hug. I never really was a hugger. I'm always at a loss, wondering how long is long enough before it's okay to back away.

"Maggie?" His faded blue eyes are concerned.

I push memories of Jake the Fireball, Nate Pearson, limestone crunching, quartz popping and my inability to handle genuine interaction back underwater, and smile at my dad.

His brow smooths. "There you are."

in all my glory

"Trip ok?"

I'm exhausted

my head hurts

and I'm pretty sure I can feel my spleen

I nod and shrug.

He peers back, skeptically. "Uh-huh. Bags?"

I nod and pop the trunk with my wireless key fob, realizing my chrome on black Range Rover trumps the douchiness of Angie's Honda by a remarkable landslide.

"So, guess you weren't kidding about the mute thing, hmm?"

I'm not mute

He winks and half smiles. "People talk too much anyway"

they really do

He pauses at my trunk as if a cottonmouth is ready to strike. He comes from a generation that believes wear and tear means something. That something that can stand the test of time was fundamentally worth whatever it cost. My new leather duffel that's been subtly pre-patinaed to look aged is essentially committing fraud in his eyes. He grabs my weathered Filson duffel instead.

"This the duffle we bought you for when you left for FIT?" I nod, and huge smile breaks across his face.

"Look at that! 26 years. Can't fake true craftsmanship"

"Maggie! Oh, you made it!" My mother, flitting down the porch stairs waving to me like I might not recognize her. My mother is a paradox. She believes anything homemade automatically makes it delicious, can clean your clock at Texas hold 'em, believes every word of the bible but never pushes anyone to do the same, adores Waylon Jennings, and is the current county fair square-dancing champion. She also brings a rip tide of worry wrapped in a cloud of Emeraude wherever she goes.

Mom humming making waffles

old french fries

exhaust

cotton candy
Dylan's hands like wet dough

pipe tobacco   cloves   roses

Mom pulls me into a fierce hug. "Oh, sweetheart, what a drive-I hope you took enough breaks. Did you take breaks? Did you take 95? Isn't it awful? I won't go near it anymore-it's so good to see you!"

I pull out of her vice grip, smile, and shrug, trying to convince her it was uneventful. It was. Except for the section south of Baltimore through Quantico. That's a preview of hell.

Her brow ripples dramatically. "You look exhausted."

"Give her a break, El, she just drove eleven hours."

Mom shoos him off and threads her arm through mine, gripping me like a manic hummingbird. "Are you hungry? I saved you some dinner-but maybe you just want to go right to bed-your room is all ready for you-I bought a few new things just to perk it up."

As we climb the porch stairs, Angie slides out from a shadow offering me a laconic wave.

"The prodigal daughter returns," she says.

good to see you too Ang

"Mom was starting to wonder if you were dead. You should replace your assistant."

"Oh, Gigi, I said no such thing," Mom says breezily. Which means that's exactly what she said. Mom, despite her earnestness, prefers to ignore acrimony between the people she loves.

"Or I made cheesecake. You still like cheesecake, right?"

"Sure she does, Mom. Don't you, Maggie?" Angie replies. I ignore her and nod, smiling at Mom.

I hear Dad say "Cool it" under his breath.

Angie responds with a quippy, sour faced "What?"

She catches me catching her. I look away before she can add this moment to her list of grudges. I've never been able to decipher what I did to make her hate me with such tenacity. She seems to have had an entirely different experience of our relationship. For her there's tons of water under this bridge to re-examine and account for. For me the river never existed.

maybe that's why

Angie slithers in behind us. My sister is undeniably a snake. I don't mean that as an insult. Snakes get a bad rap.

They're smart. Keenly observant. They often take care of things we don't want around. They also live by an acquired knowledge rarely shared with others. Also, they become the temperature of their surroundings. She does that. My sister becomes the temperature of her surroundings. But if you step too close, she won't hesitate to draw first blood.

I let whatever beef she has go for now, and head into the living room. Same deli mustard yellow couch with pea-green chenille throw pillows. Same hutch with mom's collection of Time Life plates from across the globe. Same mammoth Pine bookcase. I remember when Dad brought it in from his workshop still smelling of the fallen tree and beeswax from an abandoned hive he'd finished it with. Same books on the shelves, waiting to be read just once more before crumbling to dust. Same weathered leather ottoman, same side table, same wooden bowl, same pipe, and no doubt the same tobacco my father has smoked for longer than I've been alive. All the same. Like a museum.

I catch Mom looking earnestly at me. "Honey?"

Apparently, I've stopped mid-step.

ground control to Major Mags?

Major Mags isn't here right now

she's preparing to be spaghettified

haha

shut up

I begin to walk again. Mom and Dad instinctively sandwich me between them—gladiators ready to battle any and all comers, including any demons I've brought with me. Dad gently pulls the duffle from my hand.

"Someone needs to put her feet up."

Mom squeezes my arm "And have cheesecake!" She scurries into the kitchen.

I sit on the couch, grabbing one of the pillows to plop it across my stomach. I immediately feel better. Anchored.

Angie coils onto one of the uncomfortable chairs, opposite me, staring unblinkingly.

bit on the nose there Ang

Dad bellows "PETER!"

I hear a deep male voice reply "What!?"

no way that's Peter

that's Marvin Gaye

"Your sister's home!" Dad barks.

A large thunk, followed by faster thunking down the stairs brings my once gangly, pimple-faced 13-yr-old now tall, muscular, slightly awkward 20-yr-old brother. He lopes over to me, picks me up off the couch and gives me a bear hug.

"S'up city lady?" He releases me. "Oh, man! You're really doing the silence thing?"

A sarcastic "Apparently," slips from Angie.

Peter takes me through a series of handshakes I can only imagine have something to do with being #forreals. I follow along lamely. He finishes his assessment with "Badass!"

"Peter!" Dad yells.

"What? Come on! She is. Most people can't shut up for two minutes and she's been at it for...?" He turns to me eyebrows raised.

I shrug and hold up a finger.

"A week?" Peter exclaims.

sure let's go with that

"Of not returning messages, then driving alone? Amazing." Angie says.

"That's so," Peter confirms his assessment, "badass!"

"Peter," Dad rumbles.

From the kitchen Mom singsongs, "Anyone want deeee-caaaaf?"

I raise my hand. Angie tries to hide a scoff.

Peter covers me with "Maggie wants decaf," then elbows me in the ribs, adding "I got your six, Link."

got your six?
got your six
       rruuuuuummmmbuuumbarnmoonpeachpie
I have no idea who Link is, but I don't care. My little
brother is my new favorite person.

****

Mom spinning plates juggling and pulling different kinds of
spatulas out of a hat in between each magic trick she tosses
glitter   a studio audience ooohs and aaahs

Dad Sam Spade leaning on a lamppost carving a wooden bird

Angie cross-legged on the floor with two wild haired sock
puppets who keep biting each other

Peter playing Mozart on a tiny plastic piano   a hawk cries   a
plastic seagull on string

    wait, that's not right

    Dad says *wait, that's not right*

the audience laughs

    am I dreaming?

Angie starts to sing *which one of these is not like the others*

the hawk cries   the ceiling is different not really a ceiling huge
skylights how did I never see those? windy dormant tree
thrashing spiraling   taller than I remember so tall twisting
swirling spiraling spiraling too much the skylights will break

am I dreaming?
Dylan's making coffee in the-
I open my eyes.
oh right
My teenage Felix the Cat alarm clock says it's 11:30am. I
slept twelve hours. Usually I'd be surprised, but last night was
exhausting in the way only family can be. After Peter joined us,
it was 55 minutes of cheesecake, coffee, and awkward smiles.
One of the more interesting things I've learned in the past
month is silence is contagious. It spread like a virus last night.

Finally, Dad saved the day saying we should call it a night
because I was probably exhausted from the drive. Angie was
out the door within minutes saying she'd see us all tomorrow.
Peter left to go meet some buddies at what Dad called a
'privileged whiner's group'. That covers a lot of territory with
Dad, so there's no telling where Peter went.
It still took a while to get into bed because Mom kept going on
about the new sheets she'd bought, saying maybe she should
have gotten green instead. Or white. Or a different blue. Or
stripes. How she hoped they were soft enough but not too
squishy. Then she'd pull me into another desperate hug saying,
   "I'm so glad you're here." Her vinegary panic sweat
slicing through the cloud of Emeraude.

Finally alone, I lay in my old twin bed in the dark looking
at my teenage posters. The Eurythmics, Dune, Big Trouble in
Little China, Bowie, The Thompson Twins, Blondie, Peter
Gabriel. Thoughts of Nate Pearson, Jake the Fireball, and
building hay forts in the barn watching the sun glint through
giant orb weaver webs. I don't remember falling asleep.

I roll onto my back and look at the popcorn ceiling.
Someone's outside doing something that sounds like pounding
dirt with a giant mallet. Fump Fump Fump.
Dad

Someone puttering in the kitchen, trying to be quiet.

Mom

Muffled alt-indie rock down the hall.

Peter

The sound of a thousand grudges awaiting repayment.

Angie

I get out of bed and go to the window. Dad's clearing a patch of the garden. When I was little, I thought he'd been put into a human's body accidentally. That he was supposed to be an animal or a tree instead.

"Maggieeeee, honey? Are you uuuuup?" Mom singsongs, tapping gently on the door.

I take a deep breath and try to exhale the sensation of being hunted. Warm maple syrup, coffee, waffles, and breakfast sausages. My stomach rumbles.

"Hi honey, I hope I didn't wake you?" she asks anxiously when I crack the door.

I shake my head and try for a warmer smile. Mitchel once told me whenever I try for warmth I look like Mara, the Germanic witch of nightmares.

"Oh, good, good! I made waffles. You still like them, right?"

"And coffee. I know you still like that. Oh, and those Johnsonville links. You used to love those. Couldn't eat enough of them. I hope that's okay?"

I give her a thumbs up. It does sound good.

"Okay," she says, "well you just take all the time you need. No rush here. No rush. You just take all the time you need sweetie."

here we go

I take a few more deep breath/exhales before I follow her downstairs, heading straight for the coffee. I plop down onto one of the barstools tucked underneath the counter that

divides the kitchen from the dining room. Dad built it in the
70s. It's very Brady Bunch.

I take a sip, preparing for Folgers. But it's actually
fantastic. Like smoked cherries and caramel. I catch her
watching me hopefully. I give a hearty thumbs up.

"Oh, good! I couldn't remember which kind of coffee
you liked so I just got Larry's Smokey Mountain Roast. Larry's
is great, right? Isn't it? They're local. I know you love fancy
coffee so, you like it? It's ok? I got it at that cute little Ten
Thousand Villages store where they have that little sample
section in the back. I tried it and thought you'd like it and the
lady—they have volunteers there, did you know that—isn't
that just lovely—they volunteer—anyway, the volunteer was
the nicest lady and she told me Larry's is very popular, so I
thought I'd try it. $12 for a bag though! Whew, nelly! I
remember when coffee was a dollar a pound—but she said it
was fantastic, so I thought why not because it's such a treat
when you visit. They have the funniest little string people
keychains there. I was going to get Peter an Alexander
Hamilton one for his birthday because he loved that show, that
Broadway show, though you probably saw it, right? But Peter
went with some friends to see the tour when it came to
Charlotte and he just went on and on about it, so I was going
to get him the little string person keychain but I'm not sure I
should because now he's going on and on about the
unpunished crimes of the banks—did you know everything
they sell there helps a person from a third-world country?"

breathe Mom

Mom has three speeds: cautious, anxious, asphyxiating.

"So, I was chatting with Mrs. Dahlgren the other day,
about your—what is it called—a quiet pledge?"

now everyone in the county is going to know

"She was saying she'd read all about it in Reader's Digest. Something about taking a break from talking is a sign of a turning point or a …"

She keeps talking but it's all starting to sound the same. A violin playing a single, quavering note. She continues as she passes me a stack of Mrs. Butterworth's saturated waffles, already well on their way to gloopy disintegration, nearby sausages shriveled and despondent. I had a Winnie the Pooh divided plate as a kid. I wish I had it now.

"...can be very confusing, and everyone could use someone to talk to. Everyone needs that, don't they? It doesn't mean anything's wrong. I'm not saying anything's wrong. You know that, right, you know that sweetheart."

I gently rap my knuckles on the counter. She looks up from the batter.

it's okay
I'm okay
breathe

It would be easier to just talk. Maybe I should. It would make things easier. But I've told the lie and now I have to uphold it.

or maybe you're still too chicken noodle chicken shit
or maybe we only get one real chance to get things right
or maybe you can talk yourself into just about anything
shut up
you shut up

"—so glad you're here. I don't want to do anything to make you regret coming home."

I'm not home   I'm visiting

"If you ever feel like going to someone who comes highly recommended and is very open-minded, Dad and I would be happy to pay for it."

She pulls a card out of her pocket and slides it over to me.

Dr. Gustov Nahimana
Clinical Psychologist

I don't need a shrink

Then I remember the night I quit my job. And following Dana and Patricia. And that the only thing I've felt any kind of connection with for a very long time is a dormant tree. And how Mitchel said I was disappearing.

but so what?

when did not being okay become unacceptable?

a strong case could be made for the 80's

I push my plate away, refill my coffee and start toward the stairs. Her panic fills the room like ant spray.

"Honey, I-I'm just trying to understand. It's just that-I-I-I'm wondering if-if-I think it might be-if it might be your way of-of, I don't know, distancing yourself from people again? You-you-I don't know if you remember this-you were so young-but after that awful summer..."

what? WAIT that awful summer?

so you remember?

of course she remembers idiot

who'd forget something like that?

shut up listen to her

get out of your head for a fucking second and listen

"It was—we were worried at first because it went on for quite a while. Almost a year. But then we thought maybe it was your way of dealing with everything."

I rap my knuckles gently on the bar again and give her as confused a face as I can muster.

"Well, it was-you always handled things your own special way, honey, and there's nothing wrong with that. You were always such a porous child."

porous?

what the hell does that mean?

I feel my blood pressure rising. Time to go back upstairs. I take the little notepad and pen by the phone and write, "Mom, I'm fine. I'm just practicing for the retreat, remember?" I pass it to her.

"Right, yes, honey, of course," she says returning her attention to making more waffles. I can tell she's about to cry. It's exhausting. Now I remember. How her emotions, her constant state of feeling is exsanguinating. I always feel anemic around her. I've never been able to tell if that's because she's too much or I'm too little.

I head back to my room. Halfway up the stairs, I hear her behind me. "You know you can tell me anything, honey. You know that, right?" she asks.

sure

as long as it isn't scary for you

I try to fake a grateful smile before I close my door behind me.

what the hell are you doing?

I guess I thought I'd have some kind of memory-unlocking epiphany before I visit Ohma. Shake something loose. Not drown in maple waffle sausage mush or my mother's suffocating need for me to be okay.

oh honey have more waffles

I hope you like the sheets

I'm so concerned about the sheets

you're so porous you might absorb the damn sheets

I'm not sure I can do four days of this. A hotel would have been the smarter move. But what was she talking about? She was talking about that summer.

does she know why you're here?

no   no way   how could she?

I look out the window. Dad's still working in the garden. It's so simple. I envy him. Just dirt and a person. No conversations or misunderstandings or unmet expectations. Or scorecards. Just dirt and a person.

He stops as Mom walks up to him, looking bereft. They exchange a few words. Dad glances up at my window then back to her, saying something as he touches her cheek.

shit shitshit

I must have been nuts to think this was a good idea.

****

I've now been hiding in my room like a kid for an hour, waiting for my father's knock and along with it, a gentle reprimand over my dismissal of Mom and her waffles. I can hear them talking downstairs in lowered voices, his calm, hers insistent. But instead of his solid footsteps up the stairs, the side screen door closes with a slap-slap. Then two truck doors closing and the wuh-wuh-wuh-wuh-wuh of his truck backing up to the lane and rumbling away. Now it's quiet. In a way I forgot is possible on this planet. No cars or horns or subways or millions and millions of mouths talking and eating and fighting and laughing. No scrape-clang-thump of construction that's never once stopped in the twenty-five years I've lived in New York.

But none of that is here. Singular sounds are here. Small ones. Surrounded by so much air and trees and wild things that their edges are translucent. I feel weightless and invisible. How heavy the sounds of human industry are. How they latch onto us as we go through our day, slowly pulling at us, until body no longer syncs with soul. Until your life revolves around the endless thrumming of concrete and steel. At least for me. Not everyone. Not Mitchel or Dana or Dylan or Chelsea or Newton. Maybe the coffee cart owner would agree with me. I think he might.

I creep downstairs slowly—just in case mom's still here, a fretful spider waiting to talk again. But she's gone. Peter is too. Thankfully Angie doesn't live here. I'm alone.

A note is propped in front of the coffeemaker.

Hi honey, Mom and I are out to run some errands. Back by 5 for dinner. Help yourself to anything in the kitchen. Love, Dad

I make a cheese and mustard sandwich and pour some iced tea. There's always a pitcher of sweet tea in the fridge because the absence of a pitcher of sweet tea in one's fridge is immediate grounds for expulsion from the state. A gentle almost warm breeze floats in through the screen door.

bet it's still freezing in Brooklyn haha

I opt for lunch outside. Never has a cheese and mustard sandwich tasted so good. The tea is thick with sugar and makes my teeth ache, so I set it down and let the warm day work on the ice.

dormant tree would love it here

I close my eyes. Let the sun, a still early spring but gentler, fuller one than New York's 42nd parallel north, warm my face, imagining how dormant tree might look if she lived here. What kind of leaves she'd have. If she'd have flowers. Maybe she'd like to be next to a barn. Swaying in the breeze, shiny dark green leaves, and white flowers the barn starts to creak and expand doors open spilling jars filled with old keys and red wax pencils and mirror fragments arrows and U-turn signs on the walls and floor and ceiling all pointing at a birdhouse someone behind me touches my shoulder

"Maggie. Maggie…"

Dormant tree and her barn evaporate.

"Must have been one hell of a dream" Dad says, smiling. I nod.

something about jars and a tree

"Sorry to wake you," he says, "but the skeeters are already out this year and they'll eat you alive if you stay out much longer." It's just past sunset. Ruby, purple and dark blue. A skeeter buzzes by my ear.

Dad made a fresh pot of coffee, probably decaf, but I don't care. I pour a mug and follow the smell of his cherry tobacco into the living room. He's in his leather ottoman reading a Woodsmith magazine.

give him a minute
don't be like her   you just got here

I wander over to the bookcase looking for something to read. Between the books are small, framed photos of our family. I come across one of Mom, Dad, me around age seven, and Angie as a toddler. Mom and Dad are looking at the camera and smiling, but I'm crouched down, looking at something in the grass.

little weirdo

I sit down, looking through the magazines on the coffee table. Good Housekeeping, Classic Trucks, American Square Dance, Reader's Digest, and Woodsmith are the only offerings. Dad smiles but his eyes keep reading his magazine.

"Something on your mind?"

I get the message pad and pen by the phone. The urge to stop my bullshit not talking charade intensifies. But I'm concerned if I suddenly start talking, I'll revert to asshat, glib Maggie. Words are so easy to hide myself inside. Get lost in. I write, "She worries too much" and hand him the notepad.

He hands it back to me. "Sometimes"

One of the things I like about my dad is his economy of speech. Once I start talking again, I'll try to be more like him. I write, "I don't need a shrink,'" and pass it to him.

He hands it back to me. "She just wants to help."

I write, "I'm not broken," holding it up for him to see.

"No," he says. He's being careful. "But there's something bothering you enough to take time away from talking to figure it out. Which, I support, by the way. I think your whole generation could stand to take a healthy dose of quiet time. I support you, honey. So does Mom."

right

I hear myself emit a tiny sound of disbelief.

"You know, it wouldn't hurt to appease her on this. One hour with a doc-in-the-box could go a long way. Might be worth it. Nothing wrong with needing a little guidance to figure things out." He gives me the loving-yet-pointed look that always marks the end of a conversation and returns to his magazine.

I'm not a kid anymore
you can't just end a conversation

I write one last note, feeling weirdly aggressive as I tear it off, and gently place it next to his coffee mug on my way to the stairs and back up to my room. It says, "I bumped into Dana in New York. It's why I'm here." I look back to see if there's any reaction. Nothing looks different. It looks like he's still reading his magazine, drinking his coffee, and smoking his pipe, but the room has contracted. Like it's watching us.

He picks up my note, folds it once and puts it in his shirt pocket then resumes reading his magazine. I've never once felt uncomfortable around my dad. Until now.

August 1979

she's lyin I KNOW IT I KNOW IT SHE'S LYIN splinters n
spiders in my head n had to get em out so I opened my mouth
to spit em at her

*I DON'T BELIEVE YOU I DON'T BELIEVE YOU
YOU'RE LYIN YOU'RE A LYIN LIAR N I HATE YOU* **I
HATE YOU FOREVER**

for a second they were gone n I was startin to be a tree again
but then they came right back bitin harder   makin me into
splinters pokin in my head then she said it again
    Dana's gone sweetie her mamma died and Dana had to go
this time her words stayed in my head circlin like a twister
swallowin everythin even the spiders
*what*doyou**mean**GONE*what*doyou**mean**GONE
*what*doyou**mean**GONE*what*doyou**mean**GONE
*what*doyou**mean**GONE*what*doyou**mean**GONE
*what*doyou**mean**GONE*what*doyou**mean**GONE
*what*doyou**mean**GONE*what*doyou**WAITOHMA**
Ohma'll tell me the truth
she always tells the truth
even if it's like nettles

momma's makin sounds again tryin to hug me she's all muffle
screechysticky but don't care what she says she's lyin n I don't
believe her I'll never ever believe her again

I run **FWAAP** the screen door hits the side of the house hard

GOOD hope it left a hole in our stupid house

I'm tryin to run now but my feet feel heavy and dumb like they
don't remember what to do

been runnin a long time now should be to the end of our road now but our house is still right here   momma's face in the window momma's face always in the window in the window lookin lookin always lookin at me I don't want her to look at me wanna be invisible wanna be wind

be wind

I start to run harder

be wind   be wind

no-one ever tries to fool wind cause wind can tell when you're lyin

Fap-fap-fap-fap-fap-fap-fap-fap-fap-fap-fap-fap-fap-fap

the ground's too hard it hasn't rained in weeks n that never happens n now if what momma says is true it'll might never rain again every time my foot lands it slaps makes me want to laugh n cry at the same time it would make Dana laugh then she'd try to make the same sound then I'd laugh too thinkin bout Dana laughin makes the top of my nose way inside sting I won't cry I won't cry I'm not gonna to cry not yet not 'til I know for sure not 'til Ohma says it's true I keep runnin n runnin n runnin the waves in my ears r back **swoosh-swoosh-swoosh-swoosh** the air is fulla red dust burnin my throat n crawlin round my ankles the dust makin me so slow pullin me backwards maybe runnin is too slow cause the dust don't like bein slapped grownups never tell you anythin that helps they just look at you like you don't understand stuff when you do plus a whole lot more n they do at least Ohma's just Ohma she never ever says robot grown up stuff never says anythin anyone else says just like Nathy cause trees don't lie

I'm gonna to be just like Ohma when I grow up even if I can't ever be a real saa-laa-gee n if I can't then I'll be a tree bet I could I could be a tree

I turn onto the path past eth river that'll take me to Ohma's   I can see the trail of pale red dust where I used to be hangin in the air like it knows   watchin me   like momma

be invisible

be wind

be air

be dandelion seeds

be a tree beatreebeatreebeatree

haveta run past Dana's house before I get there n maybe she'll be outside n her mom will be paintin a birdhouse n then I'll know it was a lie big fat lie her yard's empty my eyes'r burnin more n more but I won't cry

not yet not 'til Ohma says it's true

11

Dr. Nahimana, Clinical Psychologist, was able to fit me in the next day. I don't know why I agreed to this. I don't know why I do most of what I do.

chicken shit lazy bored
pick a card any card
shut up

Ultimately, I agreed it this because maybe he'll have some insight into what the overall hell is wrong with me. I decided once Mom had secured this appointment that I'd tell him everything. Treat this appointment like releasing the steam valve on a pressure cooker. Probably a good idea before I see Ohma.

Mom made a family outing of it. We're all here—even Angie—walking in formation down a taupe hallway in an uninspired office park.

"—because it is healthier, Dad," Peter says in the I know everything tone twenty somethings excel in, "and it matters."

Dad replies, "I've said all I'm going to say on the topic."

Mom's next. "Can't they do something about how confusing this building is? Imagine not being able to find your therapist's office. How upsetting!"

Angie takes a turn. "I don't get why we all have to be here, it's not like she's having a liver transplant."

if only every day could be this day

Dr. Nahimana's waiting room is filled with forgettable furnishings and inspirational quotes about the human condition. Mom quickly breaks ranks to quietly approach Dr. Nahimana's inner office door. She leans in.

"Mom!" Angie says, hushed and embarrassed. Her tolerance for the intricacies and origins of Mom's fretfulness never seems to rise above a quarter tank.

"Shhhhh! I'm just checking." Mom replies, returning to her eavesdropping with renewed vigor. "I think someone's in there."

Peter and I exchange a look.

and there you have it
our mother

Peter chuckles and starts to peruse a Mindfulness journal. Dad shakes his head, choosing a Time magazine. I've tried to make eye contact with him over the past 24 hours, but my note about Dana shifted something, and it's as if he's become more like a projection or a hologram.

sound familiar?
shut up

Angie pulls out her phone and starts scrolling. I read the quotes on the walls.

Resistance at all cost is the most senseless act there is.

—Friedrich Dürrenmatt

The first step is awareness. The second step is acceptance

—Nathaniel Branden

People don't resist change. They resist being changed.

—Peter Senge

They're good as far as quotes go. Sure. Pretty words. But they also have a tinge of "here's a lollie, sorry about the amputation" I don't know why we're expected to pretend every moment is some integral part of a glorious fucking journey. Just once I'd like to see a quote that says, "Sometimes things suck" and "Not everything happens for a reason". And where are the quotes from women? Not a single quote from Maya Angelou, Eleanor Roosevelt, Amelia Earhart, or Nawal El Saadawi. Guess the good doc isn't above helpin' the women folk, but he's not about to quote one.

strike one doc

Mom suddenly springs from the door, nabs a mental health pamphlet, spins, sits, and flips it open. Like I said, square dance champion.

Dr. Nahimana's office door opens, revealing a tall man with unsettlingly large eyes and a wild halo of hair that looks like it's orbiting him. He steps into the waiting area.

"Good afternoon. I am Dr. Nahimana."

Mom jumps up, shaking his hand, "Oh, hello doctor, thank you so much for squeezing Maggie in today. We can't thank you enough, you come very highly recommended for-for-" She lowers her voice, "unique situations".

unique situations? uuuhhhh yeah

I stand up. Dr. Nahimana's huge eyes switch to me. "Please, come in" he says.

I follow him into his office, catching my father's eye for a second before he quickly returns to his magazine. More than anything in the surreal gauntlet of the past two months, my father's reaction to my note about bumping into Dana is the most disconcerting. It tells me she was being honest about there being a lot more to that summer than I know. That either I don't know or don't remember.

Dr. Nahimana's office is a carefully constructed cocoon of care and comfort. Light streams softly through honeycomb blinds, spilling across a giant Persian rug of blue, green, and ivory. Tungsten lamps blur edges, and abstract paintings, sculptures, and small fascinating objects of unknown origin sit upon tables and nestle into large bookcases along the walls. Everything no doubt a subtle Rorschach. There to get you to spill your deepest, darkest beans if you comment on them. I switch my attention to Dr. Nahimana.

"Please, have a seat," he says.

frog eyes

I look at my options. Three chairs with three distinct styles in three distinct relations to his chair.

the chair you choose?

strike two doc

"Anything the matter?" he asks gently.

I smile and shake my head, focusing on my seating choices. I can't help but imagine large Mamma Bear, Papa Bear, and Baby Bear placards atop each one. And myself in a Goldilocks costume. And Dr. Nahimana as a large toad, wearing a snappy vest, smoking a pipe, playing the piano, and singing *Honesty* by Billy Joel.

"May I call you Maggie? Or would you prefer Magpie?"

who told you that name?

I frown. He smiles.

I sit down in the chair furthest from him. His bushy eyebrows rising like feathery smoke as he jots down a note.

it's a damn chair doc

not everything happens for a reason

"Maggie it is," he says, leaning back. Then he waits. The length of time the man can go without blinking his huge froggy eyes is quite impressive.

"So, you mother tells me you're taking a break from verbal communication?"

I shrug.

"Mmmmhmmm, understandable, understandable," he says. "The world can be a very loud place, can't it?"

I'm about to say "Yes" loudly when Angie's voice breaks through the wall.

"This whole thing is nuts," she says. "She's officially nuts now."

"Monikers of judgement only label you, G." That was Peter.

"You're all just feeding into another one of her dramas," she replies.

I don't think Angie is going for irony right now, but comparatively speaking, I'm tepid in the drama department. Certainly the least dramatic of my immediate family.

uh huh sure

shut up

"Honey," Mom says, "that isn't fair. Maggie's trying to-"

"You always do that" Angie snaps.

Dr. Nahimana is watching me.

forty minutes to go

eight miles to go

seven miles to go

    Cedar

      Hemlock

        Pine

          Oak

"Do what, honey?" Mom's anxious voice asks.

six miles to go

        funnel cake

five miles to go

    the way, way back

"Make excuses for her. You all do. You always have," Angie replies. I can almost hear her face imploding into a sullen pout.

four miles to go

three miles to go

"Angie, leave it!" Dad adds sternly.

I laugh. Angie, the dog, caught eating poo. The waiting room goes silent.

Froggimana jots down a note. This is precisely why I don't like therapists. Always observing, always taking notes, always convinced of their ability to assess.

"Do you mind if I ask a few questions?" His crushed velvet voice continues, "Your choice, to stop talking. It started recently?"

maybe you should tell him the truth
I nod.

"Good, okay. Recently. Good"
not a child having a tantrum you idiot
no?
shut up

"Okay," he continues, "If I may, was there a particular event that initiated your decision to stop talking?"

I give him a maybe, maybe not wobble of my hand. I'm dis-appointed. In him. In me. In everything in general. I'm not suicidal, but I think I might be on the verge of being nihil-cidal. Definitely exist-cidal.

"So, recently something happened that may have initiated this time of silence. Had you been experiencing any other disruptions or unease prior to this event that may have contributed to this time away from talking?"

maybe you should tell him the truth
I nod.

"For how long? A few months?"
I don't respond.

"Six months to a year?"
I shake my head.

"Over a year?"
I nod.

Mt. Rainier?
no
before that

"Have you considered—now let me preface this by clarifying I'd not be in a position, nor would I wish to attempt, assessment today for a diagnosis ..."

diagnosis?

"But, if I may, there are a few ..."

may or not you're going to aren't you Mr. I-don't-quote-women

"... signs in your selective non-verbalization choice and apathy?"

who said anything about apathy?

"And..." He looks down and reads what I assume is the southern version of intake papers: the inappropriate sharing of personal information by well-meaning family members. "Your mother ..."

bingo

"Mentioned a struggle with processing that was there from early childhood. I stare at him, waiting. "What I'm observing in our little time together is specific behavioral manifestations that could be considered ..."

oh my self-indulgent pauses Batman
just spit it out

"Have you ever gone through any assessments for ...?"
assessments?

Peter's laughter breaks through the wall. "No escaping Saturn, man. She'll find you! Shakabuku city, baby."

"All your generation does," Dad says, the tension in his voice almost warping the walls, "is drink $10 cups of coffee and talk. I've never known a generation to talk so damn much. Maybe Maggie has it right. Maybe you all should just take a time out from discussing every damn thing."

Mom rejoins. "Something awful must have happened, and she doesn't want us to know about it."

"Nothing happened, El! For Christ's Sake!" I've never once heard him talk to her that way.

"Excuse me a moment," Dr. Nahimana says, standing.
uh-oh

"You don't know that Ben," Mom says with more strength than I remember her voice having. It was the Jesus thing. Mom doesn't stand for any taking-in-vain nonsense. Dr. Nahimana opens the door to the waiting room. Silence falls.

party pooper

"My apologies," he says, "I must ask you to keep conversation to a minimum. Or perhaps, you could avail yourselves of the coffee shop across the street."

"We're sorry, Doctor," Mom says. I can tell she's mortified. "We'll just-we're so-we'll just excuse ourselves." She'll be beating herself up about this for weeks. It will be exhausting to try to make her feel better about it.

"Sounds great, man, thanks," Peter says. "Hey, you know if they have non-GMO hemp milk?"

"Of course." Dr. Nahimana says.

It's uncertain if that was meant for Mom or for Peter. The good doc clearly excels at coverage. I peek around the door. Mom, Angie, and Peter are already gone. Dad glances in at me. He looks tired. Old. He's never looked old before. I smile at him, trying to let him know I want us to be okay. Dr. Nahimana closes the door before I can see Dad's reaction.

"Now, Maggie, where were we?"

After closing the door on a tentative olive branch between myself and Dad, I decided I was done talking to Dr. Nahimana, Clinical Psychologist. Just because someone has a PhD doesn't mean they know how to use it. So, I cycled a track of nodding, shaking my head, and shrugging as he asked me stock and standards like "How does that make you feel?" and "In what ways do you wish your life were different?" His idea of assessing whatever is was he thought he was assessing. Complete waste of time.

****

Mom insisted we take one car after Peter launched into a fossil fuels diatribe over breakfast. I'm sandwiched between Angie and Peter in the back, trying to make myself small enough to not touch either of them. Angie, a fan of the same plan, has plastered herself onto the other door. Dad's driving. No-one is talking.

"Who wants Chik-fil-aaaaaaaa?" Mom singsongs nervously.

"We can't eat there!" Peter snaps.

"And why not?" Dad asks, trying to control his voice.

"Because they antagonize anyone who doesn't identify as cisgender hetero," Peter lobs back.

"Whose sister?" Mom asks. "Honey, I don't understand half of what you say lately. Whose sister are you talking about?"

"Cis-gender, Mom. Cis-gender. Not sister," Peter says gently.

"Family! Decide!" Dad barks. Anger is rare for him so it's making us all twitchy.

"I will not support fascists!" Peter yells.

"Unbelievable," Dad grumbles, "G.D. unbelievable"

"Pretty sure the big man knows what an acronym is." Peter seems hell bent on challenging the alpha today.

Dad signals to pull the Subaru into Chik-fil-a but a truck careens past, cutting us off.

"Peckerwood! Goddamn reckless!" Dad yells, speeding up, flashing the Subaru's high beams at the truck. The truck driver flips us off, pumps the brakes and takes off again.

"Goddamn bullshit alpha dog peckerwood!" Dad yells, speeding after the truck.

"Dad!" Angie yells.

"Dad, stop!" Peter yells.

He ignores everyone, tailing the truck, closer and closer, brights on, leaning on the horn.

"Ben. Ben, stop, please! BEN!" Mom pleads.

We're now close enough to see the "Driver only keeps $20 in ammo" sticker on the bumper. Mom is bearing down, both hands on the dash. Dad careens through a yellow light.

"DAD, STOP BEING AN ASSHOLE!" I scream.

The truck driver slams the brakes hard. Dad swerves, screeching to a halt halfway onto the sidewalk. The truck driver flips us off, laughs, and speeds away. Dad rolls down the window and flips him off yelling, "Asshole Peckerwood!" We're all frozen. My heart is pounding in my ears. Everyone seems to be trying to remember how to breathe.

four miles to go
three miles to go
two miles to go

Angie puts her hand on Mom's shoulder and squeezes it gently. Mom slowly releases the dash, but her hands are shaking. Dad eases the Subaru off the sidewalk and parks. We sit there for a while. No-one says anything for what feels like a very long time.

"How about pizza?" Mom asks, her voice gentle and still shaky. "Everyone loves pizza. Right, sweetheart?" She places her hand softly on Dad's. He relaxes his stranglehold on the wheel. He doesn't look at her, but his head drops.

"Look, there's the Mellow Mushroom right there," she continues, "Easy-peasy."

All through dinner I avoid eye contact with my father, which hasn't been difficult because he hasn't looked anyone in the eye since the truck incident. I don't recognize him. I've never seen him lose his temper like that. Not once.

It's one thing to have an existential crisis. I'm a 49-year-old woman. I'm due. But it's another thing entirely to have one of the few people anchoring the remnants of my identity—behaving like a stranger.

Angie is throwing me too. How she was kind and grounding in the exact way Mom needed. I had no idea she had that in her. I'd be lying if I said I'd given my little sister much thought through the years. She's always been so self-contained. So efficient and practical. Even when she was still in grade school and I was in high school, she was so much more defined.

I've never felt defined. Maybe that's why I like trees. They're just trees, so I can just be—

what?

I look over at Angie. She's staring at the untouched slice of pizza on her plate. Maybe she's asking it something. Maybe pizza is her dormant tree. Everyone needs a dormant tree. Something to hold everything that spills over in us. Something to ask questions you can't ask people. Especially family.

"I just love Mike Wallace, don't you?" Mom says, scooting another slice of pizza next to the half-eaten one on my plate that's already sprung tide pools of grease.

"You always liked Mike Wallace, didn't you?" she asks.

I don't know what she's talking about. Then I follow her gaze to one of the half-dozen flatscreens in the restaurant. *60 Minutes* is about to start.

"Don't you, Honey? Love Mike Wallace?" Mom asks again. She's hoping one session with Dr. Froggy fixed me. The hope in her eyes is almost heartbreaking. I nod and smile.

sorry Mom   still broken

She tries to hide her disappointment by looking up at the flatscreen again. I look up too. The familiar tick-tick-tick-tick of *60 Minutes* reminds me I've been here three days and have yet to visit Ohma. I was going to go see her before the retreat. Then use that time in the mountains to process whatever she tells me. But that plan means I have to go see her tomorrow.

tick-tick-tick-tick

****

When we got home, everyone drifted their separate ways, an unspoken, mutually agreed upon recovery from our quality family time. Dad went straight to his woodworking shed. Angie didn't even come inside. She gave Mom a hug, murmured something to her, and left without a word to anyone else. Peter furrowed and quiet since the Mad Max incident, retreated to his room. Even Mom seems to have reached her limit. I didn't think that was possible. She didn't say anything. Just poured herself a large glass of rosé and turned on a PBS rerun of Jacques Pépin Cooking at Home.

I headed to my room to text Dana about being here and that I'm planning on talking with Ohma tomorrow. Telling Dana means I'll follow through. But then I saw the door to the attic. It dawned on me possible insight or even evidence might be up there. Evidence of what I don't exactly know. Maybe what happened. Where I misplaced myself. Why Dad is acting so out of character since he found out why I'm here. If anything holds a clue it's the palliative care unit for forgotten yesterdays and misplaced selves.

nothing that cannot be found
if sought

I grab my emergency bottle of bourbon and head up the attic stairs. It's clean and organized. Dad's ARMY days still spring up like mushrooms in unexpected places. Books marked BOOKS, fragile marked FRAGILE. Heavy boxes on bottom, light ones on top. Not a single doll with half lidded eyes in sight. There's even a working overhead light.

It takes me less than five minutes to find the photo albums from the 70s and 80s. 1979 and 1980 are the ones I want. The years before and after Dana left. I don't exactly know what I'm looking for. Maybe I just want to see what life looked like before everything went to shit.

I open the album. Mixed in with all the birthday party, Christmas, and Fourth of July shots, are a half dozen photos of me and Dana—most seem like we were oblivious to a photo being taken. We looked happy. Not the canned happy of Dr. Pepper commercials. The invisible, deep happy of belonging.

Of eyes that still see beauty and mystery and jokes that aren't at another's expense. The ache I feel for that time makes it hard to breathe. I've lost something no amount of longing will ever bring back.

"What are you *doing?*" Angie's voice drops to the floor behind me like a slab of ice.

go away

I turn around and give my clearest buzz off expression. She doesn't. We proceed to have that specific brand of standoff reserved for mortal enemies, and sisters. She's better at it than I, but I'd never admit that to her.

Her eyes turn sharp as she leans on the doorframe. "You must know you're acting crazy," she says.

pot-kettle there Ang

"I mean, is this some new, fucked up grab for attention in the Maggie thinks she's a special, special unicorn show? I mean, mom said you pulled this silent crap before but--"
I turn around.

what the hell are you talking about?

"Oh, yeah. Apparently, you did a whole Maggie's not talking act for an entire year once."

wait what?

"Come on, seriously? You don't remember not talking for like an entire year after Dana left? Mom told me you just 'went away'."

what?

"Yeah. So, this is whole situation is kinda a been there, done that, don't you think? And p.s., it's fucking freaking her out, which is, I mean, whatever. Just maybe this could be another-people-matter-just-as-much-as-Maggie moment. You know, fine, go through whatever it is. I'm not saying-I'm just saying maybe it's not just about you, you know?"

I try to think about when I was nine. I don't remember not talking. I know I talked in Jr. high school and high school.

"Wow. Okay. Good talk." She starts to leave, then adds, "You've always been like this, you know. Absorbing everyone around you."

I'm not the fucking Dark Crystal

"You have to stop." Her voice has changed. It's softer. I turn back around. Her mask of resentment is gone. "Look, whatever it is that you're trying to figure out. Fine, cool, figure shit out. Just, this not talking closing off crap isn't the way. I mean, you're here, right? Obviously for a reason. So, you know, be here."

She's right. I just don't know how. And the thought of saying things like, "Hello, how are you? I'm fine" seem impossible, much less "Hey, so, remember that one time when Dana's mom died, and everything went to shit? Let's talk about that." Words feel pretty sketchy to me right now. Too porous. Susceptible. Mis-interpretable.

I return to the photos. Out of hundreds from my childhood (Mom was clearly a photoholic) I've found only three with Dana in them. That in and of itself is weird since she was my best friend, but what's most surprising is how different I look in the photos where she's there. In the ones where she isn't, specifically the ones after that summer, I look like some creepy ghost child that shows up only after the picture is developed—always looking at the ground or at something out of frame.

so, creepy not entirely there ghost, you started a while ago
and the opting out thing
little weirdo
second verse same as the first

I look at the few pictures where I'm with Dana. I've only found three of them. Even though I'm still never looking at the camera, I'm always laughing or smiling. I didn't know how rare that kind of friendship would be. You don't know that stuff as a kid.

I try to remember spending time at Ohma's after Dana left, but I can't picture it. It's like a huge blank space from the summer til 8th grade. Like I wasn't there for a few years and when I finally came back, I wasn't me anymore. I don't know why. I'll add that to my list of questions for Ohma.

Some decisions carry more weight than others. It sucks how much that's true.

"Right. Okay. Whatever." she says, pounding back down the stairs. All this time I've blamed New York for my being this way, but I was clearly gone long before I got there. Before I leave the attic, I take the one photo of Dana and me with her mom, next to one of her birdhouses. I'm looking at the birdhouse with complete, joyful wonder. Dana's smiling at her mom. And her mom is looking at the camera with a small smile, like she's got a secret she may or may not share. I send the photo via text to Dana with the message that I'm home and will see Ohma soon. She immediately thanks me for the photo and says she's never seen that one. That if I have any others, she'd love to see them. I tell her it's the only one I've found. I have no idea why I lied to her about that. The whole exchange makes me feel like a fraud.

September 9, 1979

the mean lady behind the counter smells like French fries n
plastic roses   she says there r no koalas in North Carolina n
keeps askin me where my momma is

> *yes there r too koalas* I tell her *our family lives with em n I'm*
> *supposed to get tickets for me n for momma to go there*

the mean smelly French fry plastic roses lady's lookin at me
with tiny beady eyes that r too far inside her head n her big
cheeks keep smilin but her smile sounds like loud brakes on big
trucks

> *don't lie little girl lyin's a sin*

I never once yelled at a stranger not ever but I wanna yell n
smoosh her stupid face in

> *you're so mean* I yell *why won't you let me see my family?*
> *WHY WON'T YOU LET ME?*

I start to cry cause she won't help me n now I'll never see
Dana again n I have feathers n special rocks in my backpack
for her momma n now the mean lady's turnin purpley-red n
the other people in the station r whisperin

a nice lady comes over to me she smells like Christmas n iced
tea

> *What's wrong honey lamb?*

she's so nice it makes me cry harder

I-I-I'm su-su-pposed to buy a-a-a ticket for-for me n my momma to the ko-ko-koalas but-but-but she w-won't let me

I've never lied before it's kind of excitin but I also feel bad bout it n maybe the mean smelly French fry plastic roses lady knows I'm a bad person she looks like she knows

the nice old lady starts to talk with the mean smelly plastic roses French fry lady   then the nice old lady comes back over to me n shows me a schedule to a place called the Qualla

this where your momma needs tickets honey? the Qualla? sounds just like koalas though don't it? in't that sweet? must   be a nice place if it's named after little bears that hug trees

I nod

this young lady needs two tickets to the Qualla   then the nice old lady looks at me *you need the tickets for the bus at 4:30 today or another day?*

today   thank you ma'am

two tickets for the 4:30 please she says to the plastic roses lady

that'll be seven dollars smelly plastic roses lady says face all bunched up like she's gonna sneeze

I pull seven silver dollars out of my pocket that I saved from the nine granpa gave me for my birthday this year he always gives me silver dollars for how old I am I put seven of em on the counter   I wish I could just buy my own ticket n save the rest but I know they won't let me buy one just for me

*there now see? everythin worked out just fine your momma'll be
very proud of you honey lamb* the nice lady squeezes my arm

thank you ma'am thank you for helpin me I say

I feel bad bout lyin to her but maybe sometimes it's okay to lie
when it's for a real good reason

12

The problem with epiphanies is the expectation that once one sees the light, they'll be ready to change. And capable of it. What bullshit. Seeing a tidal wave coming doesn't have anything to do with stopping it, much less surviving it.

I haven't once thought what I'll do if what Ohma tells me includes something I don't want to know. Or if she won't tell me anything. Or if she doesn't remember the way Dana thinks she will. I haven't thought any of this through. All of it's been living in the nostalgic, slightly tragic fable of Maggie. A story about a best friend who disappeared after her mom died, and how life changed, and then I changed. But it's real now— the photos in our attic showed as much. My father's bizarre behavior and learning of my former non-verbal choices only further underscoring it. I need a better plan. I need to figure out some contingencies.

****

Two hours, a thermos of Larry's, and my guilty pleasure 70s and 80s road trip mix later, I'm winding my way up a narrow dirt road with a sheer half mile drop to a better to burn out than fade away scenario. Not that I'd consider it. At least I don't think so. I'm too much of either a coward, or a closeted idealist, to go that route.

It almost feels like summer. The air is buzzing with wild things stirring back to life under honeysuckle and hemlock.

A carved wooden sign strapped to a pine tree reads 'Conscious De-verbalization Retreat'. As I pull into the small dirt parking lot, The Doobie Brothers are trying to remind me about the pitfalls of fools and their beliefs. The few people milling about at a trail head on the opposite side of the parking area glare at me as if I'm blasting Motörhead.

deverbalization doesn't include music folks
wait does it?
that would suck

I can see us all, sitting music-less around a gasping campfire that can't burn because our stifled joy has swallowed all the oxygen from the Smoky Mountains. If I wanted stifled and joyless, I would've stayed at The Bridge Group.

I stuff half a volleyball sized Stick Boy cinnamon roll with cream cheese frosting into my mouth, back into an open spot, pull my duffle from the backseat and follow the music gestapo into the woods. I may be a disintegrating, pointless master of avoidance, but I'm no quitter.

As I hike the path, a feeling I haven't had in a long time stops me. It's hard to describe. Something about the air. Deep green and purple with flecks of bright yellow. Like when you're a kid and something happens that makes you so happy you think you might explode or laugh or cry, but you're not sure which one will happen. I'm pretty sure the summer before Dana left was the last time I felt this way. It makes me want to stay here, halfway up this trail, forever. But I can't.

promises to keep and miles to sleep haha

I finally cross wobbly legged onto a high mountain meadow with a breathtaking vista of the Smokies, the fading light turning sky and mountains into a kaleidoscope of green, gold, and lavender. Just a wisp of blue. Like smoke.

A circle of colorful blankets creates a mandala around a crackling bonfire where a man who looks exactly like Kris Kristofferson is playing an acoustic guitar. It's nice. A bit heavy handed on the picturesque, but nice.

I drop my duffle and default to gauging the whos and whys of the other people here. A few are easy to tag. The ones chucking amicably around the fire—not their first de-verbalization rodeo. The two or so dozen hovering between the edges and inner bonfire sanctum—first day of junior high.

Then there are the few like me. Edgers, ready to bolt if needed. They probably all backed into their parking spots too.

Everyone seems already on the de-verbalized clock, save the few near the fire who are murmuring softly to each other, completely at ease. Their low voices, mixed with the rustling trees is almost narcotic. It's such a departure from my usual experience of the human voice. In the city, making your voice heard over the din is an important part of the deal, and lends itself to a certain level of harmonic aggression. But when you're surrounded by ancient mountains the human voice at normal volume sounds a lot like a jack hammer.

just a few days
then I'll keep my promise

For now, I don't have to explain myself or listen to a constant torrent of words or drown in the tension at home. It'll also give me a week to get my questions together and plan what to do once I talk to Ohma.

I start to look at my fellow De-Verbalizers more closely. See who else paid this kind of money to not talk for a week. Everyone here seems somewhere on the spectrum of existential crisis. There's a couple hovering at the edge, arms crossed, mouths latched, no eye contact. This retreat must be the Hail Mary for a disintegrating marriage. Opposite them, a pod of thirty-somethings stands together, shuffling in spotless hiking boots. Corporate team building. At least they'll bring some comic relief.

I try to remember the last time I laughed. Belly laughed. Years. At least.

The rest of the attendees seem like variations on a theme of lost. Only one person seems delighted to be here. An impish girl in all black, with a vibrant red mouth. The love child of Audrey Hepburn and Edward Gorey. She approaches the small group of corporates.

this'll be good

She cycles through several stances, playfully mocking their uptightness. And their new boots.

I walk to the far edge of the clearing to look out over the golden outline of the Smokies. I close my eyes, smelling the woodsmoke from the fire, and the earth releasing the last of the day's warmth. Calls of cardinals and robins echo gently off the mountains, joining the crackling fire, and faint guitar.

All the questions about Dana, that summer, the answers Ohma might have, losing Mitchel's friendship, and the crunchiness between me and my dad ease their grip. I feel light, and invisible. Then a new smell enters my bubble. Rose.

I open my eyes. Mime girl is standing in front of me, smiling, her eyes closed. She's looping her head in a figure eight.

hey mime-ette not cool

She opens her huge round eyes, bows, then she points dramatically to her right eye, winking it.

uh huh you betcha

pretty sure you're at the wrong retreat doll-face

She swiftly leaps to my side, mock elbowing me in the ribs and proceeds to point out, and mimic, the people she's met so far.

every single time they find me

I'm trying to edge away from her when a wave of murmurs ripples through the clearing. The Kris Kristofferson lookalike has stopped playing his guitar and a statuesque woman is walking through the circle of blankets towards the fire. Some people have a gravitational pull. It's rare, but these two have it.

"Hello. Welcome. I'm Jendro," The woman says. Her voice is equal parts grit and honey—low and rich but since no-one else is talking it carries a surprising distance. "We're so very pleased to have you with us."

"And I'm Calah," Kris Kristofferson says with a voice so tinny and cartoonish, his commitment to a de-verbalized life seems a reasonable choice. "For the next week," he says, "through the simple act of conscious de-verbalization, you'll not only discover new ways to communicate, but you'll also learn how you use verbal communication. Everyone's different. Some use it as a dagger, some as smoke, some as a mirror. Hopefully you'll start to see your own patterns."

"And we know you get that." Jendro says, "What you might not expect is how many of you will experience some anger in one form or another this week. Talking is an effective distraction, but take those words away, and the truth rises to the surface pretty quickly, especially anything ... unresolved."

Dana's waiting   *so, fine, figure shit out then*
Dad waiting   *Keyser Söze piles*
Ohma's waiting

still just a husk

"And I promise," Jendro's voice pulls me back, "this is the most we'll speak this week."

Several people who have moved in and chosen blankets to sit closer to the fire, chuckle amicably.

"Good, good, you *are* alive in there!" she says. She's exactly who I imagined would be running this retreat. Hippie circle of trust meets tough as nails English teacher who thinks you just need to apply yourself.

"So, without further ado, or conversation," Calah loops back in squeakily, "please come with us! It's time to begin your conscious de-verbalization journey!"

Jendro adds, "We ask you to sincerely try non-verbality during your time here, but if you have an emergency or feel overwhelmed, let us know. Speech isn't prohibited here. We're just trying to explore its overuse."

Calah's cartoon laugh joins her rusty one adding, "Now, time for your three-hour orientation, hehehehe, just kidding!"

Groans and chuckles. More groans, more chuckles.

Then, with all the grandeur of opening day at the Kentucky Derby, they join for "Alright! In three…two…one…LET'S ZIP IT!"

The herd goes silent, following Jendro and Calah towards a path as "zip it!" echoes across the clearing, off the ledge and into the violet mist.

My new mime buddy beckons to me but I hang back. She cocks her head, shrugs, and darts toward the verge-of-divorce couple, joining them arm in arm, a triangular caboose for the de-verb chain gang.

A few minutes later I'm finally alone. The mountains come rushing up to meet me bringing the branches of a million trees softly rushing in endless waves, joining the gentle rustle of wings finding nests for the night. Crickets and Katydids chirp. I close my eyes and listen to the diminishing footfall of the retreat participants, and a distant bthhhoooo-hooooo of an owl. Humans take up so much space. But other things are here now. Better things. My chest is reaching in every direction at once. My eyelids stop twitching. I want to stay here in this place and this feeling forever. This is where I belong. People don't understand what they're missing.

Before I realize what I'm doing, I take out my phone, snap a picture and text it to Mitchel with the caption "Some Purple Mountains Majesty for your viewing pleasure". I watch it change from 'delivered' to 'read'. No response. No dancing dots. Nothing.

coward

I get it. We've all been tenderized by life or the choices of others. Not sure that's an excuse to throw friendship away like a disposable cup, but who am I to say? I just wish he'd had the stones to tell me why. I try to get back to the feeling I had before I let documentation suffocate experience. I close my eyes and try to recapture what I felt just a moment ago.

forget forget breathe
mountain air rustling wings crickets owl crackling embers
But I can't get back.
nothing gold can stay
which sucks

****

I've been pretending to still be asleep, waiting for the creak-slam of the screen door, signaling the departure of my two cabin mates, and my ability to avoid charades before I've had coffee.

Creeeeaak, slam-slam. I push my sleep mask up. Helene, a.k.a mimette, is perched at the foot of my bunk, silently imitating a rooster. Seeing I'm now awake, she jumps down, bows, and sweeps out the door. Creeaaaak, slam-slam.

I grab my phone. Check if Mitchel's responded. Nothing. This—the actual end of my friendship with Mitchel—stings, and given my still relatively emotionally necrotic state, that's saying something.

I throw my phone into my bag, claw into a sweatshirt and jeans, shove my feet into my own spotless hiking boots and head to the dining hall.

Two bowls of Cocoa Puffs, and one very cold shower that cemented a pale layer of soap film to my body later, I head to the schedule board to see what fresh hell awaits.

Today's workshops
Gesture: Movement and Intention
Explanations: a toxic addiction
Heightening: a journey into the senses
Sounds are Words
Masks

They all started at 10:00. It's 11:00.

I venture out, hoping to quietly view each of the workshops without having to commit. Creepers of the world unite.

First up is 'Gesture: Movement and Intention'. It looks a lot like telenovelas I watch when I can't sleep. Pass. Next is "Explanations: a toxic addiction." Calah is passing around what appears to be a questionnaire to the participants as his now tiny cartoon mouse voice whispers, "Real change begins when self-deception ends."

I believe a hearty helping of self-deception is required to function. Some things are better left interred, and I'd rather not add to the already formidable stench of unkept promises and disappointed dreams in my life just now.

Ten or so yards up the path comes the 'Sounds are Words' area where a Calah and Jendro acolyte is encouraging participants to use sounds to express their thoughts and feelings. The verge-of-divorce couple seems to be working through some issues. Best leave 'em to it.

Around the next bend is "Heightening: a journey into the senses." Participants are blindfolded. They're passing around bowls of things to smell, taste, and touch. Hard pass.

Only one more workshop. It's got to be close to noon now. Maybe I should just head back to the cabin or the clearing and wait this one out. I'll just visit this last one so due diligence is handled.

'Masks'. Jendro is standing next to a large white board, writing: 'Later we'll mold a Janus mask. Right now…creating expressions' She looks around, waiting for all to read it. Then she erases the board and writes the word CONFUSION.

interesting

She writes: 'create the expression with your face'.

A few participants try as the corporate bonding group sits in a row, looking at Jendro blankly. The real hit is Rhona. She's euphorically creating numerous versions of confusion.

Jendro holds her hand up to pause everyone. Well, mostly just to pause Rhona.

Jendro looks at me. Then everyone else looks at me. There's no cloying invitation. Just a clear expression of please join us or, if not, please move along. I decide I like Jendro. I join the ranks as she erases the word CONFUSION and writes HOPEFUL.

I look around. Lots of lifted eyebrows and closed mouth smiles. So, I lift my eyebrows and smile, closed mouthed. Deja vu sweeps through me. Not about the moment itself. What I'm doing. Like an entire swath of forgotten childhood conjured by smelling something familiar. Like play doh. Or the chalky-sweetness of a chocolate scratch and sniff sticker from your 5th grade Pee-Chee folder suddenly reminding you how 5th grade felt.

Jendro is looking at me again. She's entirely unreadable. I've always wanted to be like that. Unfathomable. A keeper of secrets. She turns and wipes the board clean.

****

After a dinner of meatloaf, over bell-peppered vegetable hash, and a spitefully cantaloupe dominant fruit salad, I trekked down to my car to stash my phone in the glove box. Over the course of the day, it had become a monument to Mitchel's lack of response. I didn't want to keep peering into the gaping hole where our friendship used to be. It also represented the continued stalling of my promise to Dana.

Everyone else is at the fire pit. Integrating. I'm integrating with a bottle of W.L. Weller Old Kentucky Straight, trying to reshape the Janus mask I created in Jendro's workshop. But the damn Granny magik hoodoo clay keeps reverting to my original choices.

The mask was supposed to represent our two faces. Public and private. One side is barely a face—like one of those Pink Floyd Brick in the Wall kids. The other looks like the edge of a volcano. I didn't have which was which in mind when I made it. I just started shaping the clay. At some point in the process, I closed my eyes. I'm not sure why.

I take another swig of bourbon and set the mask on the window ledge to dry...start to slip toward the branches of the rustling trees outside. Where she's waiting, waiting to chase me down the stairs to the big lawn through the sprinklers and the million tiny sticky rainbows she's on the other side of the mist, dancin and twirlin I want to dance and twirl too so I run into the rainbow water but the water is gone I'm in my Bridge Group office Mitchel's hiding under my desk saying shhhhhh she'll see you then you'll have to tell her he gives me a bunch of rosemary I don't think that'll help I say he points to the door and says you're already late so I leave and I'm at the elevator but a detour sign points to the stairwell where a red sneaker is lying on its side I pick it up it's a dead cardinal I'm in the forest the cardinal flies out of my hand towards a tiny woman digging in the soil next to a giant rosemary bush the woman turns around to look at me I'm next to the giant rosemary now looking across the lawn at myself

Puh-tumppuh-tumppuh-tumppuh-tumppuh-tump

My heart's pumping adrenaline and every nerve feels it, snapping my eyes open to walls of the cabin, blue grey in the moonlight. The shadows look distorted and amplified, like looking at the room through a microscope. My Janus mask is still drying on the window ledge, the moonlight exaggerating the two halves.

breathe   calm down

Rhona's face slowly appears upside down from the bunk above, an exaggerated frown etched upon her face.

DON'T

DO NOT

She slowly retracts from view.

Most dreams evaporate when I wake up and despite Rhona's intrusion, this one clings.

> *a garden   rosemary   a red sneaker*
> *a cardinal that was dead then it wasn't*
> *sprinklers   or maybe sparklers   Dana twirling*
> *Mitchel hiding under my desk with rosemary*
> *Ohma*
> *Maaaaagggggiiiiieeee waaannnnaaaaa beeeeeeeeee aaaaaaaaaa iiiiiindiiiiaaaaan*

I stayed up the rest of the night, mind cycling from Dana to Mitchel to dormant tree to Ohma, always landing back on Dad's erratic behavior. I don't want him to have anything to do with what happened. I kept thinking *maybe he has early dementia*, as if that would be a better option. Then realizing it might be a better option. Then feeling shitty about thinking that. The only conclusion I was able to reach was that not knowing is now worse than whatever the truth may be. By 6:00 a.m. I'm packed, dressed, and out the door. I leave my Janus mask behind. I don't need it.

As I walk past the meeting area, Jendro and Calah are already up, talking softly. Calah waves, smiling widely at me, but Jendro walks to meet me, bringing her clear, hazel, no-bullshit eyes with her.

After a moment of looking at me, she says, "May your words reveal more than they obscure. May they be guided by your heart." She pauses to make sure I'm listening, then finishes with, "The real one."

13

Another hundred yards.
pine oak cedar hemlock
My feet remember.
pine oak cedar hemlock
The cicadas rattle-thrum in undulating waves, an invisible orchestra echoing the indeterminate origins of my memories. Secret patterns not ours to understand.

Caught up in wondering how such a small creature can obliterate all other sounds and attempts to reintroduce myself to the voice that seems to no longer belong to me, my feet have brought Ohma's faded yellow farmhouse to me.
maybe I've learned enough
maybe I won't backslide
click clack sparklers click clack
I woke up today holding my breath. Felt like I'd spent the entire night doing it, over and over, reenacting the stillness before a storm. As I drank my coffee and picked over Mom's syrup-drowned pancake and Scrapple offering, the air around me grew more still, its only movement an invisible wake behind me as I've walked these two miles from our house to Ohma's. Just enough to push me forward. Enough to push me past Dana's old house, which was unavoidably on the way.

I don't know what I expected. Too many years in New York has my mind skewed towards reclamation and renovation. That's not what's happened there. The house that used to hold Dana and her mother has half melted into the ground. Buckled walls covered in layers of faded graffiti. The sole acknowledgment of its former life, a rusted "For Sale" sign sleeping in overgrown weeds. The reclamation here is the Kudzu pouring through broken windows and gaping doors like a giant octopus, as if the wood and stone always belonged to it, and that two people called Dana, and Dana's mom, were allowed to stay for a while. But no-one else ever would.

I'm not sure what I expected to feel when I saw it. Nostalgia. Maybe indignation over the waking of my sleeping giants. But what I felt was regret. And guilt. I couldn't tell if it was the usual everything starts and ends with me deal, or a genuine sense of responsibility.

I waited there, in front of Dana's old house for something to happen. A sign or a memory. But standing where Dana used to live—where her mother used to live—did nothing. I tried to be very still, so the memories would feel welcome. After a while it felt like I was just standing in front of a house that could have belonged to anyone. I even tried talking. It seemed a good place to officially end my silence. So, I said, "Hello." My voice sounded flat and obvious. Still, I thought maybe the house would say something back or I'd catch a glimpse of Dana's mom's ghost inside, making birdhouses. But there was nothing. No wind. No trees rustling. No instinct. No house saying, "Hello, Maggie." No ghost. Just a green octopus pulling plaster and wood into the earth. So, I walked on. I'm at Ohma's now with my toneless voice and five questions. What really happened? Why did Dana disappear? Why wasn't I told any of it? Why did you both disappear from my life? Was my father involved in what happened?

I scan her property, listening and watching for signs of life. I spot her 1973 station wagon covered in a gauze of red dust.

> *the way way back*
> *windows down*
> *hair whipping*
> *laughing   singing*
> *what was that song?*

I can't remember. Sometimes I wonder if the moment itself is all we get. I feel my chest tightening and the swuuuunch swuuuunch of blood careening past my eardrums.

breathe

I breathe. The spicey-licorice mix of wild rosemary, dandelion, honeysuckle, and fennel lining Ohma's front yard brings everything I expected to feel standing in front of Dana's house. I feel like that lighthouse keeper in La Jument Phares Dans La Tempete—nothing to do but wait to drown or wait not to drown. The sea doesn't consult us.

If I hadn't put this off a ridiculous number of times already, I'd keep walking. But drumming up another excuse is insane even for me, so I brace against the sweet-spicey-earthy rip tide and breathe. The air is just air again. No magical undertow of lost things. Just plants and dirt.

Ruuuuumbuuuummmmbuuuuummmmbuuuuummm low rumbling behind me. For a second, I think it's another huge wave coming for me. But then I hear tires grinding limestone into dust. Just a truck. A big one. I step to the side so it can pass. It eases to a crawl next to me. People tend to be neighborly here, so I prepare for a hello.

The truck slows to a stop next to me. The driver, a middle-aged white man with brown hair and eyes inhaled by folds of sallow, slack skin gives me a look before cutting his eyes to Ohma's house, then back to me. A furrow etches deep gullies between his brows. Something complicated in his eyes, like he's been waiting for me to show up exactly at this moment.

I offer him a nod and a half smile, followed by a surge of self-loathing. As he pulls away, I see a faded Army sticker on the back window. I've seen that before. Not just the Army symbol. That's because of Dad. But *that* sticker on *that* truck.

got your six Link

got your six

I wait for the dust trail behind the truck to subside. Let the sun burn my ears and the back of my neck. Let it sear every thought of him behind a wall. Sweat pools and trickles down my spine and under my arms.

A breeze stirs, cooling the back of my neck, shifting the weathervane on a birdhouse in Ohma's yard. It reminds me what I'm here to do. I push open the gate to her property. The moment I'm through, I feel different.

****

Carvings of the man in the maze, a circle painted red, blue, green, brown, black, yellow, and white, and a medicine eye hang along her front doorframe. I reach up to knock. My hand stops. She never tried to get in touch with me either. Maybe there's a reason.

"Hello, Maggie." Her voice is clear and low with the circularity of Cherokee peppered by the twangy lilt of Appalachia.

A rumbling shake starts in my chest. I remember this feeling. I'm going to cry.

Jesus don't cry you're not a kid
just stick to the plan
turn your head

I turn my head. Ohma's standing about ten feet away. Wide brimmed hat, white hair, red bandana around her neck, button down shirt, sleeves rolled to the elbows, waxed cotton pants, old boots. A look of stoic incredulity. Maybe a fraction of a smile. She's holding a basket of herbs. I can smell the lemony rich sharpness. Freshly harvested thyme. Strange to remember that. The cicadas begin another round.

rainbowmistmuddyhandsbusstationheadlightsthewaywaybackjakethefireball
feathersrosemarypineoakcedarhemlockarrowkeyMaaaagiiieeewannaaabeeea
justahuskjustahuskjustahusk
breathemaggie
breathe Maggie

She's waiting. Her eyes are like those pressure washing hoses used to pry barnacles from boats. Once she sees I'm back, she turns and disappears around the corner of the house. I follow her, passing a large garden with another weather-beaten birdhouse marking the center. I remember this garden. I remember her telling me plants know secrets. I also remember stomping on all the plants in this patch. Maybe that didn't happen at all. Maybe what I think are memories are little more than fog changing the shape of trees.

I follow her around to the back. Her old conservatory. It's dry, rich, and spicy. It smells real. Honest. Row after row of flowers, roots, and herbs hang from long metal rods along the ceiling, mortar and pestles worn smooth by time and use sit on a long, narrow table, and amber, clear, and green glass bottles on wooden shelves along the longest of the four walls. A large wooden stick leans against the wall next to the back door with what looks like wool or maybe fur bound by twine tied to it. A giant grey wolfhound is sleeping in a patch of sun under a bank of windows overlooking another huge garden behind the house. All of it is incredibly familiar. I spent a lot of time here. Until I didn't.

Ohma approaches me and takes my hand in hers. I can't remember the last time I had another person's hand in mine. I've always wanted more distance, not less. But I don't mind hers other than the fact that it makes it harder not to cry.

She looks carefully at the skin on my hand, then runs her finger along a few of my nails. Her skin feels smooth but also sturdy. Like birch bark. She releases my hand, shifting her attention to my hair. She touches the ends, then my hairline. Touch is usually about connection or reassurance. Or intimacy. Something the other person believes you want from them—or hopes you can give them. But she doesn't need anything from me. She's gathering information. It's surprising how much a relief it is to be undefended. Then I notice how quiet it is. But what is there to say? Everything or nothing. Maybe we're opting for nothing because everything isn't possible yet.

stop hiding

"I-I-it's good to-you seem good-I-I'm sorry to just drop—" My voice sounds strange. Thin. Too loud.

just start with it's good to see you
mintrosemaryhemlockoakfoursevengotyoursix

"It will take time." Her voice is gentle, but not soft. She gathers various jars from her massive collection, inspecting each one before bringing it to the large table in the center of the room.

"I-oh, uhm, okay." I stammer. "I didn't-I wasn't-I-I mean—" I don't want to break the jars with my voice. Ohma continues bringing jars to the long table. Once she's done, she pours some into individual mortars, crushing them into coarse powders before pouring them into pieces of folded cloth. Others, she leaves whole or bound with twine. It's lulling to watch her. She's a part of this room. Her movements the well-worn precision of ritual. Nothing exaggerated or performed. A sense of place and belonging, not necessarily to this room, but of the trees and mountains and wildness that hold the edges where this room belongs. And, also, to this room. As if I could touch the air itself and it would say there you are, I've been waiting for you.

"We should start with East," she says.

"East? I, uhm, okay. But I'm here to, I'm-"

"I know why you're here," she says, pulling a small wooden box from a shelf. She retrieves a worn piece of what looks like burlap from inside.

"Do you remember the other three?" I don't, other than basic deduction pointing to if one of four things is east, the other three are probably south, north, and west.

"I-I think there's a mix up about…," I say quietly.

"Once the four are balanced. Not before," she says. She sounds stern but her smile is gently chastising.

Half of me thinks that smile is the best thing I've seen in a while. The other half is irritated. I want to remind her I'm not here for some chuckle, chuckle, balance-cleanse. That I was only a kid when whatever went down, went down and can't someone just please remember that?

"If there's no balance, you'll only hear what you already think," she says. "When balance returns, you'll be able to hear more. I'm very old and very wise, you should do what I say." She gives me another stern grimace then starts to chuckle.

"Uh okay," I say. I attempt a light chuckle. It goes sideways and comes out as a sort of "fwwwerf" sound.

She looks at me, eyebrows raised.

I have no idea how to read her. I just know if I want to hear the whole story, I'm going to have to go along with this. Maybe I should let her help me. Given my father's recent behavior, there's a density to all of this I'm not sure I can maneuver alone.

Ohma unwraps the burlap and hands me a small wooden disc painted Red, Black, Yellow, Blue, White, Green, and Brown. It looks familiar. It feels familiar.

"There's seven, not four" I say quietly.

"Seven is later. After four."

"Uhm, okay."

"Good, so we agree."

"Uh…yes?"

"You don't remember, do you?"

"I'm sorry. I-it's been a really long time." My reference to the four decades it's been since we've seen each other is like some jerk passing gas in an elevator.

She nods in acknowledgement of my idiot comment, then points to white, then red, yellow, and black as she says "Body, Mind, Heart, Spirit. You already started with north.

Now east. As you find balance you'll remember more." She makes a circle on the table with twine and places her finger along the inside edge of the twine. "Within," she says, then moves her finger to the center of the circle, "Not center."

the THERE there?

"You placed yourself center," she says. She's not smiling.

"Yeah, my sister'd agree with you there," I say.

She nods. "Imbalance. Numbness, sadness, stuck-ness?"

I nod. No point in pretending anymore.

"Good. Okay. So, we agree," she says. She puts her finger next to the inner edge of the circle again. "Within. Not center. Understand?"

I nod. I'm surprised at my relief over having permission to not try to be the center anymore.

She places her finger along different parts of the circle "West, spirit. East, body. South, heart. North, mind."

wait a minute

"Wait, you said I've already started with north?" I ask. "That probably isn't right. I'm kind of a mess. My thoughts are. They're not ..."

She chuckles. "Messy is good. Confused is better. Big mess means big clearing. Space for new knowledge. You've made a big mess?" She pauses to look at me pointedly.

"Yeah. Very."

"Good. Okay." She places items into a basket. "These will help. It's hard to clear space in the mind if your blood is imbalanced. Messy and confused are good but clogged isn't." She continues, writing instructions for each item, "Your liver is also clogged. How are the hormones?"

"Uhm, I don't know. Indifferent? Uhm, sorry, I don't mean to, I mean, are these? What are these?"

She stops and looks at me. Her power washer eyes are back. She looks at me for a long time. Then she sets everything down and says "come," then walks outside.

I follow her. Once we're outside she pulls a pack of cigarillos out of her pocket. From her other pocket a cell phone and a lighter. She sets the phone down inside the door and lights her cigarillo.

"Dana said you didn't have a phone."

"I try to keep my minutes low."

"Oh, right. But you have one. Does she know that?"

Ohma doesn't say anything. Just smokes in silence. The sweetness of the smoke hovers around us like everything we're not talking about. She seems to be thinking through something.

After a few minutes she says, "You've forgotten."

I don't know what to say so I don't say anything. I look across her property to a grove of oak trees.

"You're tired. Tired that sleep can't heal."

I nod. "But I have a prescription. So, it's-is anything you want me to take going to, you know, interact?

"No. But you should try to stop taking those. Slowly though. What I'm giving you will clean your blood. Rebalance your hormones. Your pills aren't letting your body remember what it needs to remember."

Again, I'm unsure what to say, so I don't say anything. She finishes her cigarillo, tosses it into a large pail of smoked and stubbed carcasses. She goes back inside. I follow her. I feel like a stray puppy, but I don't know what else to do. This wasn't one of the scenarios I thought through.

She offers me one of the jars. "For sleep, as you slowly stop with the other," she says. It smells like peppermint and lemon. But also, kinda like feet. She picks up another. "This one for day. For energy." I take tentative whiff. Like cucumbers and dried hay. "For the next two weeks, only nettle soup, two cloves of garlic each day, beans, mushrooms, berries, apples, sunflower seeds. No meat. No sugar. Only water and teas from the jars." She pushes the basket towards me.

I'm so tired of being shaky and burned out. If this helps even a little, it'll be worth it. I can go back to bourbon and doughnuts after I'm better.

"You'll feel sick this week. Poisons built up will fight you. They'll sing you songs and scream at you. But if you stay clear with them, they'll leave. Understand?" Her scrutinizing look softens. "You knew something was wrong. It's why you're here."

"I'm here because—"

She looks at me, a challenge in her eyes. I can't help but be impressed. But I also want to tell her to knock it the hell off and just tell me what happened.

"Anger is part of it," she says, chuckling.

Everyone I've ever met has at one point or another learned to fear my temper. Maybe because it so rarely surfaces and when it does, it's a burn-it-all-down scenario. But not Ohma. Being mad at her is like a speck of dust screaming at Half Dome.

"Anger has been inside you too long," she says.

She's right about that too. I'm surprised I haven't had a heart attack. Or a stroke.

"It won't want to leave," she says. "Anger is fat and lazy now. Believes this…," she taps my heart, "is home." She puts her warm, soft birch bark hand on mine, and looks me in the eye in a way that makes the tremor in my chest return. Then she turns and leaves through the door that connects her house to the conservatory. The giant wolfhound trots after her, large claws clicking on the clay tiles of her kitchen.

"Oh, okay. Uhm, thanks," I say to the now empty room.

I walk home with the basket she gave me in a kind of daze. The sun is low. Dark blue trees and fields, quiet and waiting.

Bronwen Carson

September 9, 1979

dark n blurry pine oak cedar hemlock pine oak cedar hemlock
maybe the world belongs to em in the dark n we're not
supposed to see it not supposed to be here maybe we get to
see it the way it really is after we die

maybe Dana's momma sees it now maybe she's with the trees
n the owls whisperin secrets n learnin wind dances shadowy
arms stretchin n pullin edges brushin night black huggin blue
n balancin on silver where owls r trees n trees r sky like my
blue-black coat with silver buttons maybe they're the same
thing or somethin that can be in a few different places at the
same time I outgrew it last year I bet it'd fit Dana she's light
n fast like the raven feather I found last year I'll give it to her
I'll bring it next time thinkin bout next times makes my chest
feel like it doesn't have belts round it anymore

I watch the trees swooshin n swirlin as the bus speeds by I
wanna see Dana n tell her I'm real sorry bout her momma n
give her the feathers n the special rocks I found but I also
kinda wish we'd stop for a few minutes so I can put my hand
on the trees to watch the wind dances n hear the songs they're
singin Nathy told me they sing all the time all kinda songs
he said people can't hear em anymore that they used to but
that almost all of em can't hear trees anymore he's not sure
when they stopped but he said it's been a while he also said if
I don't practice every day I'll stop hearin em too even maybe
stop hearin him though that would take a bit longer it scared
me a lot when he said that cause he's somethin bigger than a
best friend somethin we don't have a word for so even
though the bus is goin too fast n it smells like feet n bologna
sandwiches I have to practice listenin I take a breath so big it

almost hurts then I let it out in a long silent whistle to join the
music the trees can hear   only silent sounds can join

I stretch my neck as long as it can go watchin tree after tree
swish n swirl n disappear back to their silent music n secret
dances back to all that's silver n black outside of headlights
outside names like pine oak cedar n hemlock Nathy says
people mostly get their names wrong but that trees don't mind
they think it's good that we try

click clack click clack click clack click clack

someone's knittin I peek around the seat in front of me

click clack click clack click clack click clack

navy-blue yarn with little silver threads I peek through the
crack tween the seats so I can see more I see hands knuckles
slippin back n forth one finger loopin yarn over the needle
blue ropes under skin like maybe the yarn might start inside the
person like maybe the person's knittin themself into a scarf for
someone the person must love em a lot I watch the hands for
a long time knuckles movin like an ocean of blue ropes under
tracin paper it makes me sleepy n tingly   like when I had fever
two summers ago n I could see through the walls of my room

click clack click clack click clack click clack

silver n dark blue I feel real big n real small too like everythin
that ever was n ever will be is happenin right now n I could slip
through the space between the bus doors n disappear into
forever forward n forever back watchin trees dance n hum old
songs my eyes begin to sting I don't know what time it is but
it feels a lot past my bedtime

Bronwen Carson

the bus rockin n trees swooshin pull at my eyelids I'm playin
hide n seek with Dana n we're laughin the forest is full of
dancin trees n red n black striped spiders hummin songs n
gigglin n spinnin silver n blue webs in huge birdhouses

click clack click clack

click clack click clack

click clack click clack

235

14

Three days. Without coffee or chocolate. Or cheese. Two days of twigs and leaves and sautéed root vegetables. And a tea that smells like feet. Now I understand. Time really is just an illusion. It sounds so trite. I feel trite. I am trite. Still, it's one thing to get the concept, another thing entirely to get. the. concept.

I wish I could fast forward to the part where I've done the detox, asked my questions, learned what I need to know and finally get to leave the past behind. Where it can dissolve. Feed the trees. Though, the malignancy of those years might pollute the ground water. There should be a dedicated recycling center where one can drop off their expired, toxic self. I wish dormant tree was here. I miss her.

maybe I could go get her
transplant her
give her a chance at a good life

The thought of dormant tree forever surrounded by concrete, unable to be in rich red soil or reach up through soft warm air or entwine her arms with other trees as they rustle together in a giant green ocean is heartbreaking.

I try to catch the tears in time, but I can't. Something about the air here, the lack of walls to push against. The trickle turns into a gasping, snotty, raging river. I'm so tired of feeling broken. Of feeling shitty and angry and lost. Most of all, I'm so tired of being tired, but I can't remember how to be any other way.

I don't know how long I cry, but when I'm done, I draw a sketch of dormant tree and lean it against my nightstand lamp. She was the one thing that kept me from the abyss, and I never knew it. Never thanked her.

****

I've decided not to text Dana for a while. Now that I'm beginning to be aware of how broken and lost I am, it's hard to trust myself, or anyone else. I feel like I just got a chemical peel over my entire body and need to be careful what I expose myself to. I'm also starting to think she and Ohma planned this whole thing, which is irritating. Probably a good thing, but irritating. Like I'm a misguided child. I'm also not ready to share my newly ended vow of silence with my family. The avalanche of questions from Mom, barbed tête a têtes with Angie, and opening the field of play for the brooding in my father that only intensifies the more time I spend with Ohma are all unappealing. Peter's the only one with no hidden landmines. His inner pretty much matches outer. Sometimes I think he was secretly adopted.

I just need to play everything close to the vest a while longer. If they all think I'm still practicing non-verbality, I don't have to explain things I don't understand. My primary means of self-preservation has always been avoidance. I doubt that'll ever change. Truth is, I wish I didn't have to deal with people at all. Trees and wind and birds and soil are better. Clearer, cleaner, purer. Around them, I'm better. Less me, more like them. I'm tired of being a boring broken human. People always want me to be happier, pithier, laughier, sexier, care-free-ier. Engaged, but not too much. Just enough. Just enough to not be vapid, but not so much that I'm a downer. Nobody likes a downer. But I've never really understood that balance point and I'm tired of pretending all the time. Trees and wild things don't seem to care about any of that. They don't hold me against me and because of that, I stop trying to be anything.

****

I'm not well. Last night, Mom was watching *60 minutes,* and the tick-tick-tick sound was so loud I thought the windows might shatter. My eyes are playing tricks on me too. The space between my bed and the door, expanding and contracting. And last night when I woke up in the middle of the night, Mitchel was sitting in a chair wearing a white coat asking, "Did someone call for a doctor?" Then I'm pretty sure I started being able to see through walls.

****

I'm clammy, and shaky. And I smell like sauerkraut. Five days since I began this detox rebalance east basket of Ohma's, and the new and improved Maggie Morris is emerging like a damn magical butterfly.

In a few minutes I get to go downstairs for the adventure of an ancient grains salad while everyone else devours fried chicken and hush puppies. I let myself have a little bit of bourbon yesterday because—adding to the list of Maggie's flaws—apparently there's a bit of an alcohol situation going on.

maybe a walk will help

maybe I'll go see Ohma

If I go see her, maybe she'll say something wise and meaningful. Or not. I just need something to distract me from driving to McDonalds and gorging on fries. Though, they are technically a root vegetable.

walk yes fries no walk yes fries no

My stomach rumbles. I focus on the sound of my footsteps and the trees brushing together in the breeze. They sound like the ocean. Maybe they are. Maybe I'm at the bottom of an ocean, surrounded by strange, beautiful sea creatures entirely unconcerned with my progress as a human—little starfish that look like passionflowers, and bright red fish with feather fins. Kelp trees swaying gently. I close my eyes and imagine staying forever in my new underwater world. rummmmummumumblebuumblehummmummumumble

truck

rummmmummumumblebuumblehummmummumumble

truck   *funnel cake*

calm down

                                    sparklers

Dana's mom dead rotten peaches

I listen hard, trying to track where it is and where it's going but the thick bank of trees between us diffuses the sound too much. It sounds like it's idling. Somewhere nearby.

breathe   calm down

five four three two one

five

five   five   hemlock trees

four   pinecones

three   quartz rocks

two   cardinals

one truck

no

one truck

NO

one ... ... squirrel

that can't be found if sought

A squirrel scampers across the path ruffling through pine straw.

"Hello squirrel."

He ignores me.

I try again. "Squirrel?"

"Sa-lo-li knows you're there, he's just busy."

Ohma's done her out of nowhere act again. But instead of startling me, her appearance is calming. I listen for the truck engine. It's gone.

"Hi. I didn't see you there, hi," I say, trying to stand despite the noncompliance of my legs. I ease back down to my seat on the quartz rock. She stays where she is, a few yards away on the trail. She's assessing me again. After a few moments she smiles a tiny smile and turns to continue her trek to wherever she's going. It's familiar. She must have done this when I was a kid—not hover or try to make a moment longer than it is. When she reaches the trail fork, I hear her say, "Come by tomorrow." Then she's gone.

I stayed on my quartz perch a while longer. I'm not sure exactly how long. I've stopped wearing a watch. Walking home, hot salty French fries and cream soda still sounded good, but I was okay just thinking about them.

****

My fever broke sometime in the night. I woke up dreaming about Jake the Fireball as a lionfish swimming under the house.

I feel better. Shaky, but better. Ohma gave me a tea for my fever yesterday morning when I went to see her. It's got ginseng, elderberry, vervain, wild ginger, and a few other things in it I don't remember. It tasted amazing. Like purple secrets.

She also gave me a pouch with lavender and dried lemon peel to put under my pillow "for sadness." Then we watched a John Travolt-a-thon of Saturday Night Fever and Grease on VHS, Sedi's giant wooly head on my lap. I'm not sure if we talked or not. Ohma's a huge fan of John Travolta. "The early years." And musicals. She's got an extensive collection. She also likes Humphrey Bogart, both Hepburns, and Hitchcock.

More memories are surfacing. They're vague though, like smoke in a distant valley. Spending time at her farm, and with an oak tree near a barn, and going to the Hallmark store with Dana to get her mom a birthday card. I'm starting to remember how I used to see things. It comes and goes. It's always stronger around Ohma, and when I'm by myself in the forest, surrounded by wild things that notice me but don't expect anything. I become translucent around them. It feels nice. Not center.

****

It's been a little over ten days since I started my detox. I thought I'd be back in Brooklyn by now, questions answered and onto the next chapter. But, despite the weird pretending that all is okay going on with my dad and the disdain Angie's brought along the few times she's come to dinner, it's nice to be here. I go over to Ohma's a lot. We watch movies. Or I watch her make remedies. Sometimes we talk. Sometimes we don't. Today we talked about how Sedi found her. He trotted up to her once day when she was fishing trash out of the river. She said he sat next to her as if they'd always planned to meet up there at that exact time. Apparently, he has quite a dry sense of humor. Brings her all sorts of jokes. Old wigs and sock puppets and mismatched mittens.

When I get back home around sunset it's clear Mom's been baking all day. It's one of her go tos when she's anxious.

I'm starting to wonder if fear and hope have precisely the same amount of gravity. How it's almost impossible to not be stuck between the pull of each. I'm not sure what's pulled my mother towards fear today. Maybe it's become a habit. Like a tic. I don't mean that flippantly, just truthfully. Maybe it's my being here. Or that after so many years of wanting me to "come home", I have, but that it's to spend time with Ohma. Maybe it's Dad's tension that surrounds him like a cloud of rancid patchouli. That one concerns me the most. Is she reacting out of the novelty of his tension or out of an understanding of where that tension leads?

I look at my mom trying so hard to seem cheerful and fine and supportive. I've been so fixated on my own crap I hadn't considered how what happened might've carried consequences for her too. Stirring up old smoke long settled in distant valleys.

She's sitting at the kitchen table, enjoying a freshly baked lemon bar, the unmistakable tang of Sanka in the air. She's reading *The New Jim Crow* by Michelle Alexander.

am I dreaming? I must be

She looks up and smiles. "Hi, honey, I made lemon bars, your favorite, right? You seem so down I thought they might perk you up."

A mudslide of now is not the time to talk sloshes toward me. My window is closing.

"Oh, uh," I say, "thanks, but—"

"Oh, honey! You're talking! Oh, that's wonderful, so wonderful."

"Mom."

"Oh-sorry, sorrysorry," she says, "I just—it's so nice to hear your voice. It's been years."

Which, sadly, is entirely possible. Text and emails are my preferred mode of communication.

"Yeah, I'm sor—"

"It's okay, honey. It doesn't matter. What matters is that you're here now."

She's doing that Maggie is fragile and porous and is therefore excused from all shitty behavior thing. It's irritating.

"Here," she says pushing the plate of lemon bars towards me." Have a lemon bar, and we can have a nice chat."

"Mom!"

She freezes.

"Sorry. Sorry," I say, "I-I didn't mean to yell, I just …"

think I shouldn't always be forgiven

was hoping we could skip the small talk

don't care about the damn lemon bars

"I'm getting used to my voice again."

She smiles, marking her spot in her reading and closing her book. I look at the book to make sure I didn't imagine the title.

"New book for the club?" I ask.

Mom flushes and laughs nervously. "Oh, this, no, no—I-it's something your brother gave me."

"Yeah. Very Peter. And?"

"Well, I have to say, it's interesting. Though a bit—how do they say? Above my pay grade?" She titters again. "I just— it's terrible to think all of this still exists."

I love my mom, but sometimes her obliviousness shocks the hell out of me. I decide not to pursue the topic. She scoots the plate piled with forbidden buttery citrus joy my way. "Tell me if there's too much butter."

"Not sure there is such a thing," I say.

"We have so much to catch up on, honey, I don't know where to start!"

"Uh-huh."

do not look directly at the lemon bar

"How's work? Such an interesting job."

"Uh-huh."

lemonysugarybutteryheaven

"And that nice boyfriend of yours?"

be stronger than the lemon bar

can't

"How long do we get to have you? Dad was so excited when he heard you were coming for a visit."

I stuff half a still warm lemon bar into my mouth. The silky tang makes my throat jump as euphoria rolls through me.

oh God   oh my God

I finish the other half in two bites and reach for another.

"Aww, that makes me happy," she says with the pride of a dealer that's roped a recovering addict back into the fold. "I just knew they'd cheer you up."

I finish the second one. I don't remember eating it. I should stop. But my hand doesn't belong to me. It belongs to the lemon bars. All of me belongs to the lemon bars. I reach for another.

The drug dealer's face turns wary. "Maggie, honey, slow down, there's plenty."

"Uh-huh," I say reaching for another.

"Sweetheart?"

just one more

She pulls the plate from me, runs to the screen door, flings it open, and hurls the lemon bars and the plate they're on outside, her face frozen in horror.

I can't stop laughing. I'm so happy. There's a parade in my brain. I don't ever want this feeling to stop.

"Thanks, those were A-MAZING!"

I wipe the crumbs from my face and head for the stairs, Mom still frozen to her spot by the door. Before I even make it to my room my stomach starts to cramp. Twenty minutes later there's a war in my gut that would give Stalin pause.

I've undone almost two weeks of detox in a matter of a few lemony, buttery minutes. I run to the bathroom and throw it all up amid flashbacks of throwing up on my happy horses pajamas. Rotten peaches.

****

Clattering and thumping. Coming from the kitchen, I think. I listen, trying to figure out if I'm lucid dreaming, having an insulin event, or if something is, in fact, happening downstairs.

Then I hear Dad's voice. "El? What's this plate doing outside—El? Ellie?"

"In here," my mother shouts. She's not one for shouting. She sounds angry. No, not angry, determined. "How did I not notice? And she's trying to—it's not okay—and that's that!"

"What's going on, did Maggie do something? Did she say something to you?" His voice is thick with tension.

"She's trying to get better or change or I don't know what, and what do I do? I dangle a plate of lemon bars in front of her. That's what I do."

"El, Ellie, can you stop for a-what's going on?"

The sounds of boxes being flung across the floor.

"Junk, junk, junk!" she proclaims.

"You're not making sense—"

"Oh, yes I am! Maggie needs our support, and that's all there is to it!"

"But how-what-I don't understand how throwing out perfectly good food is helping." He sounds anxious now.

"I never thought she'd—well, it's a sign is what it is, and all of this? No, it's not right. And just when she started talking again."

"She—what did she say?"

"Sometimes no matter how hard we try, it's not okay, you know? You can't pretend it is when it isn't!"

"Is that what she said?" Dad asks.

"No, Ben! That's what *I'm* saying. I won't let her down again. Not like before. That's all there is to it!"

Then it's just the sound of junk, junk, junk being thrown out. A few minutes later I hear someone quietly climb the stairs. A quiet knock on my door.

"Maggie?" My father's voice asks.

My heart starts pounding uncontrollably. I should open the door. He wants to talk. He's ready to unburden himself of secrets kept for almost four decades. But I don't want to hear his side of the story. I want to hear the whole story. From Ohma.

September 9, 1979

eeeeeeeeeeeeeeeeeeeeeeeeeepfffffoooooooooooommmmp

I open my eyes people r shufflin to the front of the bus with their purses n backpacks n duffle bags I wait til everyone's gone   the bus driver is gettin his green metal lunch pail n thermos we must be at the koalas now I pull the ticket out of my pocket it says Qualla my heart starts thumpin

what if this is the wrong place?

what if there's more than one place with koalas?

the smelly french fries plastic roses lady was so squishy n mean maybe she sent me to the wrong place on purpose no it's okay the nice old lady helped this has to be it it has to be

you okay? the bus driver is lookin at me funny

say somethin

uh-huh I say

I can't look him in the eyes but he's waitin so I tell my eyes to look up n tell my mouth to smile my mouth does okay but my eyes jump up to his face n bounce right back down to a dirty spot of smooshed gum next to his shoe he's got a nice face maple-y   like fall

is there someone supposed to meet you? he asks

uhm I-I I'm visitin someone she just moved here I say

uh-huh he says peerin outside the bus windows at the rest of the passengers wanderin off *n you say she's comin here to getcha?*

I feel my face get hot

stopitstopitdosomethinsaysomethinmakehimbelieveyou

maybe she's outside waitin for me I should go so she doesn't-

uh-huh okay he says peerin out the windows again *well I'll
just wait with ya if that's okay*

I nod n get my backpack n check my pocket for the special
quartz rocks I brought for Dana they're still there

the driver follows me out n we sit on wooden bench next to
the bus   the cars with the other people from the bus drive
away   it's real quiet cept for the trees whisperin to each other n
owls hooohoooohooooin somewhere the yellowy streetlamp
makes everythin look the same sortof color it's kind of pretty
in a weird way the bus driver keeps lookin around n clearin his
throat he sounds like daddy does before he says stuff like *eat
your broccoli* or *stay where I can see you*

he knows   he knows you're lyin

I have to make the bus driver think I'm not lyin that Dana's
gonna be here any second n that he can go I try to remember
how grownups sound

I'll be okay I say *I come here a lot all the time she's gonna be
here any minute*

I should've asked Ohma to come with me

stupidstupidSTUPIDSTUPIDMaggie

he looks at me his bushy caterpillar eyebrows goin up then
together then up again

you wait here just a minute okay?

I look at my shoes my favorite red sneakers with the doodle of
feather on it that Dana drew at the Firefly Festival it feels like
it didn't really happen that it was a lot longer ago than two
weeks

okay? the bus driver asks quietly

I nod he gets up n walks over to a phone booth it's far enough away that he couldn't catch up to me if I run cause Dana taught me to run real fast

go go go now run runrunrun

I have to wait til he's talkin then he'll be thinkin bout what he's sayin n then maybe he'll look away then I can run

he looks down at the buttons n starts to push numbers

now run runrunrun GO

Fwap Fwap Fwap Fwap Fwap my sneakers slap the road

HEY HEY the bus driver calls *HEY LITTLE GIRL*

I make my sneakers go faster **FwapFwapFwapFwapFwap**

just gotta get past the yellow streetlamp into the line of trees at the end of the block once I'm in the trees he'll never find me

I hear his shoes followin me **Fump Fump Fump Fump** but I made it I'm in the trees now I keep runnin but not too far in just far enough then I hide I'm good at hidin I can always be all the way invisible whenever I need to

I hear him callin little girl hey little girl it's okay no one's gonna hurt you you're not in trouble hey little girl come back

but I'm not gonna not til I find Dana after a while I don't hear his voice anymore then a little after that don't hear his feet crunchin in the woods anymore I wait a little more after that just to make sure when it's been nothin but trees whisperin to each other for a while I creep out of my hidin spot I'm not scared but my heart's still beatin fast it's the first time I've been by myself in the woods at night I like it but I also feel kinda itchy like it's not a good idea bet Nathy'll be proud of me though I start to make my way closer to the road just a little just so I can see it n get to it if I need to

Dana taught me how to walk without makin barely any noise
it's one of the lots of cool stuff she showed me I thought
maybe she'd know that I was comin n that she'd be here at the
bus stop waitin for me she can always read my mind I don't
know why she's not here she always knows what I'm thinkin

I wish Nathy was here I don't know any of these trees

hi excuse me hi I'm Maggie I whisper to em

the trees rustle

do you know where Dana lives?

they keep rustlin n talkin to each other decidin if they should
tell me

*I-I just need to know if she's okay see her momma died n you
prolly already know that?*

my chest feels like it's gettin smaller

but I think prolly Dana is sad n I have these for her

I show the trees the quartz rocks n the feathers I brought they
rustle n then they say don't know where she is exactly but they
reach their arms in the wind pointin down the road

thanks I whisper

branches swayin dippin brushin whisperin

stay with us

leaves n needles laughin happy n quiet pullin me so strong n
deep passin through me n back out again into the deepdeep
of the earth n the deepdeep of the sky all at once

stay with us

stay with us

I lean my head against em my ear to their dry skin listenin to the secrets they know toad stools n flecks of silver dust at dawn n fat summer rain n spiders that wear striped socks

before I start walkin to where the trees told me to go I close my eyes n think real hard bout the secret jokes n the feathers Dana n me collected n runnin to get cream sodas n plantin crunch berries n helpin Ohma in her garden I swirl em all together n think of Dana real hard

if I can think of everythin that belongs to us she'll hear my thoughts n she'll meet me halfway that's what I'll do n then she'll meet me halfway

15

Ohma's knowledge of plants and medicine is intimidating. The equivalent measure of her expertise would be doctorates in ethnobotany and plant pharmacology. She checks each herb she plans on using by smelling it, listening to it, and sometimes tasting. If it passes inspection, she adds it to the mix until the balance is right.

"It is the way of right relationship," she says. "Each plant helper has its own way, but some are stronger together. Just like people. Like you and Dana were. Opposites strengthen each other. When they are in balance. Understand?"

It's the first time she's brought up Dana.

"Ohma ..."

"Soon," she says, smiling at me then returning to crushing the dry elements into a powder. She begins adding melted beeswax, slowly mixing it with the powder to make a thick salve. She scrapes the salve into a glass jar and passes it to me. It's pungent and earthy.

"Sores, stings, bites. Willow bark if there's pain. This was what I put on your arm."

"The day I met you! The wasp stings. My father, he-"

She nods, smiles.

I reach for my little moleskin journal to make note of the ingredients, but she shakes her head and puts her hand on it.

"Knowledge comes from understanding. Understand the plant, and you'll know how to use it."

She's overestimating me, but the thought of going back to Brooklyn knowing how to make remedies is appealing. If only to keep how I feel here with me when it's time to return to real life.

"Catnip, fennel, ginger."

She crushes them gently then adds them to a small tin cup and pours hot water from the kettle.

"Nervousness, sour stomach, cramps." She hands it to me. It smells incredible. "Go ahead" she says.

I take a sip. It warms my throat and tastes bright and spicy.

"I'll make more for you to take home. For anytime you feel nervous, or your stomach is sour."

"So, anytime I see my father? Or Angie?" I ask.

She looks at me, eyebrows up, small smile, then resumes her work.

Angie came over the other day. It had been a while, at least a week. I came home from Ohma's to find Angie sitting alone on the porch swing, smoking, her face tense. She seems to have developed a habit of raking her fingers aggressively through her thick hair when she's stressed out which makes her look like a troll doll. I tried very hard not to laugh. Which, of course, made it worse.

I still can't pinpoint the exact source of Angie's grudge, but I think it has to do with Mom always hovering over me. It was always so suffocating and irritating to me, I never considered how it must have made Angie feel. Probably invisible. Which is what I so desperately wanted to be. Maybe more than any other defining quality that makes a family a family is in its members' unwavering ability to misperceive and mislabel each other.

"You were right," I said to her out of the blue. "I was a shitty sister and kind of an oblivious asshole in general.

She looked at me, but I couldn't read her expression.

"I am sorry about that", I continued, fumbling. "And my overall inability to operate like a normal person in the world sort of soaked up all of Mom's attention, whether I wanted it or not. That must have sucked. I think I'm just different in a way that made her concerned about me or maybe-I don't know-I'm trying to figure all that out, but I'm sorry about how that must have sucked for you."

Her expression changed to confusion. Maybe that's what happens when someone finally says the thing you always wanted to hear.

Ohma's power washers are waiting patiently for my mind to circle back to being here, with her. She understands my thoughts come when they come and go when they go and I'm not anywhere near being able to manage them. So, she waits. Once she sees I'm back, she continues.

"To strengthen the body and build resistance?"

"Oh, uhm, I don't think I—"

"This knowledge is in your mind," she says.

"That was almost 40 years ago."

"You might surprise yourself."

I look at the dizzying array of leaves, flowers, stems and roots in mason jars along the wall. I approach them hoping some sort of bibbity-bobbity-boo proximity factor will save the day.

"It's there," she says, "Trust yourself."

She still has no idea how much of an ask that is.

"I'll be in the kitchen. Come get me when you're ready."

I look at the wall of jars for a few minutes. Nothing. No clue. I've even forgotten what remedy I'm supposed to be making. Something to do with strength. I think. I know some things that do that. But just from the section labeled "Immunity" at Whole Foods. Elderberries, echinacea, goldenseal, rose hips, and, I think, oregano? But that's only five and I'm supposed to use seven. Maybe lemon balm or ginseng. Maybe nettle. No, nettle's more for allergies. Maybe burdock. She puts it into almost everything, though I'm still not sure exactly why. I add the ginseng and burdock to the others on the table then go to get Ohma.

"Now," She sorts through my choices quickly, a smile slowly pulling a corner of her mouth, "from most to least."

I try to sort them. I get it about half right. Then she sits in a worn wooden chair next to Sedi and waits. It takes me an hour of checking in, trying to read her expressions, but I finally get it right. I made something. No demographic analysis or shaping optics. I just made something that can make someone stronger.

My heart starts to pound but not from panic or stress. It's been a while, but I think this feeling might be happiness.

****

It's been a little over three weeks since I started Ohma's fix Maggie plan. I didn't know it was possible to feel this clear. This steady. Sometimes I miss the jet fuel of Adderall or caffeine, but on the few occasions I've cheated and had a cup of coffee, it left me feeling jagged. The less bullshit I have in my life, the less I need serrated edges to cut through it.

I still occasionally write emails to Mitchel. He never responds, but I don't expect him to. Maybe he's a tether to a life I'm not sure I'm ready to release. Maybe I'm chronicling. I don't really know. I just do it. I've done so much self-examination over the past nine months that I feel a lot like a Mobius strip. I still don't trust myself. But it might be possible someday.

I've texted Dana a bunch of times. Mostly sending her pictures. Of Ohma. Of Sedi. Of Ohma's conservatory and the gardens we used to spend so much time in. Of her mother's old birdhouses that are still standing. She always texts back, except once. I thought I'd seen Emilynn Martin walking into the Dollar Store, I followed her thinking I'd take a photo and send it to Dana. A nod to the triumph of we-got-out-and-she's-still-here. I'm not sure why I knew it was her. She was different. Really thin. The not well kind of thin. But her eyes were exactly as I remembered. Small, hard, swallowed up by her face. I knew it was her. I didn't have the nerve to snap a photo, but I did text Dana that I'd seen Emilynn outside the Dollar Store and how she might be a meth addict now. It felt mean and left me a bit nauseated, but I wanted to tell Dana about how someone who had been vicious to us as kids was clearly not living the dream. Dana didn't reply. Weirdly enough, the next day I could have sworn I saw Emilynn again backing out of Ohma's driveway in an ancient burgundy Toyota Camry. I asked Ohma if it was Emilynn Martin that I just saw leaving. She looked at me with her power washers, though they seemed a bit less barnacle obliterating than usual, then she just returned to sorting through some lemon balm. When I texted Dana again, saying I'm certain Emilynn was at Ohma's, she finally did respond with "No, that's not possible." When I asked why, she didn't reply. I wanted to push the point but it didn't seem a good idea to poke that particular elephant. Not yet.

****

I've been spending almost every day at Ohma's lately. She's like the high country air she's spent her life surrounded by. Air understands everything because it touches everything. It gives hundred mile vistas and dense fogs, erasing markers between

257

the way through and the way back, forcing whoever got stuck in it to rely on deeper instincts. Hypothermia will kill you up here, especially on days you think everything will be fine. Ohma's like that too.

A few weeks ago, after we'd foraged for wild nettles and replenished her jars of goldenseal, licorice root, hops, and passionflower, she told me she'd like me to do some tasks for her. And that after I completed them, I'd be ready to learn about the night of the festival and what happened after. She said each task would take the exact amount of time that it would take and not to think about "getting through the list." She can see right through me.

So far, I've done five, including my detox. She only tells me the next one when I've finished the one before. They've been simple things.

My most recent task was to find a feather. Specifically, she said, "Think of it like if you were a feather, that's what you'd be." To bring her that one. Before I began searching, I already knew which feather I wanted. A blue jay.

At first, I couldn't find a single blue jay feather which was weird because they're common here and we're well into the first summer molt. The more I looked the more I fixated, the more nothing else would do. I was sort of aware I was fixating, but that didn't change my need to find one. Then I realized I was looking for a feather New York street style. Scanning and speed walking. Covering as much territory as quickly as I could.

Ohma saw me once and started laughing. Full blown laughing. She said, "You look like a robin." She puffed up her chest and scurried one way then the other. It was funny and I tried to have a sense of humor about it, but mostly I was embarrassed. Then I said, "I thought I was a Magpie". She liked that. Her eyes crinkled, and she chuckled, "Yes. Yes, you are." Then I

258

asked if I could move on to the next task and she said, "No. You haven't brought me your feather yet." I both love and hate that there's no getting away with corner cutting with her.

So, I tried slowing down. I started to see feathers everywhere. But not one from a blue jay. I expanded my perimeter each day, walking farther and farther into the woods. Sometimes I thought I could smell exhaust, and I'd get flashes of holding my green Jansport backpack and running through trees at night.

Almost a week passed, and I'd still not found "my feather". I started to feel numbness creeping back in—like piles of kinetic sand that had been pushed to the corners of a room slowly spreading back to the center. The resumption of an inert state of flatness.

I kept going out and looking. I wish I could say it was out of a higher self-operating mode but mostly it was fear of completely reverting to my former Dr. Scholl's gel insert glory. I did finally find a perfect blue jay wing feather, resting in the middle of a trail. Not a speck of dust. Not a single spine missing. The jay must have just dropped it moments before. It was stunning. Exquisite. And utterly not me. But I was tired of looking for feathers, increasingly irritated with Ohma, and disheartened at my remaining proximity to apathy, so I brought it back to her.

She didn't look at it. She looked at me. Then she raised her eyebrows a fraction before turning away to continue whatever remedy she was making.

I marched home, indignant. On the way, I let it flutter to the ground at the foot of Dana's old overgrown front yard and didn't look for a feather or go back to Ohma's for three days.

The morning of the fourth day reality caught up to me. I could go back to New York and resume an apathetic life of little helpers, a best friend who won't talk to me, failure at honoring my promise to Dana, and a job that allows me to collect lots of stuff. Or I could stay and try Ohma's way. I resumed my feather search, but this time with no specific feather in mind. Just a hope I'd know it when I saw it.

I found it before I'd even made it past the drive. A raven feather, still wet and muddy from a storm that had careened through the night before. But it was still mostly intact and, once I found a puddle to rinse it in, still so black it was almost blue. It was absolutely, and utterly the one. When I brought it to Ohma she didn't say anything, just smiled and nodded as if a rumor she'd heard a long time ago had finally been confirmed.

Each task has been different. There was one where I had to log my thoughts for a week under "Then" "Now" and "Soon" columns (more illuminating than I wanted), and another where for a week I had to place a small stone into a pail each time I got angry (I thought I'd have one full pail by the end of the week. I had three). That one was followed by tossing those same stones one by one into the pond at far end of her property to listen to what the ripples had to say (at first nothing, then a lot about inextricable connections ... so, surprisingly deep for a pond—haha). Then there was the one where I had to examine every leaf, needle, bud, flower, and stalk in each of her four huge gardens (the first day I kept losing track of what I'd done and not done, but by the end of the week I wanted to start again to see how the ones from the first day had changed). I liked that task the most, which was surprising.

With each new task, I feel the moorings of indifference loosening, drifting closer to being unable to adjust the valves. I need my valves. Without them, I become Ouroboros—an infinity of everything to the point of nothingness, to the point of everything-ness. Again, and again. All those sayings about the journey starts with leaving the familiar shore. They're great when you're packing. Beginnings are easy. The I-don't-want-*this*-anymore is always strong enough to get you started. And at first, it's so filled with hope. The wind, the view of what you had the courage to leave getting smaller and smaller, the vast deep blue mystery gently pulling your boat farther and farther. The seagulls wave at you. The dolphins laugh and cheer, "Good for you, Maggie!"

Then, after a while, the dolphins are off playing somewhere else. And the seagulls have turned back to the familiar shore. And you're alone. No land in sight. Just water, water, water, water. And you think, okay, tomorrow I'll see my next shore. But you don't. Just water. That's when the reality of a decision made from a moment of conviction sinks in. And all you want to do is turn back. You think *it wasn't so bad, I'll appreciate it now, I'll be different this time.* But it's too late because you have no clue where the old shore is anymore.

Most of my life has flown past me because I wasn't there to notice it. Years of counting minutes on clocks til I could escape to another place with another clock. But when I'm working in Ohma's gardens or foraging or learning about plants and remedies, I don't notice time at all other than the slow stroke of the sun. The more time I spend with trees and earth and plants, the fewer questions I have.

I'm not healed or fixed. Nowhere near my next shore. I know this. Scratch the surface and anger is right there. That one's going to take a while. It's been a trusted companion to navigate the world. Even when I thought I was indifferent, it was still anger. Just obsidian instead of lava. I hope someday I'll stop trying to be something I'm not. Maybe not all of us are meant to be in a human tribe.

Surprisingly, the person who seems be doing okay through all of this is Mom. The other day after another one of my strained interactions with Dad, she just smiled and said, "It's okay, honey. When one person changes the steps in the middle of a square dance, people can get frustrated. Try to make you go back to the old steps. Sometimes they must sit a dance or two out before they return, but they'll catch up." It shocked the hell out of me. I've never given her nearly enough credit.

She was talking about Dad, but it's really me who isn't ready yet. I can't change and apply changes simultaneously. Maybe some people can. I can't. So, for now, I spend my time with Ohma and go to the wild things to practice. To the resin and iron—the smells of a forest untouched by man. Wild smells. The ones simultaneously near and far. The ones that always make sense to me. Asphalt and steel bludgeons the wild parts of me, the only parts worth having. The crush of feet in greased and grimed sidewalks, the thrum that awakens so many, neuters me. I know that now.

****

Today I'll complete my seventh task, which means Ohma will finally tell me what happened that summer. I'll finally be able to put it behind me. I texted Dana last night and told her. She said to call her in a day or so and she'd tell me what she couldn't say at lunch that day. That lunch feels like years ago.

It's only 8:00 a.m., but I've already been at Ohma's for an hour because she asked me to stop by before I head out to help her fill some jars and check the draying racks for mold. I've been thinking about the possibility of opening an herbal apothecary in Brooklyn. I could hold weekend workshops on how to grow medicinal plants and make basic salves and tinctures. I've been playing with the idea for a few weeks. It seems like the perfect solution to the what-should-Maggie-do-now conundrum. But there's something that doesn't feel right about it. Maybe it's too close to the plastic shaman thing. I don't know. I'll ask Ohma.

I'm about to head out the back door to the old barn and the oak tree I used to call Abernathy as a child, where my last task awaits, when Ohma stops me. She takes my hand in hers.

"If you have the courage to look directly at fear, you can see it is a friend."

I smile and nod, but I suddenly feel apprehensive. I can't put it off though. I don't want to. It'd be nice if one big leap took care of all the little ones, but I'm starting to believe it's the smallest ones that span the deepest crevices.

okay old oak tree and dilapidated barn

do your worst

****

I haven't visited this spot since I was ten,

pale violet sky

golden clouds

maple leaves

secret trails

within, not center

almost invisible

yet my feet knew exactly how to get here. I trust them now. They're much smarter than my head.

The white oak tree I used to call Abernathy and spent every afternoon with as a child was giant thirty years ago.

up n up n up

he sounds like the ocean

Overwhelmingly majestic barely covers it. Everyone has left this tree alone. One thing about the forest and the mountains, and the people who choose to make it their home that I'd forgotten, is a fundamental belief in sacred things. That some things are, in fact, sacred. Not all ancient things are. Abernathy is. I can feel it.

match my breathing with the breeze

creamy lemony spicy-sharp

And the old barn is too, though now little more than the remains of walls buckling with mossy decay.

fingers skimming   flecks and curls

from the day before that   n the day before that

n the tomorrow after that

I'm almost there when I stop. I'm revisiting Ohma's mention of fear. Is this task about fear?

faded yellow paint

violet soul

I wait for a few minutes telling myself it's just a tree and a barn. Just a tree and a barn. My feet start walking again.

I stop just short of the boughs because Abernathy's five main arms are each the size of large tree trunks, drooping down to the ground with their sheer weight, hovering along it for another few feet before gently curving back up to the sky again, to branch off into smaller arms, again and again, then huge fingers, again and again, holding both sky and the earth. A tree like this can't possibly exist in a world where Laffy Taffy and emojis live.

Though Abernathy's enormity temporarily stunned my brain, I'm slowly noticing other things. Silver lichen that covers most of his bark and crimson, yellow, and purple wildflowers spring like cartoon polka dots out of a lush carpet of bright green moss, curling up the sagging side of old barn.

I hear a funny sound somewhere close. I look for a woodpecker or even a raven because they often sound like they're laughing. Then I realize it's me. I'm laughing. There isn't a word to describe how a single spot on the planet can feel like it's where you completely and utterly belong.

I decide to venture into the barn first. Abernathy still feels overwhelming. Carefully walking so as not to step on anything or anyone, I make my way through the opening that used to be the barn doors. The roof did fall in, but it must have been a long time ago because a few small trees have made old barn their home. Abernathy's children by the looks of them.

It's cooler and quieter in here and even though it's quite possible one or all the remaining walls will collapse in at any moment, I don't care. Not in my usual I don't care way. More in an I've found a kind of peace I never thought I'd have again way.

I close my eyes and listen. Nathy's leaves, branches swaying, wings fluttering, wild, tall grass rushing in waves, the breeze like water—they all merge and fold through each other—an a cappella choir of a hundred voices. Nature, wild and unrefined.

I'm ready now. I wander back outside and straight under Abernathy's arms, touching the rough bark of his trunk. I rest my forehead on him.

he sounds like the ocean up and up and up

don't blink don't blink flame colored leaves piles of fire tossing flames with Dana

little stone circles   twigs and feathers

around his trunk

Crunch Berries

I think maybe my soul's been here. Waiting all this time. Buried with the bits of quartz and feathers and Crunch Berries. Waiting while I went to junior high, then high school, then FIT, then The Bridge Group. Waiting while I screwed up my reunion with Dana and took vows of silence and language of the body classes and conscious de-verbalization retreats, and scraping the courage together to contact Ohma, and through her, finally found my way back here again.

Sometime just now I started crying. Decades of nothingness are pouring down my face. All those years without my own soul. All those years Nathy and old barn kept it safe for me. Trusting one day I'd come back for it.

****

I must've fallen asleep. A no holds barred cry out is like general anesthesia. I lie on my back and look up through Nathy's huge arms. Up, and up, through a thousand yellow-green tipped leaves, to the sky. I have no idea what time it is other than somewhere around noon. Doesn't matter. I stretch. My arms and legs feel light. Like all the rust fell off while I was sleeping.

I sit up, running my hands along the velvety moss then across Nathy's bark, its roughness reminding me he's solid and here, and that I'm here too.

"I'm ready now."

My voice sounds like it belongs to me again. I stand up but don't brush the moss and dirt off my pants. I like that they're there. A gust of warm wind lifts the hair off the back of my neck. The air smells flinty. I look up and see the sky turning grey green. It's going to rain. It's not going to be the soft summer rain that falls like lace, evaporating the moment it touches your skin. This one's going to crack and rumble and shake the ground. I can't wait.

New York has intense thunderstorms too. Rain glancing off buildings, sidewalks washed of dirt and urine, sky illuminated with the forked tongues of urban dragons. But in the city, we forget how incredible it all is. We forget this planet doesn't belong to us.

Out here it's different. The push and pull of trees as they swirl in anticipation of water that will replenish them. And me. Gauzy mist will weave and dance though hemlock trees and the places I stop, and they begin, will overlap. For a while, nothing else matters.

I close my eyes and hear the rush of leaves giving in to the air that lifts them. Then the *shhhhhhhhhhhh* of water meeting pine straw and patent leather holly bushes. Then the rumble and crack, reaching into my bones, making me jump, and laugh.

I pull the rich red soil, Nathy's bark, the lichen, and the dense earthy smell of wild mushrooms into my lungs and feel it pass into my bloodstream. I've been separate for such a long time. How lonely I was. Not lonely for human companionship. For this. For trees and soil and plants and animals. For quiet, strong things. I don't feel alone anymore.

Walking back to Ohma's, my rust-free limbs take long, light strides towards my next shore. Just a few more steps from what was to what will be. My seventh task is complete and I'm ready.

Steam from the storm-soaked earth is hovering above the fennel and rosemary along her property giving it an otherworldliness. The pungent sweet sharpness still has an undertow, but it doesn't bother me. I like it.

The lights aren't on in the conservatory, but sunlight streams, smudged and soft, through rain glazed windows. I slip out of my mud slathered boots and set them outside. This room is so much like Ohma—so still it vibrates with life.

I sit in what has become my chair, listening to the silence, and watching water drops transform into luminous snakes sliding down the windowpanes. I look around for Sedi, listening for the gentle click, click, click of his easy trot, but he's not here. Which means Ohma's either foraging or on a house call. I'll have to wait just a little longer.

I've often heard people describe contentment like a gentle fullness. I breathe in the smells of the herbs, flowers, bark, and roots in various stages of drying. The anger and emptiness I felt is gone. How strange. How indescribably wonderfully odd.

If she's foraging it could be a while, so I decide to get to work. Even though we replenished many of the jars earlier this morning, she likes to have a second jar of the ones she uses the most. Chamomile, burdock, lemon balm, rosemary, thyme, ginger root, wild garlic, nettles, turkey tail, comfrey, and mint all need a backup jar. I should also check everything we hung to dry a few days ago for mold. It's tricky to dry things here. The Carolinas rarely dip below 60% humidity, but Ohma always has a way of working with the environment without asking it to change for her. Sometimes she uses drying trays and a portable fan, but only if absolutely necessary. Mostly she binds the herbs in loose bunches then places them in worn burlap pouches. It helps catch seeds as the plants dry and keeps the dust off them but is breathable so air can circulate. I never notice time passing when I'm working in the conservatory. Everything stops.

Bright sun streams in through the windows, opening the corners of the room, and the colors and textures of a hundred mason jars. It's breathtaking in an immense and hushed way. A thousand arrows in my soul pointing to this room. This moment and this room.

I look out the window across the back yard—the pockets of steam clinging to the dandelion bushes she allows to grow unchecked because of their potent medicine. The mist makes the bright yellow puffed flowers look like they're floating. I love that nature doesn't care if you witness its beauty. It's just there. It just is. Spending time immersed in it snaps the delusion that everything is about humans. It almost always isn't.

As I sit at the window and watch the steam drift, I hear the click, click, click of claws on the clay tiles. I turn around. Sedi's sitting in the doorway to the kitchen, watching me.

"Hey Sed, hey, buddy" I offer my hand. That usually results in a relaxed trot to me, but he doesn't move. "Whatcha doin?"

I'm slowly getting used to the sound of my voice. It still sounds too loud, but it no longer sounds hollow or alien. I like that I don't talk unless I truly need to. It makes me feel like I'm part of this place instead of outside trying to get in.

Sedi chuffs quietly and trots away, back into the house. I've been expecting Ohma to materialize in that way she does, but I don't think she's here right now. I wouldn't be surprised if she knew that last task would send me for a loop and that a bit of time back here on my own would settle me.

I close my eyes and try to follow Sedi's footfall into the recesses of the house to find other sounds. All I hear is silence and the gentle stirring of Ohma's weathervane.

Ridding my body and mind of all the toxins I'd gouged into myself over thirty years, has slowly freed up room to notice things outside myself. Like how all living things have a presence. Humans, animals, trees, plants, air, water, fire, earth. The elements are alive. At the very least they're filled with tiny living creatures or chemical reactions that shift and breathe and exist. How presence is the place where one thing meets another. And at that meeting place a vibration exists. All living things have it. It's taken a while, but my sense of those vibrations is returning.

It went away, or I ignored it in the city. It's easier there. The clear, unmovable edges of concrete and metal. A certain kind of ever-present hum. But now I'm away from them, the in-between places are swirling and overlapping again, like when I was young. Right now, as I follow Sedi into the house, I can see deep indigo smoke curling behind him. It's not actually there, but my mind sees it. And whenever I think of Dana, I see sapphires and smell dried eucalyptus. Certain people have specific sounds or textures around them like a kind of membrane or cloak. A staggering number of people remind me of American cheese slices. It's hard to explain. But it's something I had as a child that I forgot about. Until now. Because a small book of secrets I don't remember losing found its way back to me.

I step into the kitchen and look out the front window, just in case Ohma's coming in the front carrying anything heavy, but I don't see her. Truth is she's probably stronger than I am but being aware of other people is part of my rehab.

Her kitchen is simple. A space for preparing food just like any other kitchen, but it's also a place for healing, laughter, and understanding. Of safety and solace. It's filled with dozens of wooden utensils, worn smooth from use, resting in wide mouth clay jars. Large pots hang from hooks along the walls.

They're all dented and patinaed various shades of brownish red from decades of simmering roots and berries. Not a single bowl, saucepan or knife is for show. It's the most beautiful kitchen I've ever been in. A space of undeniable, and unadorned purpose.

I check the front yard once more, but I know Ohma won't be back for a while. She often makes house calls back-to-back then does some foraging near the lake.

I follow Sedi's indigo wake to the living room. The brown leather sofa along one wall, and the shelves filled with pottery and carved wooden animals on the other the same as 40 years ago. Me and Dana sorting through feathers, stones, and twigs, inside where it was always cool and not as bright, playing finding faces in things . Fresh strawberry lemonade and corn cakes for lunch. More and more memories have been returning lately. Just a few holes left. Those are the ones Ohma and Dana will fill.

I listen again for Sedi, but he must have gone back to napping somewhere cool and dark. He does that. Some people that Ohma visits have dogs that react in unexpected ways to Sedi's wildness. They get overexcited or agitated. Reminded of wilder paths not taken.

Sedi now settled, I go back to the conservatory to resume counting elderberries. The ones we harvested over the past few weeks must last through the winter. Ohma's elderberry tincture is a flu season staple here. She adds a little lemon balm and valerian to her nighttime tincture to help with sleep. It's my favorite.

"Uhm, Hi?" A young woman, maybe late teens, or early twenties, it's hard to tell with skin that age, is standing in the back doorway. "I, uhm, I'm looking for, like, Onee?"

"Ohma," I say

"My mom sent me. I have these." She shows me a few angry wasp stings on her arm. "She said I could get this, like, ointment stuff here? I'm heading back to NYU on Saturday, so she said to get it today."

I motion for her to give me her arm so I can see if any wasp stingers are left. One is. I take the smooth edge of a small knife and run it across her skin. It pulls the stinger out.

"Whoa, like whoa!" she says, pulling away.

I lay the stinger in a tiny bowl. Ohma might want it. Sometimes a tiny amount of one thing helps heal other things.

I go to the shelf where she keeps the prepared salves but the drawing salve I need isn't there so I quickly gather marigold, balm of Gilead, arnica, goldenrod, witch hazel, broad leaf plantain, and lobelia, setting them each on the table in order of amount used in the recipe. I light the candle under the small ceramic pot and set a chunk of beeswax in to melt then start crushing each of the herbs and roots individually to make sure I keep the amounts correct. As I crush each into a powder and set them aside, the young woman chatters on.

"Yeah, so, like, I was just here for the summer. I go to NYU"

you mentioned that

"I wish I could have just stayed there. I mean, the city is SO much fun in the summer. The festivals and the culture ..."

the hot garbage and urine

"Oh, wait you have to see this. I mean, so much like racism and like inequity is finally being addressed. This is from a Native Nights fundraiser I organized last year. To raise, like, awareness, you know?"

She shows me a picture of her very pale self with a few others, flashing the peace sign, wearing feather headdresses made of brightly dyed feathers and shiny beads.

"Don't do that," I say. I feel power washers in my eyes.

"Uhm, what? Raise awareness? Raise funds to donate to like Indigenous children?"

I wish Dana was here. She'd set this My Little Pony straight. The thought makes me chuckle.

"It's not, like, something to laugh about," she says.

"So, we agree," I say

I refocus on what I'm doing. Broad leaf plantain, marigold, arnica, goldenrod, done. Balm of Gilead, done. Tiniest pinch of bloodroot. Bloodroot's serious stuff, but great at drawing out toxins.

The beeswax mixed with the thick, camphoraceous woody-vanilla scent of balm of Gilead ripples through the room. It's a heavenly smell. Rich and smooth.

"Whoa, like Pine-SOL!" she says with a scrunched moue, "Anyway, I was like, Mom, just get that pink stuff from Rite-Aid, you know? But no, she's on this whole go natural kick ever since Dad left her for Marcos, their ballroom dance instructor, so whatever."

She starts picking up jars, inspecting them suspiciously, then setting them down in the wrong spots.

"So, like, of course I had to get stung by friggin' wasps the day before I go back. So embarrassing! Like, hello country bumpkin! Ugh. I can't wait to get back to civilization."

I finish the salve and hand it to her. She takes a huge dollop and smears it across the wasp stings. I take the jar back, shaking my head.

"Like, wait, what're you doing?" she asks indignantly.

I take my pinky finger and lightly dab a small amount of the salve onto it and tap it across my skin lightly.

"A tiny amount is enough," I say. I'm trying to be goddam four directions balanced here, and this Manhattan-obsessed, bigoted child-woman is trying my last nerve.

"Oh, uhm, so like *spar-ing-ly*?" she says clearly uncertain I know what sparingly means.

I smile and nod. "That's right"

"Wow! This stuff, is, like, a-mazing!" she says, "The pain is, like, totally gone! You sure you didn't add like, Novocain?"

"Many prescription drugs are derived from plant compounds."

"You should totally market this to, like, Whole Foods or something ..."

I let the silence be my response. The Crickets. A distant hawk. The gentle clack-clack-clack of Ohma's weathervane.

"Okay, then," she says, handing a $20 bill to me.

"I don't think Ohma charges," I say. But maybe she does. I don't know.

"Tell you what," she says winking, "I'll just, like, leave this here." She puts the twenty on the table. "As, like, a thank you"

I shrug. Not my call.

"So, like, okay," she says, popping the salve jar in her purse, then examining her arm. The redness is subsiding, and the swelling is reduced. Her mask of entitlement slips for a moment and genuine surprise emerges.

there you are

"Wow. That's incred—wow, they really feel—that's amazing. You really should talk to Whole Foods!"

I almost tell her she'll be able to find me and many remedies like this in my Brooklyn apothecary next year, but I don't. After she leaves, I decide to make a few more jars of salve. They go quickly this time of year and once made, hold their full medicinal properties for around nine months if kept cool and dry. That may not sound like very long, but nature is different. Life is cyclical and ephemeral. It's a huge part of the beauty of it. I'm trying to accept that. The more I do, the lighter I feel. Expectation is like looking in a closet filled with light, silky, cozy options. But they're all lined with lead.

I hear a soft chuff. Sedi's in the doorway again. I walk over and reach out to pet him. He trots back into the house.

something's wrong

I follow him into the house. He looks back at me then trots down the hall into a room to the right. A small lead fist forms in my chest as I walk to the edge of the hallway and pause.

"Ohma?" My voice bounces off the narrow hallway.

I can imagine her emerging from the room with Sedi, a small, secret smile on her face as she says, "I knew today would be the day. So, I waited in here 'til you were ready," but the hall remains empty. It reminds me of walking in the financial district after 9/11. No birds. Too still. Like a black hole.

"Ohma, did you fall asleep watching Casablanca again?"

My feet start to walk to the room Sedi entered. I can't get my eyes to look up, but I can see Sedi is now lying on the ground next to a bed.

Pthump Pthump Pthump Pthump Pthump Pthump. My blood is crashing in my ears.

pleasepleasepleasepleasepleasepleaseplease

Ohma's in the bed, her eyes are closed. But not entirely. She's just communing with the ancestors. I've seen her do it. She goes somewhere else for a while and her eyes look like this.

that's not what this is

SHUT UP

FOR ONCE JUST SHUT UP

*she's fine she'sfineshe'sfineshe'sfine***she'sfineshe'sfine**

I knock on the doorframe. It's too loud. It echoes through the house.

"Ohma?" I whisper.

I'm next to the bed now, but I don't remember walking across the room. Sedi is lying very still. His head on his paws. I reach out to touch her arm. It's cold.

I'm supposed to do something now. Scream or cry. Curse the heavens like they do in the movies she loves. But it's so quiet and she looks peaceful. It doesn't feel tragic. It feels empty. My eyes are getting blurry. My cells are forgetting what to do again. I'm sitting on the ground. Now I'm lying on the ground. Next to Sedi. Water is flowing out of my eyes. No gasping, no struggle. Just water flowing from my eyes.

I'm in the road in front of my parent's farmhouse now. Looking in the windows at mom's book club meeting. I don't remember how I got here. My father's out at his woodworking shed. Instead of all the tension and awkwardness there's just water. Maybe I brought the water with me. Rushing water from my eyes carrying trees and houses and me and Ohma.

He's next to me now, saying something but it sounds like he's talking through a wall. His voice keeps getting louder, but not clearer.

"MMMMMAAAAEEE!MMMMMAAAAGGEEE!"

His hands are on my shoulders, but I don't feel them other than the weight of them pulling me closer to the earth. I see him. I know he's there. But it doesn't matter.

"MMMAAAAGGEEE? Whaaasssrrrrraaaaawwg?"

I should tell him. I should say something. But then it'll be real. Right now, it's just me and Sedi that know. But if I tell them, it's real. But it is. It is. I have to say her name now. I don't want to, but I don't want him to guess. I don't want him to say her name. He doesn't get to.

"Ohma," I say.

His face changes. Drops. Slides off his bones and into his hands. My mother is next to us now. I didn't see her come out of the house. She's just here now.

"What is it? Is she ok? Is she hurt?" she asks.

I look at my father. His eyes are older and paler than I remembered.

"Weathered sea glass," my voice says.

I feel an arm around my shoulders and now we're walking to the front porch. Hands and voices setting me down on the porch swing. It's too wobbly. I'm going to be sick. Too much funnel cake and cream soda. I walk to the porch edge and throw up then I sit down on the top stair.

My father's voice says, "I'll be right back. I'm going to get you something to drink, okay? And make a call."

I'm staring over the lawn to the row of trees across the street.

tree *tree* *tree* **tree** *tree* *tree* *tree* *tree*

September 10, 1979

the room's dark but I've been in here for a while n there's a little bit of light comin from under the door so I can see more than when he put me in here   I'm not sure how long ago that was cause I forgot my scooby doo watch I think that was yesterday but I don't know feels like a really long time ago everythin isn't what it was so I don't know God picked the world up n shook it really hard n nothin's in the right place anymore

I hear a chair squeakin on the other side of the door sometimes soft footsteps   sometimes the clu-clackclack clack clack clack of a typewriter I recognize the sound cause a reporter man was typin in an episode of the credible hulk I got to watch once momma never let me watch it again after that one time cause she said she didn't like that color green I thought the credible hulk was a nice color green I wonder if he's still walkin along the highway all alone

I shouldn'ta tried to find Dana by myself but I had to come I had to but I didn't find her n she didn't find me now I'm in trouble they only take you to jail if you're bad I didn't know it was so big here n I thought people would know everyone knows everyone at home now they'll never let me come back I'll never find Dana my eyes start to get prickly I don't wanna cry

not yet not yet not yet

278

if I cry it means I won't find her n I'm gonna find her I will I
haveta come back I stare at the floor to give my eyes somethin
to do so they won't cry   the floor is grey with red speckles so I
try to connect all the speckles and make pictures maybe the
police man will take me to the bus stop in the mornin maybe
they won't notice I was gone I could say that I was with Nathy
n that I was sad cause of Dana n her momma so I wanted to be
alone I could say I was with Ohma when I get back before I
go home I'll go to her farm n ask her if it's okay to say I was
there but they prolly looked for me there maybe I'll say I just
needed to be alone cause I was sad my plan makes me feel
better n I don't have to cry anymore if they don't know I came
here I can try again it's almost dawn   the black edges round
the curtains r startin to turn grey I can go to the bus stop soon

a door opens in the other room clickclickclickclick fast feet in
click-y shoes

> *Maggie? Maggie honey?* momma's voice *Magpie? Where is she?*
> *WHERE IS SHE?*

my heart starts poundin she's gonna ruin everythin

no nonononoNONONO

> the police man says *ma'am she's fine ma'am she's okay*
>
> *where is my daughter?* momma's voice sounds like it belongs
> to someone else
>
> *she's asleep in the break room through there* the police man says
>
> *thank you for taking care of her for us* that was daddy

he's sayin somethin else now but all I hear is momma's click-y
shoes gettin closer I flip to face the back of the couch n pull
the blanket the police man gave me with a big bear n a moon
on it over my head I don't want to talk to her   no-one will tell
me anythin bout why Dana left but they know I know they

know but they won't tell me so I'm not gonna talk to em til
they tell me   I should have tried harder

stupidstupid babybaby Maggie

now you'll never find her

the door opens momma's feet skitter like a spider apologizin
before it bites you anyway she's gonna try to pull the blanket
off my head but I won't let her   I squeeze all my thoughts
together n make em all think the same thing

don't don't don't Don't DON'T DON'T

she sits next to me making the couch droop I fight hard not to
let the couch make me roll towards her   she rubs my back but
I don't want her to she always does that when she's upset she
never ever notices I don't like it

> *honey? sweetie? wake up everything's okay daddy n I are here we're*
> *not mad sweetie*

my belly starts to shake n tears run out of my eyes even though
I have em squeezed shut

> *oh honey sweetie honey honey it's okay it's okay*

it's not n she doesn't even understand why it's not goin to be
okay ever again

> *we picked her up wanderin along route 19 said she was on a*
> *campin trip n got lost*

the police man's voice sounds louder n clearer they're all in the
room now talkin bout me n lookin at me

be invisible

be invisible

be invisible

280

thank you for finding her-for taking care of-thank you daddy says

she's okay she's okay she's just tired she's okay momma says

keep the blanket the police man says *she seems to like it*

daddy's pickin me up blanket n all rollin me into his arms his old spice aftershave I curl up as tight as I can like a roly poly bug

don't cry don't don't DON'T

he kisses my head n it makes me cry he carries me out of the jail station while momma scurries next to us   the air is cold n clean   mist n pine sap n leaves

I don't wanna go I say tryin to sound clear like a grown up *I wanna stay I'm supposed to find her I-I- w-want to-to-to stay   I have-haveta f-f-find her*

I think I said it out loud I wanna say it out loud but I'm not sure I did cause God sometimes changes things into somethin else n I think he maybe took my voice away cause I lied n so he made it so I couldn't find Dana either

so what

SOWHATSOWHATSOWHAT

I don't care

I'm never ever talkin everever again

I don't wanna be a person I wanna be a tree

pleasepleaseplease let me be a tree

bark n branches n moss

pleasepleaseplease let me be a tree

but it isn't workin

you have to catch it earlier my blood whispers

no we can do it we can be a tree my bones say *we know the shapes but we haveta get rid of the other parts first before we can be a tree*

daddy puts me in the backseat n closes the door

gonna be a tree

gonna be a tree now

let the other parts go away so the tree has room

momma gets in n reaches back to sweep hair away from my face

     everything's going to be ok she says

swunchswunchswunchswunchswunchswunchswunch

slower

swwwwuunch swwwwwuunch swwwwwuunch

slower slower slower like sap

swwwwwwuunch ssswwwwwwwuunch ssswwwwwwwuuunch

16

They say acceptance is key when facing the irreversible. There are master plans and better places. Ways too mysterious for us to understand. Sleeping helps. But then comes waking and a feather crushes the world once more. There is no word for life without her.

Everything's a tableau. The cars in the driveway, the soup cans at Harris Teeter. The Morris family breathing in and out, pretending it's all going to be fine. Here are Angie and Peter playing Scrabble. Here is Dad reading a Woodsmith magazine. Here is Mom pretending to read her book club book. Here is me in a seated position on a chair.

"She was a badass mammajamma," Peter says to the silence.

"Wonder how many people she helped over the years?" Mom asks, "Must be—"

Dad finishes her sentence, "Hundreds. At least hundreds"

Angie doesn't say anything. She makes eye contact with me and leans her head slightly into a sad smile.

"The goddamn real deal is what she was!" Peter's voice bounces like a pinball off the walls.

Voices are too loud. Words are just Ziplock baggies of stupid, ice-burned platitudes pulled out and offered when someone dies, then stuffed into the backs of freezers again. Until the next time they're needed.

"Peter!" Dad barks.

I flinch. They're all just trying to help, but they're all so nervous that Maggie's not okay. Again. Except Angie. Like with Mom after the Dad-goes-Mad-Max incident, once again she's the most in touch with what is truly needed. My sister is kind of incredible that way.

Silence thickens the room again, so I head outside to sit on the porch. Less than a minute later the front screen door creaks.

"I want to be alone," I say to whoever it is.

My father sits down on the stairs, leaving distance between us. His eyes drift across the lawn to the tree line. "I didn't know when the best time was to give you this. She gave it to me last week. It was the first time I'd...it had been a long time."

He hands me an envelope. Maggie is written across the front in Ohma's straight-forward handwriting. Seeing it is strange. It's so normal. Almost mundane. Someone's handwriting. But it's not someone's. It's hers. And she's gone now. She'll always be gone now. I glance peripherally at my father. I want privacy. But he stays where he is, looking out across the yard to the perch pole birdhouse.

I tuck the envelope into a pocket. I've worn this jacket— Ohma's waxed tin cloth jacket—for the past 48 hours. It smells like cherry cigarillos, Ivory soap and sweat. I must have put it on sometime between finding her and walking home. I tried to take it off last night, but when I did, I started to spread into the air like my skin was missing. Blood and fat and bones leaking into space, a planet without gravity.

where's Maggie?

she's in the walls with the oregano

"She was going to tell me," I say to a robin in search of bugs in the overgrown grass of the front lawn.

"Tell you what?" my father asks.

I don't say anything. He knows exactly what I'm talking about.

He sighs heavily. I wouldn't be surprised to find him halfway submerged in the stairs. Maybe this was Ohma's plan all along. That would be just like her.

"It was such a long time ago." His voice is like mud. "Does it really matter anymore?"

"It does," I say.

"You're grieving," he says. "We all are. Dredging up the past won't bring her back. I'm so, so sorry you lost her. She was a great person."

A hard, spiky place in the center of my chest stirs. All the broken and mean parts of me, everything I thought I'd worked through over the past months, are back.

"I expect platitudes from Mom, not you."

He nods almost imperceptibly.

"Sorry," I say. I'm being cruel and it's not fair.

For such a bear of a man, he's astonishingly fragile. I want to yell at him about how secrets have infected everything between us. But I need answers more.

"Dad," I say, trying to soften my voice, "I'm trying to help myself move on from something I didn't even realize has shaped most of my life."

"Nothing can do that unless you let it," he says so softly I'm not entirely sure it was meant for me.

"I have to figure out what went wrong. Where I went wrong."

"I thought you were doing well."

"I wasn't. Seeing Dana again and being here—being with Ohma again—reminded me of stuff I buried a long time ago.

Not just about that summer, but before it happened, how I've become someone I don't think I'm supposed to be."

"Mary died is what happened," he says.

The expanse between us widens.

"Maybe if I know what really happened, that night and after, with Dana, I can finally let it go. Finally find a way to be..."

We're both quiet for a few minutes. Finally, he says, "Okay." It's barely a whisper.

****

Ohma's letter didn't say much. Typical Ohma. She wrote she believed I'd balanced my four directions and was beginning to remember myself. That she was proud of me. And that she'd decided to leave the farmhouse and her station wagon to Dana and me and that she'd asked Sedi if he'd be willing to watch over me for a while and he had agreed. She didn't write anything about that summer.

When I called Dana, she was quiet. So was I. What is there to say when someone you love dies? There's no point in filling silence with things that don't need to be said yet. I thought I heard her crying, but I'm not sure. She said she'd be there as soon as she could. Tomorrow or the next day. Then she hung up.

So, I'm here now. I walked. My Range Rover would look grotesque here. And very much like that first day, I'm frozen at her front gate. A small pile of cards, notes, flowers, carved figures, and, I think, preserves—which is odd—are blocking the front door. They should be left undisturbed. They're not for me. Maybe Dana will help me sort through them.

I'm not sure how long I've been standing here. Doesn't matter.

I'm glad Dana's coming but grateful she's not here yet. I just want to be alone with Sedi. He won't judge me or tell me how to grieve or what to think. He won't ask me to be something I'm not. He won't need to explain or use words then hope I understand them enough to move on. I don't want to be around people. Especially my father.

I'm having a hard time wrapping my brain around what he told me yesterday. It wasn't just what he said, it was how he said it. As if he was reading the ingredients on a jar of mayo. "It happened around 10 p.m.", "The police report filed her death under a hit and run.", "They never found the driver.", "Ohma believed it wasn't an accident.", "We all felt Dana would be better off with her uncle."

When I asked him why Ohma thought it wasn't an accident, he got quiet again. Eventually he said that even though there are a lot of good people here, some things are more complicated than we think they'll be, and that people disagree about how things should and shouldn't be done. Then he asked if we could go for a walk.

I'm not sure either one of us planned it, but we ended up at Dana's old house. Looking at their home melting into the ground, the damn broke. He told me that he loved my mother, but that Dana's mother was the love of his life. That he knew it from the moment he met her. And that Mary had felt the same. That if he could, he'd go back and do everything differently. Then she'd still be alive. He couldn't talk beyond that. I wanted to ask a thousand questions. Why would she still be alive? Did they have an affair? What did he mean by differently? But his face was so contorted with the pain of ripping through thirty years of scar tissue, I couldn't bring myself to ask a single one.

Instead, I let him say what he could. He talked about contacting Mary's brother who lived on The Qualla to tell him what had happened. How they all decided Dana probably shouldn't stay here. I asked him why Dana couldn't just live with Ohma, or even with us, but that's when he shut down again. He kept saying, "I-we-we made the best decision I could at the time." Maybe having a constant reminder of Mary around was too much for him. Maybe he's Dana's father. My mind can't fully grasp it, but the possibility is a shard of glass stuck in my thoughts. Maybe people suspected the same. Not much gets missed in small towns. I couldn't help but think if Mary had been white, everyone would have gathered around Dana to make sure she was taken care of and didn't have to move away. I don't understand why Ohma didn't just take over. Why my father had a say in what happened at all. Every time my mind drifts there, the shard of glass digs deeper. Maybe Dana will know but I have no idea how to ask that question.

My father then switched over to talking about what happened after I'd taken the bus to The Qualla to find Dana. How he decided it was best for me to stop seeing Ohma for a while. That he went to her and said he wished things were different but that what happened to Mary was his fault and he wouldn't allow anyone else to suffer the consequences.

It didn't sound like him. It sounded like someone else. I kept picturing that old truck with the Army sticker. How I knew I'd seen it before. And the eyes of the man driving it. How they didn't look menacing. They looked more like he'd been expecting me for a while, but too much time had passed, and he'd forgotten what he was going to say. I wasn't sure what made me think of him at that moment, but I did.

Before my father and I returned home, he asked me to not tell my mother what he'd said. The first thought I had was *she already knows*. When we got back, I told my mom I wanted to stay at Ohma's so I could be there when Dana arrived. For the first time in my life, her face was unreadable. The air around her became very still, then she simply nodded, gave me a hug, and said to let her know if I needed anything. I wanted to say I was so sorry. That she was so much stronger than I ever knew. But I just hugged her back. I didn't count the seconds until I could let go. I just hugged my mother and meant it.

A gentle chuff greets me from the side garden. Sedi. I'm not sure who took care of him for the past few days. Probably Sedi. Once he knows I see him, he turns and trots to the back of the house. I follow him. I wonder if he learned that trick from Ohma or Ohma learned it from him.

His food bowl is empty, and the water bowl has a filmy inch of reddish-brown water in it. I wash it out with the garden hose and refill it, then take a scoop from the giant bag of dog food inside the door and fill his bowl. It's strange that it's there. That the last time it was opened was three days ago, by Ohma. She always mixes in raw chicken or venison. Sometimes river trout. I watch him tuck into his kibble. I still don't feel entirely here, but Sedi's a tether and that's enough for now.

As he eats, I look around her conservatory. It's exactly how I left it. The ceramic melting dish has the remnants of the wasp salve I made that day—a faint smell of camphor stirs as I set my duffle down. The smell. It's still here. It still just happened. I still have to stop myself from thinking about when I was making it. If that was the exact moment she died. I've tried to resist thinking about it. If it was when I was making this damn salve. Or if it was earlier. Maybe when I first got back from my time with Nathy. Or maybe when I was checking the drying racks. I know nothing can be done, but part of me seems to keep searching for something to be done. Something that might change it. Like if I can somehow figure out the moment it happened that will somehow change it. Make me worthy of her not leaving.

But she did leave, and she's gone now. The stillness and quiet and the slight slowness of Sedi's movements confirms it. She knew it was coming too. Giving my dad that letter a week ago. I'm not surprised she knew, but I don't know why she didn't tell me. I don't know. She would've made one hell of a chess player. Leaving her farm to both Dana and me. It makes sense, of course. She was a medicine woman and medicine isn't just a prescription for little helpers. It's not even just tinctures and poultices. She showed me it's mostly hard-core spirit and mind work. Changing how you think. Forgiveness. Drinking some tea is the easy part.

I keep expecting the soft scuff of her shoes on the floor as she quietly sings *Boogie Shoes*. Then my mind spits out the moment I found her. How the sleeves of her pajamas looked like they'd been recently mended. And how her eyes were just a little open—like she'd been, for some reason, looking at her feet the moment she died. I might have told Dana about those things. I'm not sure.

I thought I'd be able to feel her presence. People so often say that. That they can feel their loved one's presence. But Ohma took all of her with her when she left. No unfinished business.

But I am. I'm unfinished. There's a gap between my skin and soul that wasn't fully bridged before she left. I hate myself for wishing I'd finished my seventh task just one day earlier. That I hadn't taken days obsessing over a damn blue jay feather. Or that I hadn't wasted nearly four decades pretending she didn't exist.

****

It took me until after sunset to make it into the living room. Sedi helped. Invited me into each room. He understands.

On the walk over here, I'd decided to stay in the second bedroom. The one she kept available for those who wanted to be near her as they healed. On special occasions, when Dana and I would get to sleep over and sort the feathers and stones we'd found, we'd get to share that spare room. My eyelids getting heavy as Dana whispered stories she'd made up about people we'd seen that day. But now I'm here, I'm not ready to walk down the hallway. Dana can have it while she's here. I'll take the couch.

It's strange how these structures we build and burrow into and fill with objects define us. I don't belong in my loft, I don't belong at my parent's house, and I want to belong here. But I don't yet.

Bronwen Carson

October 1979

> *does your father know you're here?* she asks me

I don't answer I don't care if he does all I want to do is pull
this dandelion outta the ground I know she's waitin for me to
look at her but I don't want to she takes the dandelion from
me real gentle

> *you'll see her again* she says *I'm not sure when but you will so
> little tsisqua you have to choose and until you choose you'll stay
> stuck understand?*

I hate it when she talks like this like rocks n splinters rn't
inside me like they're far away like it's easy like it's just
supposed to be easy n far away

> *they're just stupid plants they can't do ANYTHIN*

I stand up n kick em kick all the plants round me then I run
away rippin up as many as I can before I get to the gate   even
though it makes me cry cause I can feel em when I'm hurtin
em   then I turn round n yell as loud as I can

> *you let her die n you let Dana leave   I HATE YOU*

then I run I run n run n run til I'm at the river I find the
hugest rock I can n throw it in I hate her I hate all of em but
specially her   I'll never ever forgive her   never ever

gonna be a tree now

grow bark

be real still

be invisible

17

It's the day after yesterday. I've spent most of it sitting in the side garden, next to a large, raised bed of nettle, ginseng, black cohosh, and goldenseal. The shade from two giant wild cherry trees and a gentle slope creates perfect growing conditions for them.

Someone nearby is doing a controlled burn. The smell is nice, a little sad. The smell of something once loved but misplaced.

Sedi's next to me, his giant head resting on crossed paws. We're both trying to figure out how to live without her. We know we don't have to pretend we have any idea how to do that.

I spot an old garden fork next to a basket. The goldenseal roots need to be harvested soon or they'll rot.

I pick up the fork. It's old and dull, which makes it perfect for loosening the long, solid roots without disturbing the small ones. It takes time. Even with the right tool, it takes time. I'm starting to remember things taking time is normal. Growth, healing, seasons, all of it. I'd stepped so deeply into the thrum of steel and asphalt, immediacy felt normal. But it's not.

Sedi's head lifts and he chuffs quietly. He gets up and trots to the corner, looking into the front yard.

I get up, brush the damp earth from my pants and follow him. Dana's standing just inside the gate, one hand carrying a large duffel, the other buried in the dense fur of Sedi's neck. It's surprising how relieved I am Patricia isn't with her.

I want to walk up to her and give her a hug.

I want to walk up to her and tell her Ohma didn't tell me anything.

I want to walk up to her and reclaim Sedi.

I want to walk up to her and cry.

I walk up to her and say, "Hi."

"It's the same," she says quietly. She looks tired.

"I know. It shouldn't be."

"Except it is—"

I nod. Sedi returns to me, leaning on my leg. His weight reminds me I'm still here.

Dana's eyes land on my muddy garden gloves. Her eyebrows twitch. She smiles—sad, but warm. "Looks like you were in the middle of something."

"I-no-not really. She'd be-she was harvesting the goldenseal," I say.

"You were always so gifted with all that," she says.

"No, you were the one-," I reply.

"No, I wasn't. Wasn't my thing. Definitely yours though."

We stand awkwardly for a few moments. Her eyes drift to the hill of cards, notes and flowers leaning against the front door.

"So-I-the second bedroom is open," I say, "if you..."

"You're not?"

"No-I'm on the couch. Just-I mean, for now."

"Okay. Thanks."

I look at Sedi. His eyebrows are shifting back and forth. I pat his mammoth head and whisper, "It's okay, buddy." His eyes are skeptical, but he trots to the back of the house anyway. Dana follows him. I'll get back to the goldenseal tomorrow.

The rest of the day was equal parts comforting and excruciating. Lots of everything and nothing in the air. Sedi finally got fed up with us and went outside where things are straightforward. I would have joined him if I could.

After an hour and a half of stilted conversation and a greasy burrito I felt was rude not to eat after she ordered them from a Tex-Mex place in town, we exchanged the awkward goodnight of best friends turned strangers.

She's now asleep amid the indigo sheets of the spare bedroom, and I'm making mint tea to settle my roiling gut. I can hear Sedi breathing somewhere nearby. It's a little windy tonight. The trees brushing against each other in waves, like the ocean. The faint squeak of Ohma's weathervane.

"I wanted to say—I know this isn't easy for you," Dana says quietly from the kitchen doorway, "It must seem pretty unfair that she left right after you returned."

I freeze. I know I should turn around. But I can't.

"I think she'd say she waited for you and stayed as long as she could. Death is different for us. There's loss, but if the life was long and good, there is less grief. She led a good life. One with purpose. She was loved and needed. She got to see you again. You meant more to her than I think you know."

I'm trying to get myself to turn around, if only out of respect or shared loss, but I'm glued in place, water running out of my eyes again. It's surprising I have any tears left.

She waits. Gives me a chance to say something if I need to. I let myself drift back to the wind outside.

"There are some things," she continues carefully, "I know Ohma'd want us to do for her."

turn around

say something

yes, let's talk about it

would you like some tea?

spending time with her again was a gift

no-one can do anything for her ever again

say something

she's sad too

say something

I pour hot water into my mug and make myself turn around, ready to hear about the things Ohma would want us to do. But Dana's gone, the spare bedroom door softly closing behind her. Maybe I imagined the whole thing. I hold the mug of mint tea until it burns my fingers. Then a little longer after that.

****

I don't remember falling asleep. Only waking up and that it's morning now. There's no way of telling if Dana's here. I have no idea if she's one of those crack-of-dawn or noon types. The house is quiet. I strain to listen for any signs of her. Nothing.

I head to the kitchen to make coffee then take my mug outside to finish harvesting the goldenseal I abandoned yesterday. Dana's rental car is still parked in front so unless she's on a walk, she's probably catching up on sleep. It's one of many magical properties of Ohma's farm. Sleep is possible here. Far away from the sounds of man. No jackhammers or leaf blowers. Ohma cared and watched, and most of all, allowed this place to be nature's domain. Humans are guardians here, not developers. It may not be everyone's idea of heaven, but it's mine.

Between my mug of coffee and finishing the goldenseal harvest four hours passed. Dana's rental car is now gone. When I'm in the garden, everything else fades. After hanging the roots to dry, I moved on to starting a big pot of Ohma's potato, white bean, and leek soup in hopes of avoiding another take-out digestive disaster.

I hear a soft creak behind me. I flinch and turn around. Dana's leaning against the conservatory doorframe.

"Hey." she says.

"Oh, hey, you-sorry, you startled me. You're so quiet."

"Yeah, Ohma always said I missed my calling as a cat burglar."

"Right, John—" I say.

"Robie," she says.

"The cat," we say together. A sudden wave of loss crushes my chest.

"Want to watch it tonight?" I ask.

"That'd be good." She chuckles. "Her obsession with Hitchcock."

"Right? When did that start?" I ask.

"Don't know. She always was."

The room goes quiet again. Instead of leaving, she sits at the small wood dining table.

"Smells good" she says.

"Oh, yeah, thanks. Ohma's potato, bean and—"

"Leek soup," she says. "Smells just like hers."

"Should be done in another few minutes if you want some."

"Yeah. Good. And maybe we could talk about those things we need to do."

I nod then turn back to the stove. Away from the weight of things to discuss and do that Dana seems to carry with ease. She's so placid and capable. My abilities are currently maxing out at a five-ingredient soup.

Ten minutes later, Dana and I are sitting at the table with large bowls and cornbread. We let each other eat in silence. Once we're done, she lights one of Ohma's Kentucky cheroots. The smell of it makes me want to scream.

"We should talk about what we need to do for Ohma, for her ..." she trails off.

"Like rites?"

"Yeah, yes. The paperwork stuff can wait. If that's okay."

I'm trying to figure out what paperwork stuff she means when I realize she's talking about the farmhouse. I feel my blood pressure rising.

"We need to get her body released so we can bury her here."

"Here? Like here, here?" I ask gesturing to the house.

Dana nods. "Under the house, near her bed would be best, but I looked at the foundation and I don't think that will work."

My rational mind knows my say in what happens or doesn't happen or how the foundation of a farmhouse I hadn't seen in almost 40 years until a little over a month ago will allow for a traditional Cherokee burial is irrelevant. I know this. I just don't feel it.

"So, we should bury her near the house, maybe near the oak tree around back?" It's more a statement than a question.

"Uhm, okay."

I'm hoping she doesn't mean us. Us burying her. "So, how do we…?" I ask, unsure how to ask what I'm asking.

"That's where I was today. Signing papers to have her released to me. To us."

"Oh, okay. Was she? Were you guys …?"

"Related? No. She gave me power of attorney a few years ago."

"Oh, okay. Makes sense."

"I came back here on my thirtieth birthday," she says, reading my mind. "I hadn't been back since—I hadn't really dealt with my mom's death."

"Right, I mean—God, that must have been hard. I mean, even though it was a terrible accident, there's no making sense of–"

Dana is looking at me strangely.

"I thought you said your dad told you what happened."

I don't remember telling her he'd said anything to me. I must have told her over the phone when I called about Ohma. I wonder what else I said.

"He did. I mean, I think he did."

"What did he say?"

"That—he said that—" I'm panicking.

I'm going to say the wrong thing. Dredge up trauma for her. Bumble-fucking-mumble my way through the worst night of her life. Dana waits, her face looks like pieces that don't fit together anymore. Like that mask I made in Jendro's workshop.

"He-I-uhm-he said that she was-uhm-hit by a-"

"Murdered," Dana says quietly.

I continue as gently as I can. "That she was killed by someone who left her by the side of the road. A hit and run. Someone who'd been at the festival, he thinks."

"He thinks." Her voice is quiet and hard. "No. He knows. What else did he say?"

I don't know what to do other than tell her everything he said. So, I do. About her mom being hit, possibly by accident with probably a large truck, and how she was left, and how they never caught the person who did it, and how he said he and Mary had been in love. And how Ohma didn't think her death was an accident.

"Wow. I don't know why he'd lie after all this time, but he did."

My dad isn't my favorite person right now but her attacking him puts my defenses up.

"I-I don't-I mean, he's trying to remember something that happened a long time ago. Maybe he's forgotten some—"

"You don't forget something like that."

"Hey, I'm sorry. I'm sorry he didn't tell me everything or that he left things out. The day Ohma passed she was going to tell me-"

Dana looks at me as if I might be the most horrible, selfish person in the world. Not sure she's off the mark on that. I wish Ohma had some booze. I could really use a drink. I'm sure Dana could, too.

It was almost impossibly hard to stop drinking at first, but as I detoxed, and if anything, just wanted to not feel so shitty all the time, I realized I never liked the way drinking made me feel. Still, it'd be easy to fall back into that hole. The thought of simply resuming my general bob-weave-dodge fuckupedness after everything Ohma did to help me has me grateful there's no bourbon around to resist. Or not resist. Instead, I let that old crutch slide back into a corner and I wait quietly. Try to stop being the most horrible, selfish person in the world. I still have a gift for emotional stupidity.

"He probably left out the fact that the driver accidentally ran over her twice." She says it quietly, but very clearly.

I feel potato, bean, and leek soup rising in my throat.

Jake the Fireball crying

quartz pops and limestones crunches

ARMY sticker rrummmmble

Dad and the moon

I remember

The only way Ohma's potato, bean and leek soup doesn't end up all over the table is if I say something. One way or another something's coming out.

"They never told me. Dana, I'm so so sorry."

working depth of a postcard

She sits very still for a while; her eyes fixed to the empty chair across from her.

moorings and storms and lost ships

There was a part of Dana that slid beneath the surface and drowned that night. Part of her is gone now. Sometimes we lose a part of us that cannot be found again, even if sought.

"What was done to her," she finally says, her voice still quiet, still clear, "it's not the kind of thing anyone wants to admit happens in their town. The only reason why Ohma agreed I should leave is because she knew people don't like to be reminded of diseases in their community. So, they turn on anyone that reminds them of that infection."

She pauses. I'm not going to say anything. There's nothing to say. Nothing that will ever make it okay. I look at her and nod, just to let her know I'm not going to defend my father or blurt platitudes anymore. That I'm going to listen now, and she can say as much or as little as she wants. It's taken 40 years to finally get it. This was never about me.

"Remember how it was a really nice night?" she asks.

I nod. I don't remember. That doesn't matter.

"Warm and soft. Remember my mom brought us—"

funnel cake

"Funnel cake," she says. "And your dad gave us—"

"Sparklers," I say.

She nods.

I remember.

running around the festival with Dana while Mom and Dad were on a blanket near the bandstand and Dad's Army friend sitting with them and blue grass music and Dana's mom brings us funnel cake and Dana's mom dancing with us and us laughing and dancing then Dad's friend talking too loud and yelling at Dad and pointing at us Mom waving at us her smile too big and Dana's mom dancing and dancing and then Dad buying us sparklers and Dana drawing zig zags in the air waving goodbye as they started walking home

A perfect summer night from childhood where the air is soft and full of possibility, cool around the edges where crickets and frogs serenade trees, and grown-ups didn't matter because you and your best friend are laughing and dancing and sharing cream soda and funnel cake and drawing zig zags with sparklers.

Dana's watching me. Now she's the one waiting. It finally hits me. Dana was with her when it happened. And it happened while they were walking home from the festival. I'd known that, of course, but it hadn't truly sunk in until just now.

"Oh my God. Dana. I'm so sorry. Jesus. I … I didn't-"

"I didn't hear it at first," she says. "She was making funny blue grass music sounds and dancing, and I was laughing. Then she just disappeared. Like wind had picked her up off the ground. But then she was back on the ground, in front of me. I didn't understand how she got there. And a red truck was driving away fast. And I had dust in my eyes, and I didn't understand why. But there had been other cars that had passed us because of the festival, so I didn't think about it. I thought maybe she'd tripped but she was too far away, and she was in a weird position. I don't remember how I got to her, just that I was trying to help her get up, but her legs weren't right."

"She looked at me like maybe she was okay, just a little hurt. That's when a rumbling truck sound got louder, and she told me to hide. Her voice didn't sound right. I was confused. I didn't want to leave her because her eyes were changing. Like she wasn't there. And then she was, and she looked scared. I tried to get her up and move her, but it's like she was glued to the dirt. Then I saw red taillights and white back up lights coming closer, and she told me she loved me, and that I had to hide. I couldn't move. I didn't want to leave her there. So, I tried to pull her with me but each time I tried the sound she made was awful. Like a wounded deer. Then she yelled at me to hide. I ran as fast as I could to the trees nearby and hid. I tried not to watch but my eyes wouldn't blink or look away. I kept hoping the truck would stop. That it was coming to help her. But it didn't stop. I couldn't see him-the driver. Because after he'd-after he'd ..."

She stops. I don't say anything though I want to tell her she doesn't have to say anymore. That she shouldn't ever have to.

"His headlights were on her. She looked like crushed leaves. The dust and the night bugs were in the light between the truck and her. Like the headlights were showing things that weren't supposed to be there. And showing her in a shape she wasn't supposed to be in. Then the truck just drove away. I tried to move, but I couldn't. I stayed in the field waiting for her to move or call me back to her. But she didn't. I don't know how long I waited. When I finally got back to her, I just sat there and told her it was okay now cause he was gone. But she didn't look like herself anymore and she was very still. Her eyes just a little open, looking at where I'd been hiding. I don't know how long I stayed with her or how I even got to Ohma's house. I remember the look on her face, how she made a strange sound, then held me and we cried. Then she boiled water and willow bark, and we walked back to where it happened, but when we got there your father was there. He was crying and holding her, rocking her. He was making sounds like she made when I tried to move her. I remember hitting him and yelling at him to go away and how he went back next to his car, crying and crying while Ohma washed her with the willow bark water. I hated him for crying so much. He didn't belong there, and I hated him for showing up too late. When Ohma was done, she sang to her as your father picked her up. We walked back to our house. We were almost home when it happened. When we got home, Ohma sang to her so her spirit might come there instead of staying at the side of the road. After that, everything gets fuzzy. I remember your dad leaving and then Ohma and I stayed. Then she gave me tea and put me in her station wagon, and we went to your house, but I think she must have put something in the tea to make me sleep because the next thing I remember is my uncle was there and it was morning. And I thought it was just a nightmare. But then it wasn't because he and Ohma took all of Momma's clothes to the backyard and burned them. The smoke from her clothes was grey and blue. It left a long trail because there was no wind that night, and I wondered if maybe she could see it. Then we buried her next to her favorite birdhouse."

Her face melts into weary resignation. There are things in life we can heal from or learn from. This isn't one of them. Maybe she's smiled over the years, maybe even felt happy, but wonder and hope were ripped from her at age nine.

"Once the smoke from the fire stopped, my uncle took me home with him. I didn't want to leave because I knew my mother's spirit would stay here for many years before it returned to the mountains where she'd been born. Where I'd be waiting for her. But it had been decided. By your father and my uncle and even Ohma. They were afraid. Afraid I'd seen the man in the truck. In truth, I don't know what they thought. I don't care anymore. What I'm trying to say is I wanted to stay here. Stay with my mother's spirit and with Ohma. And you.

But they didn't listen to me. I was nine. They didn't listen to me."

We sit in silence for a few minutes. I feel like I should say something, but everything in my head sounds like cardboard.

"I know you tried to find me," she says quietly. "I found out a few years later. My uncle was very protective."

"I'm glad you knew I tried," I say gently. "Dana I'm so sorry."

She looks at me, her eyes red and weary. She nods.

****

She went back to her room after telling me, closing the door quietly behind her. The next day we stayed in silent orbit and once more, at dusk, she appeared in the kitchen. We talked into the night. She talked about how she still has all her mother's birdhouses in a storage unit. That maybe we could set them up in the woods for the birds because her mother would like that. I told her I thought her mother had the best smile I'd ever seen and how she seemed to know all the best jokes, but she also was almost impossibly beautiful. Then we talked about Ohma. About her dry sense of humor, how funny she'd thought it was to name a giant wolfhound Sedi, which means walnut. And her quirky love for John Travolta and Bogart movies. We talked about her gardens and how many people she helped heal and how strong she was and how neither one of us thought about how hard it must have been for her after that night. Then we talked about the day we met and how we'd become best friends over the course of a single afternoon. How kids do that. We talked about Nathy and planting Crunch Berries and how fast she used to run. The years slid away, and we found ourselves remembering more of our lives before all the after.

18

Last night we burned Ohma's clothes. Dana told me a bit about Tsalagi traditions, but mostly she led me through them. Let me participate. Which was incredibly kind. We burned her bed, her linens, her towels. Her favorite chair. The hardest for me was her foraging basket. The one with navy blue rings like water ripples and small purple stains on it from decades of holding wild elderberries. But it wasn't mine. It was hers. I'd have to get a new one. Earn the stains myself.

We decided to bury Ohma under her favorite oak near the house as the grey-blue smoke from the fire drifted into the night sky. She would've liked that—her body giving the oak what it needed—it's roots slowly curling around and through her until finally they become one.

It was strange and wonderful. And straightforward. How natural and right it all seemed.

The next morning Dana told me she'll be leaving in a few days. We've had a parenthesis of time in which we embraced our friendship again. But I could see being here was wearing her down. We shouldn't have to stay if the pain of that place has already taught us what we needed to know.

Today we walked to where her mom had died. It was dry and dusty. Quiet except for a woodpecker trilling in a nearby tree. Dana didn't say anything, and we didn't stay long. It felt empty. Just a patch of road. Not the place where the world had been ripped apart.

What happened, happened to Dana and to her mother. Maybe a bit to my father. But not me. Not really. I've ridden the waves of someone else's tragedy for most of my life. I let the undertow carry me from myself, pull me farther and farther out to sea. But none of it belonged to me.

****

Dana's leaving tomorrow and I still haven't gotten the courage up to ask her what she thinks about the apothecary idea. I still feel stuck between old me and true me. Familiar horizons still too close. Carroll Gardens, The Bridge Group, Mitchel, Zaytoons, Adderal, too much wine, the keys of Dylan Chester Montgomery. My dormant charcoal tree. When I think about them my chest tightens. I want to have been fixed. I want to be fixed enough now to return with my knowledge of the dragon and the cave and the potions that healed me. If I return in a way that helps instead of harms, maybe I'll find my way into the life I should have led. But I still don't entirely trust my choices. My patterns are buttressed by decades of hiding and fighting and denial. So, I need to know what she thinks. If she thinks it's a good plan, I'll do it.

The problem is broaching the topic feels awkward. A bit opportunistic. I don't want to dissolve the fragile new beginning of our friendship. But Ohma helped me, and when I think of how others could be helped—maybe how'd they'd start giving a crap about the planet they take for granted once they realize it can heal them—it seems like a good plan. So, I need to know. Need to know if it'd be what Ohma would want because I didn't get to ask her. And now Dana's leaving too. Going back to her life. I'm not sure I'll have the guts to bring this up later.

We're in the conservatory and I'm trying to demonstrate my knowledge of Ohma's remedies by making a couple of them by heart. It'll be a better springboard into asking. But the formula for her cold remedy versus her flu remedy when it comes to fennel or rosemary has me a bit stumped, so I'm just shuffling jars around and checking for mold on the drying rack.

Dana's sitting with Sedi over in his favorite corner near the hazy window that overlooks Ohma's massive back gardens, his giant head taking up her entire lap. She's burying her hand in his wooly neck. We've been like this for a while. Her looking out the window to the oak tree where we buried Ohma a week ago. Her with her hand in Sedi's wooly fur. Her watching me check herbs and organize jars, sometimes smiling to herself like Ohma's whispering secrets. Normally I hate being observed, even peripherally, but for some reason having Dana in the room doesn't bother me.

just ask her

it's Dana

just ask

I casually check the rosemary I've already checked three times. "Hey, so I was wondering if I could ask you-I mean if I could get your thoughts on something?"

The hand buried in Sedi's wooly neck pauses, the glow from a September morning sun through the hazy window giving Dana the appearance of the Virgin Mary blessing a wolf-bear. It makes me want to laugh and cry at the same time. She smiles an almost smile at me, and nods. Ohma's tree is motionless behind her. It's going to be a hot, breezeless day.

"I-I-sorry. I was thinking, you know how much being here kind of fixed me and how these remedies are really incredible but also really about more than just me or us or, you know people, but about..."

Dana's huge walnut eyes are unwavering. Waiting. I think she must know what I'm trying to say but she's going to make me say it. Which is kind of irritating. And very much like her. I take a deep breath.

if I can't say it, I don't have the right to do it

"Ohma reminded me I have a place here. I've never felt like I belonged, you know, like with people." Dana smiles, chuckles, nods. It's a good sign, so I continue. "The only bridge, I think the only way I can be a part of society-Jesus that sounds so dramatic, I know, but it's kinda how it's always been for me. The only way I can be a part of it is if I make these remedies and make people understand how much the plants and this planet is—crap, now I sound like an infomercial—"

She's nodding and half smiling and waiting. I take another breath and remind myself I used to direct the choices of titans. I used to know how to do this in my sleep. Pitch an idea, make people get on board with it. But as I connect to that old self, I start to feel deeply tired. But I've started now, and I'll regret it if I don't see this through.

"These remedies-Ohma's remedies are important. They need to not disappear. Don't you think that would be tragic? To have all her knowledge fade away? People need help. This world isn't working anymore. All this stuff we buy and the pills we take to *seem* like we care and the pills we take to not care *too much*. I was beyond help, but she helped me heal myself, and I just think that's something that, the more people know it and bring it into their lives the better everything will be. Don't you think? I just. I think..."

Dana looks out the hazy window. She stays like that for what feels like hours.

Then she says "Ohma once told me how everything changed after that summer. Not just for me and my mom. But for you and your father and very much for her too. She said she was sad for a long time. Because she'd lost all of us that night. She said she became still for many years. Let her gardens go, let the weeds take it. She said many times she walked the river path to your house, but never knocked. And how after a while she stopped because it kept reminding her of things that no longer were."

I hadn't thought how Ohma might feel. Children don't think of the heartaches of adults.

"This time you had with her. Healing is hard. Harder than people think it'll be. And healers are rare. Ohma was a medicine woman. All the women in her family were Red Paint clan. It was her life's work to heal. To help people heal themselves. Though, she was unique in her methods. A wild card sometimes."

I laugh. "Oh, I know. She had me do these seven tasks."

Dana laughs too. "She was a fan of those. Building your own bridge. She didn't believe people should be too reliant on her for their healing. Which happened a lot. People would come to her for a remedy for something then go right back to how they lived before. She wasn't interested in being a pharmacy. She had a bigger idea of what healing is. What it takes."

I laugh, this time more quietly. "Yeah."

My eyes start to sting again, and I don't want to cry. Not now. Over the past two weeks I've learned Dana gets very still when I cry. Which is nice, but it also severs the momentum of whatever conversation we're having, and I need momentum if I'm going to get through this.

"She had me try to find a feather, you know, that represented me. So, of course I wanted to find a hawk or a blue jay, you know. Which, in hindsight was...*anyway*, I got pissed off because I couldn't find a single one. Not one. And then finally, after a week of searching and a few tantrums, this..." I show her the feather, now tied with a piece of twine, hanging next to the back door. "This janky raven feather. She loved that. Thought it was funny and, I don't know, it almost seemed like it whispered something to her."

Dana nods, her face turns sober. "That's why"

"Why what?"

"Why your healing included bringing you back here, to this room. Reminding you of everything she taught us as kids. Everything you had such a gift for."

"I don't remember—I mean, having a gift for it."

"I know."

"More that it just, I don't know, made sense, I think."

"I do." She looks down at Sedi's massive drooling face, twitching and dreaming of squirrels. Secret trails. Fallen maple leaves. Her legs must be numb by now.

I can tell she's given me her answer, but in an irritatingly cryptic way. For someone who can be blunt, someone who is a journalist, her lack of clarity sometimes is odd. It's probably that she doesn't want to talk about it. She doesn't want me to do it. I know this. But I need her to say it and tell me why.

I continue. "How she'd sing songs from *Saturday Night Fever* when she was tidying up, and those cigarillos of hers! Once I got her a vanilla spice flavored pack and you should have seen her reaction. Like I'd just given her a pile of poo-"

"She loved you, you know," she says. "Believed in you and thought you were incredible. Gifted. Different. She saw you, the real you, and knew spending time on her farm would heal you and remind you."

"Yeah, I think maybe you both did," I added

Dana's chuckling again. "Yeah, the phone thing. Sorry. Kind of a jerk move on my part—"

"Not really. I mean, yeah, maybe a little."

"It wasn't just for you. Though it was kinda clear you were miserable and about a year away from a heart attack. It was for her too. I think she needed to see you again, and that window was closing, so when I bumped into you, I knew you two were supposed to find your way back to each other. And I took my chance."

"So, it wasn't about not being ready to tell me?" I asked

"That was part of it too. And you kind of seemed—"

"Like a world class asshat?"

We laughed and agreed that, yes, I was.

"But you're not anymore. You-you're not. But if you were to take her remedies to…"

That's when I caught up. "You don't think I should open an apothecary in Brooklyn." Then I truly caught up. I imagine this must be what base jumping feels like. A shift, a fall, the walls disappearing, revealing vast spaces previously unseen. Spaces that belong to others. And just because I see them, have been invited once or twice, doesn't mean their mine. I finish, "Because that would be me poaching her life's work after she helped me and—"

Then Dana chuckled and said, "Well, yeah."

I feel stung and ashamed. And very relieved. Which is weird.

"I think," she says, "I believe she'd want you to learn on your own about the plants here and how they can be medicine. Everything's here already, in her gardens and the forest. Maybe you could become someone who helps people too. Make your own remedies. They'll be very much like hers. But it takes time. It should. I think Ohma'd like that. She always had a reason for what she did."

"Like leaving her farm to both of us."

Dana nodded and smiled.

19

Last night, lying on the couch, Sedi's snuffly snore and the rustling hum of nocturnal things softening walls and decisions, I tried to imagine going back to New York. As the now-healed Maggie Morris. What I'd possibly do now that the apothecary idea is off the table. I tried to imagine opening my own PR firm, only representing people and companies who've made the Planet Pledge. Maybe even getting in touch with Mitchel. Laughing about Maggie's fall off a cliff and binge watching *Supernatural* over a bottle of Dickel. But no matter how I tried, I couldn't quite get beyond a feeling of forcing something to seem real because it'd be great if it could be real. The version of me that could believe in forcings has been left in other places and times.

I stayed up late–letting the stillness of the forest dissolve the remnants of my apothecary plans. I thought about everything Dana said. How Ohma helped me heal in every way a person can be healed. It still feels impossible how quickly that happened after such a long time of being unwell and unhappy. I'm starting to realize it wasn't just her remedies and the tasks; it's these mountains and this farm. I never felt this way in the city. I'd tried to be that person who could spend an afternoon in Prospect Park and be rejuvenated. But I'm not ever going to be that person. I fell into a worm hole of numbing agents instead. Trying to be that person and always failing to be that person was only part of the problem. Some people thrive in the city, some don't. I think the ones that do have a tighter mesh, one that filters out the constant onslaught. Some people are born with wider mesh than others. I'm a wide mesh-er. No amount of cleansing breaths, or Shavasanas, or mindfulness contemplations sipping cold pressed juices are going to overcome how the city affects me. The unrelenting sounds and smells and vibrations. The proximity to millions of people.

How I never stopped feeling just a hair outside places everyone else slipped into with ease. How the echo patterns I adopted became my only way through. That's not good enough anymore.

I thought about what Dr. Nahimana said. And the porous thing mom brought up. Naming a thing doesn't change a thing. But there's a kind of relief knowing I've always been this way. That I pretended not to be who I am for a very long time. Maybe there's a finite amount of pretending given to each of us when we're born. And once it's used, it's gone.

When I woke up today, it was to a feeling of belonging. I got up, made coffee, then contacted a broker about selling my loft on Sackett. I'll use it to buy out Dana's half of Ohma's farm. Not because I don't want to share it, but because she says although it's beautiful here, and that she sees what being here is for me, she doesn't belong here anymore. She said being here again, burying Ohma—she realized she stopped belonging here the night her mother died. She told me she belongs in the city where she can continue her own work building a news platform that doesn't censor or warp indigenous voices.

When I was a child Dana was just Dana, and Ohma was just Ohma. Before them I was only at home with wind and trees and animals. Sun falling through Nathy's leaves. The thick, flinty-maple smell of the earth after a storm. That was home. I didn't know people could be like trees and water and sunlight until I met Ohma and Dana. I think I was obsessed with them, though. In a way that keeps you from really knowing a person.

Then Dana's mom was gone. Then Dana was gone. But I didn't lose myself until I lost Ohma. First because I was angry, then because my father kept us apart. Time took over from there. The way it always does. The long slow departure not only from memories but reminders. They became part of the story I told myself. The people I loved who went away and an old oak tree.

Dana and I came back into each other's life for a reason. I don't think either one of us mourns the friendship we had as children. It belongs to then, not now. She'll visit, maybe. I hope. Or I'll visit her. And I'll get to read everything she writes. It gives me hope. I finally don't see hope as weakness. Real hope has grit in it—ground up remnants of the cynicism that proceeded it. Giving it heft. Making it stick.

Even though I wanted to, I didn't ask Dana if she thought we might be sisters. It was strange to leave such a huge question unanswered, but I'm not sure if she knows. And even if she did, what would it change? It would just be another way for me to claim her and I'm pretty sure I've done enough of that. Maybe she knows, maybe she wonders too. But there's only so much a person should have to delve into at once. Maybe one day we'll talk about it.

Before she left, my father did come over to see her. That must have been almost impossibly difficult for him. They went on a very long walk and when she came back it looked like she'd been crying. I wanted to do something. Say something. I made Sunset lemonade and ordered her favorite Chinese food instead. My need to know isn't the point. If she'd wanted to talk about it, she would have.

She went back yesterday. Back to Patricia. The spark in her eyes when she talked about returning to New York was unmistakable. It's her home.

As far as my own relationship with my father, it has a long way to go, but at least the distance is clearer. No amount of me punishing him will ever surpass what he's already gone through. It must be hard for him to revisit those years. Regret has deep roots. It takes a while to find them all.

I did ask him about his old Army friend. The one with the truck. The one that was sitting on the blanket with him and Mom the night of the Firefly Festival. After what felt like a long time he said, "Denny. He died last year." I wanted to push for more, but something stopped me. Maybe it's timing. Maybe it has something to do with no longer feeling more information is always the answer. Maybe someday we'll talk about it. About all of it. I hope so.

For now, neither of us is pretending everything is okay, which helps. A clearing has sprung up where we both have room to try and room not to be entirely ready. We'll keep meeting there until one day we'll be close enough to be in each other's life again. For now, it's quiet. But quiet is good. Quiet means maybe.

Yesterday he brought over a hickory drying box he'd made for me. The almanac is predicting a wet winter.

It's almost spring now. Sunlight rippling through morning fog. Hemlock groves. Cool mist and malty earth. A gentle wildness stirring within me. Dormant mycelium awakening. Something in the air. In the water. In the dense, red earth.

Soon the honeysuckle and the acacia trees will make the entire state smell like heaven. The flinty storms of summer will soon follow. Then I'll go outside, let the warm rain fall on my face, and I'll think of Ohma and Dana and Nathy, and little Magpie Morris. Then lightning will crack through a violet and green sky. And I'll laugh with joy. After a while, I'll walk home, gathering stones and feathers as I go.

Time will pass. People will begin to tell stories of me. The witch in the woods. The virgin crone of the forest. The tree keeper. I hope so. To be a part of the wild things that surround me. To be known but unknowable. I'd like that. Like Ohma weaving into the roots of her oak tree. Not separate. Part of something bigger. Something else. I'll open my hand and let go of what was because this is where I belong.

I'll breathe in, then breathe out with a whistle only Nathy can hear. I'll look up and up and up, through his arms. He'll sound like old secrets and the ocean.

I can almost hear his voice again.

CPSIA information can be obtained
at www.ICGtesting.com
Printed in the USA
BVHW052257230223
659154BV00010B/69

9 781737 519488